GAME CHANGERS

GAME CHANGERS

Dean Smith, Charlie Scott,
and the Era That Transformed
a Southern College Town

ART CHANSKY

THE UNIVERSITY OF NORTH CAROLINA PRESS

Chapel Hill

This book was published with the assistance of the Blythe Family Fund of the University of North Carolina Press.

Set in Arno Pro by Westchester Publishing Services

Manufactured in the United States of America

The University of North Carolina Press has been a member of the Green Press Initiative since 2003.

Library of Congress Cataloging-in-Publication Data
    Names: Chansky, Art, author.
Title: Game changers : Dean Smith, Charlie Scott, and the era that transformed
    a southern college town / Art Chansky.
Description: Chapel Hill : University of North Carolina Press, [2016] |
    Includes bibliographical references and index.
Identifiers: LCCN 2016023981 | ISBN 9781469630380 (cloth : alk. paper) |
    ISBN 9781469630397 (ebook)
Subjects: LCSH: University of North Carolina at Chapel Hill—Basketball—History. |
    North Carolina Tar Heels (Basketball team)—History. | Smith, Dean, 1931–2015. |
    Scott, Charlie, 1948– | Basketball coaches—North Carolina—Chapel Hill. |
    Basketball—North Carolina—Chapel Hill—History. | African Americans—Civil
    rights—North Carolina—Chapel Hill—History—20th century. | Racism in sports—
    North Carolina—Chapel Hill—History.
Classification: LCC GV885.43.U54 C425 2016 | DDC 796.323/6309756565—dc23
    LC record available at https://lccn.loc.gov/2016023981

Jacket illustrations: front, photograph of Dean Smith and Charlie Scott reprinted with permission from *The News & Observer*, Raleigh, N.C.; back, *March on Franklin St.*, photograph by Roland Giduz used with permission from North Carolina Collection, Wilson Library, University of North Carolina at Chapel Hill.

Frontispiece: Charlie Scott, Rusty Clark, and Dean Smith rejoice after 1968 Eastern Regional win over Davidson (author's collection, compliments of Hugh Morton).

TO DEAN SMITH AND CHARLIE SCOTT

without whom ...

Contents

Acknowledgments

The idea for this book began with a surprising question about a piece of college basketball trivia: How did five Morehead Scholars wind up on the 1967 University of North Carolina at Chapel Hill (UNC) freshman basketball team with Charlie Scott, four other scholarship athletes, and five walk-ons?

The Morehead Scholarship (now the Morehead-Cain Scholarship) is the most prestigious academic scholarship awarded to students at the University of North Carolina. Although Carolina basketball teams over the years have featured the occasional Morehead recipient here or there, such a concentration of academically elite students stands out as a bit odd. So what was the story?

The players from that 1967 group have remained closer than many Carolina teams over the years. Their periodic reunions are sometimes attended by Larry Brown, who was a twenty-six-year-old assistant that season; some players say Brown was the toughest coach they ever had. During one such reunion in 2013, a Raleigh attorney and one of the Morehead Scholars, Bob Bode, wondered aloud how this cluster of scholars had happened. A week later, Bode called me, since I was their classmate at UNC and covered the varsity Tar Heels for the *Daily Tar Heel* in 1968–70. Bode said it might make an interesting feature and suggested we talk to Chuck Lovelace, the current executive director of the Morehead-Cain Foundation.

After checking the records, Lovelace could not find a case where close to five Morehead Scholars from the same class had ever played on a Tar Heel team. Bode, attorney Harold Pollard, and I were in Lovelace's office, and the three of us immediately had the same thought: Dean Smith.

The 1967 freshmen shared a part of UNC history, for they shared the court with Scott, the first African American scholarship athlete at Carolina. Over the years, we had all come to revere Smith as not only a great basketball coach and cagey strategist but also a smart, sensitive man who tried to look at things from many angles. Smith liked to play the odds, and we agreed it would not be unlike him to have created an environment that gave Scott the greatest chance for peace off court and success on it.

In researching what I had experienced, written, or read about UNC and Chapel Hill in the 1960s, it became clear to me that this was more than a feature article in a magazine or for a website. It was a full-blown story that needed to be told—not only about Scott, Smith, and the teams of the 1960s, but of a town in turmoil over race relations and a university that had a liberal reputation but was far from standing in the vanguard on such matters.

Unfortunately, by the time this book began to take shape in my mind, Smith's health was in steady decline from progressive cognitive dementia that had begun to emerge after he endured complications from knee replacement surgery in 2007. The one source whose legendary memory could have taken us back there in more vivid detail than he had already provided in his autobiography, *A Coach's Life* (1999), was no longer available. Fortunately, most of the players and other notable figures from that era are still with us and were willing to talk about such a meaningful time in their lives, a period when Chapel Hill, the university, and its basketball program were in the throes of major change.

Thanks to retired editor in chief David Perry and Editorial Director Mark Simpson-Vos, the University of North Carolina Press agreed to publish *Game Changers*, which in the beginning was not going to be a book focused on the upheavals of the civil rights era. But Perry and Simpson-Vos favored a book not just about Smith and Scott but about the 1960s—the most contentious, controversial, and yes, colorful decade in UNC and North Carolina history, as well as that of much of the nation. Recounting the early careers of Smith and Scott made it a "Carolina basketball book," but it is far more the tale of a college town, a college coach, a college star, and a college trying to find their way through the U.S. desegregation era.

The book is also an attempt to set the record straight on what, in some cases, has become myth over truth. Take, for instance, the often-told story of Dean Smith helping to lead the integration of certain Chapel Hill restaurants. Yes, Smith was at The Pines restaurant when it served a black customer for the first time in the summer of 1959. But no, that was not the end of segregated eateries in Chapel Hill.

Bringing the story fully to light was possible thanks to the research help of many people. Daniel Wilco, a brilliant UNC journalism student from Atlanta, went all the way back to the Reverend Charlie Jones and his inclusive congregation at the old Chapel Hill Presbyterian Church to depict the underpinnings of true racial unrest in the college town. Wilco also spent hours poring over *Daily Tar Heel* archives to determine just what the racial makeup and climate of UNC was during the 1950s and 1960s. Susan Newrock at the Chapel Hill Historical Society provided some valuable leads and allowed me hours with more than a dozen books written about Chapel Hill as well as bound copies of the *Chapel Hill Weekly*, even while she was packing up and moving from the basement of the old Chapel Hill Public Library building to the ground floor of the new library off Estes Drive. The discovery of a documentary produced by retired UNC education professor Gerald Unks, whose students interviewed prominent black and white Chapel Hill senior citizens for a video called *Town before Brown*, was a riveting reminder of the Jim Crow system that existed prior to the 1954 *Brown v. Board of Education* Supreme Court decision and endured through the passage of the Civil Rights Act ten years later.

The interviews carried out for this project, most of them supplemented by my notes from prior conversations, were intense and revealing. Scott, who remains one of the most beloved athletes in UNC history, gave the most of himself—nearly three hours. Scott's wife, Trudy, was helpful with several follow-up texts to verify facts. Besides information from Robert Seymour's two books, a two-hour interview confirmed his memory was razor sharp at ninety; two more hours were spent with Howard Lee and one with his wife, Lillian; and two with retired Orange County sheriff Lindy Pendergrass and his former deputy Rick Smith, who were part of a law enforcement team that worked nearly round the clock during more than two years of constant protests. I also spent invaluable time with almost all of Scott's freshman teammates who are still living (plus coach Larry Brown) and with his other varsity mates, notably his best friends on the team, Dick Grubar and Bill Chamberlain, New Yorkers who settled in North Carolina.

Bishop McDuffie, whose grandparents founded the Laurinburg Institute and whose parents, Frank and Sammie McDuffie, ran the school when Scott was there, gave me the better part of a day at the now-struggling campus.[1] Bishop was clear that his family favored Scott breaking the athletic scholarship barrier at UNC rather than at Davidson or any other college, because it would mean more, historically, to Laurinburg and the state university.

Dr. Randy Forehand, a pulmonary physician in Virginia, former basketball manager at UNC, and Scott's roommate for the 1968–69 season, shared his experiences and wisdom about just what the 1960s in Chapel Hill meant to anyone who witnessed or was part of that definitive decade. For my book *The Dean's List* (1996), Forehand first revealed how close Scott came to boycotting the 1969 National Collegiate Athletic Association (NCAA) Eastern Regional championship game against Davidson. With twenty more years to think about it, Forehand had even more insights this time around.

Margaret Scott, Charlie's first wife, was more than gracious with her ninety-minute interview and several follow-up phone calls; this was the first time she had talked publicly about being married to Scott, who was then the most prominent black athlete in North Carolina. Their daughter, Holly Scott Emanuel, helped set up the initial meeting and coaxed her wonderful mother along.

Dean Smith's first wife, Ann, and their oldest daughter, Sharon, still share the family's unwritten rule of privacy, but both took my phone calls. Sharon owes her life to her father in more ways than one. When she was a year old and turning blue with a choking spell, Smith raced through the streets of Aurora, Colorado, on an empty tank of gas to get her to the emergency room for a tracheotomy. The incident led to Smith's long-held belief in basketball as just a game.

Thanks are also due to the late Chapel Hill mayor Sandy McClamroch, Delaine Ingram, Jim Crisp, Larry Keith, Braxton Foushee, Fred Battle, Joel Bulkley, Steve Lerner, Mel Lewis, Albert Long, Rick Brewer, Allen Reep, Chris Boulton, Joe Sitterson, Ruth Murphy, and Roy Williams for sharing their recollections and thoughts. Although she was a student in California during the 1960s, Dr. Linnea Smith provided a detailed account of the Presidential Medal of Freedom ceremony at the White House, where she accepted the award for her ailing husband of almost forty years.

This is my eighth book having to do with the history of UNC basketball and it has been by far the most challenging and exciting one to write. Much background information came from my prior writings and the boxes of old newspaper clippings and magazines that take up half a room in my home. Thanks, as always, to my wife, Jan, for putting up with the clutter and lending an ear and an eye to the drafts when she could take a spare minute from running a radio station and website. Steve Kirschner and Matt Bowers, UNC's exceptional sports information duo, again let me pore through files and photos in their office.

UNC Press is, by a country mile, the most thorough and meticulous publisher with whom I have worked. Simpson-Vos and staff not only demand getting the facts right but also confirm their long history as one of the top storytellers among university presses in the world. While he is a rabid Carolina fan, Simpson-Vos is the consummate professional and "firmly gentle" with his feedback and editing. It was a pleasure to work with the entire UNC Press crew on a book I hope they are as proud of as I am.

And finally, to my longtime colleagues and personal editors, Owen Davis and Alfred Hamilton, thank you and thank you. Although grossly underpaid, your work with grammar and syntax, and as wordsmiths, makes this old boy look better than he deserves. Retired newspapermen extraordinaire, they remain the best at their trade that I know.

Historical writers—unless they are very, very old—usually lack firsthand knowledge of what they write. Having experienced the end of the 1960s with the rest of my UNC Class of 1970, being able to recall and then write about a young Dean Smith, Charlie Scott, and Bob Seymour while having known them all at the time, and actually witnessing some of their experiences beyond the basketball games and sermons themselves, was surreal. I hope that rare and memorable opportunity has come through in this book.

PROLOGUE

Careful Crusaders

Late on the morning of November 20, 2013, Barack Obama stood just outside the East Room of the White House. Sixteen recipients of the Presidential Medal of Freedom strode slowly down the North Hallway toward him. Among them was Dr. Linnea Smith, an accomplished psychiatrist and noted activist on matters such as the exploitation of children. However, Dr. Smith was present on this day as a representative for her famous husband, Hall of Fame basketball coach Dean Smith. Smith, who was in declining health back in Chapel Hill, and unable to attend the ceremony.

A tall Marine, fully dressed and spit-shined from head to toe, approached Dr. Smith as she proceeded with the group. The Marine was carrying a steel briefcase.

"The marine expressed his admiration for Dean,"[1] Linnea said, recalling how she glanced down at the steel briefcase that seemed to be out of place for the occasion. Later, she learned the briefcase was the "nuclear football" containing codes the president would need to launch an attack in defense of the country if he was away from the command center in the White House. The marine with the football always had to be within a few feet of the president wherever he went. "I guess he was still close enough to Obama at the time that he could talk to us," Linnea said.

Among President Obama's many duties was to award the Presidential Medal of Freedom to citizens "who have made especially meritorious contributions or other significant public or private endeavors." In Dean Smith's case, this included countless confidential good deeds that never came to light. Reading the citation honoring Smith, Obama cited some of his most famous public accomplishments in a thirty-six-year career that had taken Smith and his University of North Carolina Tar Heels to the pinnacle of college basketball.

Smith's achievements off the court got even greater billing, however. He was lauded for graduating 96 percent of his players, campaigning for a nuclear freeze, and fighting against the death penalty. And as the honor was granted by the nation's first African American president, perhaps nothing in Smith's career stood out more than his role as a civil rights leader, represented most clearly by his recruitment of Charles Scott, the first African American scholarship athlete at the University of North Carolina.

Smith certainly deserved the Presidential Medal, but how it added to his legacy also mirrored his legendary career as a championship basketball coach and champion of equal rights. As a child in Kansas, Smith took an oath of equality and fairness that was commonly sworn by schoolchildren in that day, and no doubt he carried it with him to Chapel Hill. However, he was always a careful crusader who fought most causes behind the scenes. Smith even characteristically pushed all the credit for his 879 victories and two national championships toward his players. An inherently shy man, Smith nevertheless developed a legion of followers who marshaled their forces to give him the praise he never sought; they included influential alumni and a press corps whose support he attracted with his low-key charm and astounding memory for names and faces.

His nomination for the Presidential Medal came about much the same way—from the outside in. An online petition for Smith to receive the nation's highest civilian honor had been circulated hastily in February of 2013 and was signed by 1,091 people—far from the suggested 100,000 names but obviously enough in such a short window for the word to get to Obama, an acknowledged fan of both Smith and University of North Carolina basketball. (Early in his tenure as president, Obama once famously played pickup with a Tar Heel team and accurately picked the 2008–09 squad to win the national championship.) While petitions often start years in advance, Smith's was open for fewer than ten days in February; by then, the eighty-two-year-old coaching legend was rapidly losing his fight against the progressive cognitive dementia that would claim his life less than fifteen months later, which may have been a factor in expediting his nomination despite having so relatively few signatures. Most of the names came from North Carolina, although residents in forty-two other states and Washington, D.C., also signed the petition.

Several UNC graduates worked in and around the White House at that time, any of whom could have received a recommendation from various university administrators and alumni with a pipeline to the White House. Doug Dibbert, president of the UNC General Alumni Association, admitted that he was encouraged "to do whatever I wanted to with contacts I had in the Obama White House/Administration."

Among those UNC graduates who had Obama's ear was Cassandra Butts, who grew up in Durham and was a classmate of the president at Harvard Law School. She was deputy White House counsel during Obama's first administration. Melody Barnes, UNC Class of 1986, was a domestic policy advisor during Obama's first term. Carol Mason, who served on the UNC Board of Trustees, worked in the Justice Department and is a close friend of Obama's senior policy advisor, Valerie Jarrett. It was not unusual for such a team to unite in support of Smith. And so the outpouring of emotion in Smith's honor had started long before the Hall of Fame coach died on February 8, 2015.

A good six months after she first heard about the petition, when the first call came, Linnea Smith did not know why the White House was trying to locate her. She got the message and said it was "a little bit scary." At the same time, an Obama staff member had tracked down UNC basketball coach Roy Williams in Asheville; as Linnea recalled, he refused to give out the Smiths' personal phone number without first checking with the family. She okayed it, and then the call came from the White House saying that her husband would be one of sixteen honorees at a ceremony in November. "They wanted us to know before they released it to the media," she said. "That's why there was such urgency, which was thoughtful."

Linnea, who was accepting the award for Smith, could invite five guests. She asked the three children from his first marriage to the former Ann Cleavinger, but only one was able to attend. Sandy Combs lived in Charlotte and could not get away, and Sharon Kepley, who had remained in Chapel Hill for almost every game her father coached, wanted to maintain the low profile she had kept all those years. Scott Smith, the only son, wanted to go, and then Linnea asked the two grown daughters she had with Smith, Kristen and Kelly, if they would attend. Kristen, a government relations executive with the Chapel Hill Chamber of Commerce who had already moved home to help with her father's care, and Kelly, a pediatric resident at UNC Hospitals who was married and pregnant at the time, agreed to accompany their mother. The other two invitees were obvious to Linnea: Williams, Smith's protégé, who had returned home as Carolina's head coach in 2003, and Smith's thirty-year faithful lieutenant, Bill Guthridge, who had guided UNC to two Final Fours in his three seasons as head coach after taking over when Smith retired in 1997. With the help of his wife, Leesie, Guthridge made his last prolonged trip out of Chapel Hill; suffering from his own degenerative illness, Guthridge died in May 2015, slightly more than three months after the death of his famous boss.

There had been so many earlier ceremonies in Smith's honor, including induction into the Naismith Hall of Fame in 1983 and the Arthur Ashe Award for Courage at the nationally televised Excellence in Sports Performance Yearly Awards (ESPYs) in 1998, when a handful of Smith's African American players surprised him on stage, including Scott in a stunning white tuxedo jacket. But this one had less to do with basketball than all the others. Smith's name would be joining more than five hundred former recipients on the fiftieth anniversary of the Presidential Medal, which was created by John F. Kennedy before his assassination in 1963. Linnea, on behalf of Dean, received two invitations to the gala celebration of all winners at the Smithsonian Institution the night following the 2013 ceremony and insisted that her daughters attend and sit at the head table with the president and First Lady.

"We've been to the White House three times," she told them. "You go."

Those who know Dean Smith as a Hall of Famer, power broker, and supporter of mostly liberal causes may not remember that for most of the 1960s he was more of a struggling young basketball coach concerned with keeping his job and protecting his family. Some of the players he inherited at first did not know what to make of his demanding coaching style and never respected him then as much as they learned to later in life. Smith was clear on his personal beliefs but unsure how to act on them at what was very much a conservative state university.

Looking back on that decade, an important yet complicated period, nothing heightened Smith's challenge like his liaison with Scott, who came to Chapel Hill and the predominantly white UNC campus after living the great majority of his first seventeen and a half years in segregated black surroundings. While their relationship became legendary, it was not that close early on. Separating myth from realities, the story of Smith and Scott reveals two young men with a lot to lose, figuring it out as they went along during one of the more turbulent periods in American history, both trying to protect their people and their own potential.

Smith was a man of principle but a coach under fire for his first five seasons after succeeding the flamboyant Frank McGuire. Scott was a teenager with wisdom and experience far beyond his years, but he was understandably leery of the new environment he had chosen after growing up in the Harlem ghetto and then spending three years at an all-black preparatory school in rural North

Carolina. The coach and the prize recruit were learning to coexist in a college town that had, despite its liberal reputation, convulsed in a clash between civil rights progress and long-held prejudices. When they finally joined forces, could Dean Smith and Charlie Scott change the game? Or would they both go down together? We know how the story turned out, but few know how it could have ended very differently. The time has come to tell that story.

CHAPTER

1

The Key Players

In the sweltering New York City summer of 1961, if you wanted to find twelve-year-old Charlie Scott, you'd look for him hanging out at the schoolyard a mile or so from his tenement apartment on West 131st Street in Harlem. Scott lived in a poor, hard-edged neighborhood called the Valley, where those who could find work had blue-collar jobs, and where kids were tested on the toughest playgrounds in the city. Most housing in the Valley came in the form of dilapidated apartments, many infested with rats and roaches, and lacking sufficient heat in the winter. Activist groups such as Harlem Youth Opportunities Unlimited (HARYOU) wanted existing buildings in East Harlem torn down and replaced by rent-controlled, city-designed and managed residences that would be safer than those owned by private slumlords. However, objections by community members who would have been displaced during demolition and construction halted the projects.

For many families in the Valley, children slept three and four to a room, so they were up and out early and in the schoolyard until the sun set well behind the lowest buildings. If they weren't big enough or good enough to get in a game, like Charlie Scott in 1961, they sat or stood all day long watching their hardscrabble heroes make moves they hoped to master someday. Teenagers from other neighborhoods and boroughs walked through the gates with silent scowls that said, "lace 'em up and let's go." Before the Harlem riots of 1964 and the emergence of crime lords such as Frank Lucas who smuggled heroin into the United States from Vietnam on American warplanes and later turned to trafficking cheap crack cocaine, Scott's environment was rife with the petty crimes of low-level hustlers. All that action occurred outside the chain-linked fences, however; inside, serious contests of young manhood unfolded on uneven asphalt courts between single poles and metal backboards with broken

and bowed rims left by athletes who went hard to the hole. In parks with nick-
names such as the Battleground, outside shots might clank and carom anywhere. And in the "I got next" world of pickup games where only winners kept
playing, the surest shots were stuffed through the hoop, no matter how bent.

West of the Valley was Sugar Hill, home to City College of New York
(CCNY) and professionals and middle-class blacks who went down Harlem
River Drive or by subway to office jobs that allowed them to buy brownstones
and apartments far better than those in the Valley. Most of the black players
who went on to play for the New York Knicks of the 1970s lived in Sugar Hill,
and boxing champion Sugar Ray Robinson owned a popular bar there. The
neighborhood would later become home to Sugar Hill Records, the pioneering
hip-hop and rap music label.

Sugar Hill was also home for Bill Chamberlain, who would follow Scott to
the University of North Carolina as the second black scholarship basketball
player. The big difference was that during the week, Chamberlain's family, who
owned and managed real estate on Sugar Hill, sent their son to an integrated
high school on Long Island, where he saw an even wider range of possibilities.

That was not where Charlie Scott lived, however. "The Valley was much
poorer than Sugar Hill," Chamberlain said. "Charlie's parents were not wealthy.
He did not have an easy childhood."

Scott's parents had separated when he was eleven, and he lived in the
St. Nicholas Projects[1] with his alcoholic father, a cab driver whose drinking
would cost him his job and his life. His mother, Louise, a strong-willed matriarch, tried to hold together the family—three older sisters and Charlie, whom
she called "Charles" from almost the day he was born. From his mother, Scott
received mixed messages about commitment and loyalty, which Louise
demanded but could not follow when she split with her husband and married
another man.[2] Scott couldn't have known how symbolic a summer it would be
for a lonely kid who some day would break one of the most publicized racial
barriers in North Carolina history. But while Middle-American Yankees slug-
gers Roger Maris and Mickey Mantle embarked on their personal and epic
home-run derby, another sort of history was in motion. The first Freedom
Riders bravely boarded buses in Washington, D.C., on May 4, 1961, to test two
federal laws banning segregated public bus travel. Aboard the buses, which
stopped in Greensboro and Charlotte before being blocked and attacked in
Alabama by armed Klansmen, was James Farmer, a founder of CORE (Congress for Racial Equality), who would spend time in a Chapel Hill on the brink
of violence in 1963 and 1964 when the civil rights movement was in full swing.

But Charlie Scott knew mostly about sports. Harlem hatched a generation of African American athletes who played basketball because asphalt courts were more plentiful than football fields and baseball diamonds. Basketball became the new Harlem Renaissance, succeeding the music and arts explosion before the Great Depression. It was seen as a new way for kids to escape to a better life.

In 1961, Scott was approaching six feet tall and loved baseball best, but couldn't find enough kids to throw and catch and play stickball with. So he watched more basketball than he played that summer, wowed by the unsupervised pickup games among bigger, taller, and older guys on the Battleground courts at 140th and Lenox Avenue (today named Fred Samuel Playground). One player who started showing up was Lew Alcindor (later Kareem Abdul-Jabbar). A year older and almost a foot taller than Scott, Alcindor was a quiet, intelligent giant who went on to become the all-time leading high school scorer in New York City at Power Memorial; he would be nicknamed the "Tower of Power."

Among those local legends of their time, none was bigger than Earl "The Goat" Manigault, a six foot one guard with a fifty-inch vertical leap who would serve as an inspiration to many, even as he failed to ever play big-time basketball. Four years older than Scott, the Goat had been expelled from basketball powerhouse Benjamin Franklin High School for smoking marijuana.[3] He had disappeared from New York when word came back he was averaging thirty-one points and thirteen rebounds a game at a place called Laurinburg Institute; the school was thought to be in either North Carolina or South Carolina, no one was quite sure. Manigault would go on to all-black Johnson C. Smith University in Charlotte, but he washed out after one year of arguing with his coaches, returning to the city in 1967 to reclaim the mantle of schoolyard legend.

Scott had no idea how good a basketball player he could become, but in those early days, he had raised his expectations of a life that could go beyond Harlem, perhaps entering the armed services after graduating from high school. Then, with an inner drive he never could quite explain, his goals grew to be the first member of his family to attend college. Pushed by a junior high school teacher who apparently saw something in the shy youngster, Scott prepared for the Specialized High Schools Admission (SHSA) test that could get him into prestigious Peter Stuyvesant, one of nine high schools in New York City that offered tuition-free accelerated academics to city residents.

Scott credits the teacher he knew as Mrs. Jarrett for building some early study habits that helped him become one of eight hundred qualifiers among the more than twenty thousand eighth- and ninth-graders who took the test, giving him a spot at Stuyvesant. Once he was accepted, he knew he could also qualify for college. But which one? How would he get there? And how to pay for it? "If I wanted to go to college, it would have to be on a scholarship," Scott recalled years later. "We were poor. My parents could not afford to send me to college."

Scott said, "Basically from the time I was eleven, I took care of myself."[4] He clearly remembers being different from the kids who worshiped the streets and never wanted to leave the playground scene. He practiced intensely, often by himself, but always looking for a game, whether three-on-three or full-court, five-on-five. And he began to develop a tough, cocky playing persona that was common among the other recognized playground stars in Harlem. That attitude, seen by some as arrogant, would follow him his entire basketball career and offer a sort of safety net he could hide behind. He loved to watch Elgin Baylor on television, patenting his moves after the Lakers' star whose team had just moved from Minneapolis to Los Angeles. Baylor seemed to spend more time in the air than on the floor and inspired Scott to do the same. Scott eventually aggravated below-the-rim players with his jumping ability and hang time, as well as his blistering end-to-end speed.

In 1962, the summer before ninth grade, Scott joined a team with Alcindor, who eventually left New York City for UCLA, and his Power Memorial teammate Norwood Todman, who would go on to break the color barrier at Wake Forest, Al Hayes (Providence), and Larry Newbold (Long Island University) as five college-bound starters. "We entered some tournament and thought we'd breeze through it," Scott said of his first motivational lesson on the court. "What happened? We got kicked by a team from Brooklyn."

Scott enrolled at Stuyvesant for the ninth grade, catching a train from the 125th Street station down to City Hall and walking four blocks to his new school on Chambers Street. He continued to play well in AAU (Amateur Athletic Union) ball, which further nourished his thought of fleeing New York for another world. "I began to believe that basketball was going to be the means for me to go to college," he recalled. Scott also dreamed of playing in the Rucker League, which was started as a youth program by neighborhood parks hero Holcomb Rucker, and the famous summer tournament at Rucker Park on 155th across from the old Polo Grounds in Harlem. Hotshots from all over the country stirred up the crowd that packed the park for the Rucker, while fans who couldn't get in climbed trees or watched from rooftops. Pro stars and schoolyard legends played a brand of ball labeled by Alcindor as "flair and showmanship" that featured slam dunks, crossover dribbling, and behind-the-back passing not yet part of the college or NBA game.

Known as "Scotty" around Harlem, Scott was recruited to play all over the city for the best teams, including St. Joe's, which had the nicest uniforms and enough money for the coach to take the guys out to eat after they won. But Scotty never knew who would be playing with or against him from game to game. He watched kids come and go, and learned some New York City playground regulars were leaving to get a diploma and a college basketball scholarship elsewhere. His new goal crystallized.

The first person Scott knew well who left for Laurinburg Institute was John Barlow, who went on to play at Kentucky State in 1965 for John McLendon, an early disciple of James Naismith and the former coach at North Carolina College for Negroes (now North Carolina Central) in Durham, North Carolina. In 1944, McLendon had organized and won (88–44) the first integrated basketball game known in the South when his team secretly played against a team of white medical students from Duke; he later won three consecutive NAIA (National Association of Intercollegiate Athletics) championships at Tennessee State. Dexter Westbrook, another player Scott had watched in awe, also left for Laurinburg and then headed for Providence College on a full scholarship. Westbrook followed Boston schoolyard star Jimmy Walker, whom Scott had seen tear up the Rucker Tournament one summer. Walker had also signed with Providence, one of dozens of players Laurinburg sent on to, and graduated from, Division I colleges.

Scott was building his own brash reputation in AAU ball, having grown to a sinewy six foot three with close-cropped hair and showing off the speed and high rises that now had people talking about him. He played in the Rucker League in 1963, his last full summer in New York, but returned during and after college to fulfill his other dream of starring in the Rucker Tournament, where he became one of the Elite 24 Rucker Park Legends along with Walker, Connie Hawkins, Abdul-Jabbar, Julius Erving, Tiny Archibald, and Earl "The Pearl" Monroe, to name a few.[5] "Charlie was the most spectacular player I saw in the Rucker," said Erving, the man later known as Dr. J. "He never failed to amaze me, and no one could stop him. The only person I could compare him to was Pete Maravich."[6]

Scott had asked his AAU coaches and the men who ran the playgrounds about Laurinburg and learned that Boston Celtics shooting star Sam Jones, still banking them in for the perennial NBA champions, graduated from there and went on to the same North Carolina College where McLendon had coached. They wanted to know whether Scott had ever heard of Dizzy Gillespie, the jazz legend. Scott nodded. They told him that Dizzy went to Laurinburg, too.

The Oak Hill Academy of that era, Laurinburg was a basketball and prep school that took African American youngsters from all over the country on full and partial scholarships and educated them enough to qualify for college. Scott decided that if he went there to play ball, he could earn an athletic scholarship to a basketball school. His class rank at Stuyvesant and his SHSA test score meant he could get in almost anywhere.

Scott asked the coaches whether they knew anyone at Laurinburg Institute. One of them said the headmaster and basketball coach was Frank McDuffie, who basically ran the boarding school, which was close to the South Carolina state line. Eventually, Scott asked his coaches to write letters of recommendation, which he would include with the transcript of his freshman year at Stuyvesant when he personally mailed it off to Laurinburg.

Scott was streetwise and savvy, and not afraid to go to the South, a place that could be intimidating for a young black boy, especially one on his own. "I was already taking care of myself," Scott said, referring to the lack of support from his alcoholic father. "All the decisions that were made were made by me. It was my decision to apply to Laurinburg."

That independence eventually led Scott to believe he could handle being the first black basketball star at a predominantly white southern university. It also led to a self-reliance that could make it difficult for Scott to simply fit into a new environment.

While most of his playground heroes chose colleges in the North that were already integrated, and from where they could more easily spend summers in the Rucker League and Tournament, Scott found all the attention from a few southern schools alluring; they somehow made him feel special. It was the kind of attention he never felt in his broken home, where he lived in what he called "survival mode." This ability to build a shell around himself and subsist would come in handy soon enough.

Dean Smith was also in transition late in the summer of 1961. As third-year assistant to UNC head basketball coach Frank McGuire, Smith had contemplated going with McGuire to coach Wilt Chamberlain and the Philadelphia Warriors of the NBA. The North Carolina program was coming off an NCAA probation that had kept the Tar Heels out of the 1961 NCAA Tournament. It was a hard fall for a program only four years removed from "McGuire's Miracle," an undefeated team that thrilled a basketball-crazed state and won the 1957 national championship by defeating Michigan State and Kansas on consecutive nights in triple overtime.

McGuire's swashbuckling style and "us against the world" attitude had made his previous four UNC teams seem like playground toughies, involved in stare-downs and push-offs that occasionally led to fisticuffs and, on two occasions, all-out brawls at Wake Forest and Duke. Those were the days that "PC" meant "privileged character," and McGuire's men often acted and played the part. The fact they were mostly northerners invading the South gave them little quarter with many fans when trouble broke out. And the worst crowds, those at Clemson and the University of South Carolina in particular, did more than hurl insults. Sometimes it was, literally, a rotten apple; other times it was a "hot penny" scorched by a match or cigarette lighter.

Straight-arrow Smith was definitely the anti-McGuire, hired for his knowledge of the game learned from his father, a high school teacher and coach, and his college coach at Kansas, Phog Allen. Smith ran practices while McGuire went off recruiting; he emphasized passing and defensive drills, which the players hated, giving Smith the reputation of a much tougher coach than his far more colorful boss, who mostly let them scrimmage while McGuire sat in the bleachers with his cronies yelling criticism through a megaphone. Smith knew he wanted to do it differently, although from McGuire he learned how to dress stylishly, bait officials without raising his voice, and win over sportswriters by complimenting their stories.

Smith had met McGuire for an informal job interview at the 1957 Final Four in Kansas City, where McGuire cracked, "Whoever heard of someone *named* Dean?"[7] Smith admitted, albeit sheepishly, to be favoring his alma mater against McGuire's unbeaten and top-ranked, yet underdog Tar Heels. Thinking he might have blown the chance to eventually join McGuire's staff, the twenty-six-year-old Smith called his father, Alfred, back in Topeka, who said McGuire was more likely to have been impressed by his honesty of the moment and loyalty to his school. Alfred Smith, who had retired from a renowned high school coaching career of his own, was right on both counts.

A captain in the Air Force reserves after joining the ROTC (Reserve Officers Training Corps) at the University of Kansas (KU), the younger Smith was a player-coach for a service team in Germany that won the European championship; he served his last two years of active duty in Colorado Springs at the Air Force Academy as the golf coach and assistant to head basketball coach Bob Spear. When Smith was discharged in the spring of 1958 and had the opportunity to return to his alma mater and assist new head coach Dick Harp, Spear suggested he instead accept McGuire's offer to experience a new part of the country, another university, and a different way of coaching than

Smith had learned from Spear and the legendary Allen, for whom he mostly rode the bench at KU and studied Allen's strategies.

"Bob Spear is the reason I am at North Carolina," Smith said in 1995 while attending his mentor's funeral in Colorado Springs. Smith had visited Chapel Hill once the summer after his discharge from the Air Force to formally interview with McGuire and search for a home that his wife, Ann (the KU coed he had met his senior year), might like if they made the move. Smith fell in love with the town—with the magnolias in bloom, the sand sidewalks, and the seeming gentility of a southern college campus.

Smith and McGuire spent time together on the decisive visit, playing handball and golf, talking basketball, life, and religion. Smith considered himself an American Baptist, having grown up attending church at least twice a week as a child in Emporia and Topeka, Kansas; by his high school days, Smith's Wednesday churchgoing gave way to playing football, basketball, and baseball for Topeka High School.

The longtime connection between the universities of Kansas and North Carolina actually began when Smith was a reserve junior guard for the 1952 Jayhawks. That squad defeated McGuire's last St. John's team for the national championship in Seattle. After that game, UNC named McGuire its head coach, replacing Tom Scott, whose program had fallen into mediocrity and well behind the juggernaut built by Everett Case at North Carolina State, a few miles away in Raleigh. McGuire endeared himself to the frustrated Tar Heels fans by snapping a fifteen-game losing streak to the hated Wolfpack, although he did lose six straight and eight of the next ten to Case's teams led by Mel Thompson, Vic Molodet, and the towering Coloradan, Ronnie Shavlik.

Smith's Chapel Hill odyssey started thirteen months after McGuire's Miracle, when he and his wife moved from Aurora, Colorado, with two baby daughters and an infant son. He replaced ailing and alcoholic assistant Buck Freeman, who had been McGuire's coach at St. John's and his sage ever since. Smith took his place on the bench alongside McGuire, as Freeman had for the previous six seasons, keeping a pencil and pad in hand to record data.

The Chapel Hill Smith and his young family settled into had been in transition for decades but was seemingly dealing with the changes like the gentle breezes of summer. To many, it remained a sleepy village coined the "Southern Part of Heaven" by author William Meade Prince in 1950, when few roads were paved and Franklin Street still had mostly sand sidewalks. Because it was home to a state university with a celebrated liberal arts program, the town had become a haven for writers and artists—with a population of 1,500 in the

1920s that nearly doubled by 1940.[8] The 2,155 citizens older than twenty-five had an average of 13.7 years of education, compared with 12.5 years in Palo Alto and 12.3 years in Berkeley, California.[9] The town's population tripled to almost 10,000 residents by the 1950s,[10] expanded and enlivened by the return of 4,500 World War II veterans who received ninety dollars a month on the GI Bill to study, and sometimes to play varsity football, basketball, or baseball.

On the surface, Chapel Hill was idyllic, with large colonial homes bordering Franklin Street as it wound up to and through the village to the site that gave the town its name—a chapel on a hill that had long ago been replaced by the Carolina Inn. Officially chartered as a township in 1851, with its main drag named for Benjamin Franklin, Chapel Hill was a place where most everyone knew their neighbors. The more-established writers, poets, and painters clustered around Davie Circle. Meanwhile, the "starving artists" chose the Carrboro communes of mill houses and bungalows, where actual members of the Communist Party would come to live, holding meetings that were a threat to some but regarded as abject nonsense by most.

The mayor in the 1940s was R. W. Madry, and the first Town Council was organized in 1941 to upgrade run-down neighborhoods without losing the charm of the village (a quest that still exists today). In 1942, Madry participated in the opening ceremonies of the Carolina Theater, which had 1,141 seats. Without a balcony or other provision for segregated admission, however, the Carolina was not designed for the community's African American moviegoers. It remained that way for seventeen years until the 1959 film *Porgy and Bess* with an all-black cast played at the Carolina and drew one of the first protests in Chapel Hill by both blacks and whites. E. C. Smith, the theater's owner, ultimately allowed nineteen black UNC students into one showing. Not long after, Smith opened the Hollywood Theater in Carrboro for minority patrons. In 1950, the black-owned and operated Majestic opened on West Franklin Street.

Frank Porter Graham, UNC's president beginning in 1930, had a towering reputation despite his height of five foot three. For two decades he was the liberal face of the nation's first state university. His progressive influence was limited, however, because of Jim Crow laws that still segregated Chapel Hill as they did all of North Carolina and the South. Not far beneath the apparently tranquil surface, Chapel Hill was in turmoil. On the liberal left were figures such as "Dr. Frank" and the Reverend Charlie Jones, whose racially mixed ministry at the then-named Chapel Hill Presbyterian Church was radical for the time. But they faced opposition from the long-held convictions of southern segregationists, many of whom were prominent business leaders in the town.

Against this backdrop, in 1952, Frank McGuire was looking to leave his native New York in the wake of a point-shaving scandal that all but ruined college basketball there. McGuire was also motivated by the arrival of his third child, Frankie, who was born with cerebral palsy. Doctors told McGuire and his wife, Pat, that Frankie should be moved to a healthier climate with round-the-clock care or be institutionalized. Familiar with UNC from having been shipped to the Chapel Hill Navy flight school ten years earlier, McGuire picked the Tar Heels over coaching the Crimson Tide of Alabama. He immediately landed his most important recruit, Lennie Rosenbluth, sent him to prep school, and began laying the tracks for what would be his version of the "underground railroad," running basketball recruits from North to South.

McGuire did not take long to figure out whom he should know in town. For example, when money was needed to build the original St. Thomas More church building on Gimghoul Road, the collections from the relatively few fellow Catholics were made by Bill Carmichael Jr., UNC's comptroller and patriarch of the influential Carmichael family. Carolina's Irish American basketball coach, who recruited mostly Catholic kids from New York, joined Carmichael and helped push the funding over the top. Soon enough, UNC basketball became the "preferred religion" of all sects.

In 1957, McGuire's dream team of New Yorkers captivated Chapel Hill by winning all thirty-two games, including the championship victory over Wilt "The Stilt" Chamberlain in triple overtime. With the game played at Municipal Auditorium in downtown Kansas City, the biased and boisterous home crowd made it seem like a David and Goliath rematch. David won again when Joe Quigg sank two free throws in the final seconds of the third overtime and UNC knocked away the intended pass to Chamberlain as time expired. The final score after fifty-five minutes of play was 54–53.

Largely thanks to a broadcasting entrepreneur named C. D. Chesley, thousands watched a soundless black and white telecast of the Final Four games while listening to the radio call. On the afternoon following the championship victory, Sunday, March 24, a crowd estimated at 10,000 awaited UNC's Eastern Airlines propjet at Raleigh-Durham Airport. The swarms of people crowding the tarmac forced two aborted landings before the aircraft touched down and a throng rushed to carry the players from the stairs of the plane to the station wagons waiting to take them back to Chapel Hill.

McGuire had constructed his all-white powerhouse behind Rosenbluth, an All-American Jewish forward, and four Catholic fellow starters, Pete Brennan, Bobby Cunningham, Tommy Kearns, and Quigg, all five from New York or New Jersey. McGuire's teams, and other successful athletic programs, were among a variety of factors masking uneasy race relations bubbling beneath the surface in Chapel Hill and other southern towns such as Tuscaloosa, Oxford, Knoxville, Lexington, and Athens.

Upon his arrival, within the confines of the university and his wider points of contact in the community, it would make sense that Smith did not immediately notice these tensions. Time away from work for a young assistant was scarce. On Sunday mornings, when he and his young family went off to worship, their early experience likely recalled their midwestern roots, with church bells ringing and people strolling to the congregation of their choice.

The influence of church remained deep in Smith's soul. His father, Alfred, was a deacon in his home church, and his mother, Vesta, was a guidance counselor who taught Sunday school and played the church organ. The Baptist congregations of Smith's youth were inclusive and tended to be more progressive in an otherwise conservative state. This religious environment complemented Dean's time around the kitchen table, where he had grown up listening to the emotional accounts of how his father integrated high school basketball in Kansas at great peril to his job security and his family's safety.

The Baptist tradition in North Carolina was different from that in Kansas. Nevertheless, while meeting various members of the UNC administration and faculty, Smith was told by Baptist student chaplain Jim Cansler about a new liberal congregation that had organized in Gerrard Hall on campus. Cansler suggested that Smith might like the young pastor they had just hired. The Reverend Robert Seymour, then in his early thirties, had gone from a liberal congregation at Myers Park Baptist Church in Charlotte, to poverty-stricken Warrenton, North Carolina, where he caused an uproar by urging the all-white police force to hire a black officer in a town that was 60 percent black. From Warrenton, Seymour had moved to Mars Hill College in western North Carolina, which was so conservative that hardly anyone noticed Seymour's liberal-tinged sermons. Seymour was relocating in a place where everyone would notice everything he did.

Choice of church in Chapel Hill was as much a conflict of subcultures as race and social strata. Sermons from the pulpit and sentiments of the congregations stirred an undercurrent in a town of assorted ideologies and long-held prejudice. Most congregations, like schools and neighborhoods, were segregated. Black churches on the outskirts of town were supported by clapboard frames and simple columns, unlike the in-town churches with towering steeples and austere bases of brick and stone. Those characteristics exemplified the differences and relative dangers that separated the lives of their respective parishioners.

Seymour would not be taking over the town's first racially inclusive ministry. That distinction belonged to the Reverend Jones, whose Presbyterian congregation on East Franklin Street had added to the drumbeat for change for more than twelve years. An upheaval was coming between those born into a segregated South with little freedom of choice and a minority of whites like Jones whose native southern ancestors grew up questioning the separate-but-equal doctrines of an 1896 Supreme Court decision and became activists of their time.

It's hard to imagine Carolina basketball and Chapel Hill if Dean Smith had never come, or if he had turned down the head coaching job after the UNC program suffered what looked like a catastrophe. Despite McGuire's Miracle, football was still king in many ways, generating more revenue and garnering bigger newspaper headlines. Football coach Jim Tatum, the former Tar Heels two-way tackle who had won the 1953 national championship as coach at Maryland and returned three years later for his second stint coaching UNC, held sway over an entire corridor of offices for his assistants at Woollen Gym. Meanwhile, the basketball suite was a converted two-room ticket office at the front of Woollen, looking out onto Raleigh Street. Office space aside, McGuire operated much like Tatum, with friends all over town who told him and Freeman where their players were hanging out and what they were doing.

Tatum and McGuire were both type-A personalities whose egos clashed repeatedly. That came to a stunning end, however, when Tatum was bitten by a tick during the summer of 1959 and died from a form of Rocky Mountain spotted fever. Their last disagreement was over the starting salary of McGuire's new assistant coach. "Frank offered me $7,500 a year and I accepted," Smith wrote in his 1999 autobiography *A Coach's Life*.

> The money was of little consequence to me; I would have taken the job for $4,000 a year. What I didn't know was that Frank had to get the salary approved by the administration. . . . Basketball wasn't yet a big

revenue producer, and most programs had to skimp to make ends
meet, so head coaches could afford only one assistant. When Tatum
heard what McGuire had offered me, he protested to (Athletic
Director Chuck) Erickson, "You can't pay him that much because
it will mess up the pay scale on my staff."

In those days there tended to be a bias toward football because
most athletic directors had come out of that sport, and it received
more attention in the sports pages. Feeling certain that Erickson
would side with Tatum, McGuire circumvented them both by going
straight to the top, to William Aycock, the dynamic university
chancellor.[11]

Smith got the salary McGuire offered but later learned that Dr. Chris Fordham had come to UNC the same summer as a faculty member in the medical
school and was also paid $7,500. "There was something inherently wrong that a
young doctor and a young assistant basketball coach could arrive at the same
time at the same university and make identical salaries," Smith wrote in his
book of the late Fordham, who became dean of the UNC School of Medi-
cine and later the university's chancellor. Fordham Boulevard, a five-mile
stretch of the main bypass around Chapel Hill, is named for him.

As golf buddies and power brokers, Smith and Fordham turned out to be
giants in Chapel Hill in the 1980s; indeed, they launched the building of the
biggest on-campus basketball arena in the country from private funds and
fussed over what to name the 22,000-seat Teflon-domed octagon. By then, the
town was fully desegregated and far more deserving of its reputation as a liberal
bastion.

After climbing to the top of the mountain, McGuire's program suffered three
seasons of slippage from colorful to controversial, despite the Tar Heels' first-
place finishes in the then–eight school Atlantic Coast Conference (ACC)
each year.

William Aycock was a law professor forced to use his legal training to try
to keep McGuire out of hot water with the ACC as well as the NCAA. The
NCAA had been founded by President Theodore Roosevelt in 1906 over concerns of professionalism in collegiate sport. The organization's scrutiny fell
on McGuire's program for what they called "excessive expenditures." More
simply stated, the NCAA believed he was paying scouts in New York City to
find players for McGuire's "underground railroad" to Chapel Hill.

McGuire stonewalled the first NCAA hearing in the fall of 1960, claiming one of the committee members was an old New York adversary out to get him. When Nicholas McKnight, former dean of students at Columbia, who was on the committee, read that McGuire had spent thirty-five dollars for three dinners in Manhattan, he said, "Coach McGuire . . . I know many good restaurants in New York where I can get an excellent meal for three dollars." McGuire smirked and said, "I wouldn't eat where you eat."[12]

Since McGuire used cash advances from the university and was embarrassed to ask for receipts, he sent Smith to South Building to help put together a defense. Smith produced some paperwork and statements from those on one of the 1957 road trips in question to show that McGuire was really spreading his money around by wining and dining friends, sportswriters, and players' families who were on the bus to games in Charlottesville and College Park. Smith then accompanied Aycock to San Francisco for an NCAA Council hearing to refute the charges. Aycock presented a strong defense to the NCAA, based largely on the research Smith had done. Smith stood by silently and handed Aycock documents to support their case. The Council was impressed and said so. But the infractions committee still hit UNC with a six-month probation and banned the Tar Heels from the 1961 NCAA Tournament that was to begin in six weeks.

McGuire had hoped all the charges would go away or at least be delayed until after the tournament. All-Americans York Larese and Doug Moe were seniors, and McGuire figured this was his best chance for a second national championship. Convinced the antagonist from Columbia had screwed him, a fed-up McGuire decided that his team should also sit out the ACC Tournament and not eliminate any other school with the chance to move on. The Tar Heels' absence from the tournament in Raleigh further rankled Carolina alumni and fans, who at least wanted to see their team compete for the conference title. When Aycock wrote McGuire a letter dated the following April 21, informing the coach that a decision about extending his contract in 1963 would not depend on the number of wins or losses by his team, McGuire was on his way out. Once arguably UNC's most popular and revered employee, McGuire stewed while on vacation in upstate New York and then resigned abruptly the first week in August 1961. He recommended Smith for the job while at the same time telling his assistant to jump the sinking ship with him.

In the meantime, a point-shaving scandal had touched the consolidated university (Tar Heels Moe and Lou Brown had tertiary involvement but avoided charges by agreeing to testify to what they knew), moving UNC system president Bill Friday to abolish the beloved Dixie Classic Christmas tournament in Raleigh and reduce the schedules of both UNC and N.C. State to sixteen regular-season games for 1961–62. Friday also limited the number of recruits the two schools could sign from outside an "ACC area" that stretched only as far north as Maryland. Friday wanted no easy contact for recruits with the point-shaving perpetrators, who were in New York and under federal investigation.

It was obvious that McGuire would advise Smith that the new scheduling restrictions and being locked out of the fertile New York and New Jersey recruiting areas had dug too big of a hole for any incoming coach to fill. It seemed that Friday was de-emphasizing basketball at both state schools, but that was not his intent. He merely wanted order restored.

McGuire expected that Aycock would offer Smith the position because he had quickly elevated assistant Jim Hickey as head football coach when Tatum died two years earlier. Furthermore, Aycock wasn't interested in forming a search committee and kowtowing to fat-cat alumni who were pressuring Chuck Erickson to hire another big-name coach. But as McGuire told the Raleigh *News & Observer,* "I tried to talk [Smith] out of taking the job in the first place because I thought it was going to be impossible to get anything going again after what we'd been through with the point-shaving ordeal."[13]

For his part, Aycock was so impressed with Smith's work ethic during the NCAA investigation that the chancellor had already thought about promoting him if he needed to make a coaching change. "It was during all this that I came to discern that he was a man of great character," Aycock said in a 1995 interview. "He was more like a teacher than one who was solely interested in coaching to get results on the scoreboard. I could see those qualities in him. I knew Coach McGuire would never have brought him here if he hadn't known a lot about basketball, because Frank McGuire wanted someone to do the hard drills. So I knew he knew basketball, and I said to myself that if the occasion should arise, he would make a good head coach for the University of North Carolina."

Fortunately, Aycock meant what he said in the letter to McGuire about wins and losses and reinforced that to Smith when he offered him the head-coaching job the same day McGuire turned in his official resignation. Aycock was far more concerned with the arrogant image the basketball team had developed and a downturn in the academic standing of some players. His job description to Smith was simple: Don't worry about your record, run the program correctly, keep the university out of trouble, and present a model image.

"I will never fire you for losing games," Aycock said, according to Smith, "but if you cheat I will fire you in a minute." Aycock had already handled criticism on athletics. In 1959, he rebuffed three prominent boosters who wanted to fire Erickson over his feud with McGuire. And in 1960, after suspending McGuire's star player Doug Moe for poor academic performance, the chancellor had greeted a group of protesting students at his doorstep and then led them to Gerrard Hall for a question-and-answer session that lasted late into the night. So he was prepared for an uproar over the now-unilateral decision to hire a no-name assistant amidst the fear that UNC basketball had been ruined by the gambling scandal and NCAA probation.

Smith, meanwhile, did not envision himself as an NBA coach, and despite the bleak picture McGuire had painted, believed he could get the program back on track. He had learned to love Chapel Hill, although it was not quite as liberal in thought and action as his first impression led him to believe. On August 3, 1961, thirty-year-old Dean Smith was officially named the University of North Carolina's new basketball coach. Everybody made nice, at least with reporters, the day McGuire resigned and Smith took over. Aycock said that the university "agreed to release McGuire (from the two remaining years on his contract) with regrets but with our deepest good wishes. . . . Coach McGuire has been an outstanding coach in this institution since 1952, and we are most reluctant to lose him."[14] Smith's appointment was big news in North Carolina, but it was buried in the eighth paragraph of the story on McGuire's departure that ran in the New York *Herald-Tribune* on August 4, 1961.

Nearly six decades later, it is difficult to imagine the challenge Smith inherited for likely not much more than the $7,500 he earned as an assistant coach. McGuire was a bigger-than-life character, with the sort of presence that lit up a room. Smith was shorter, quiet, and homely compared to the regal redheaded Irishman—a mild-mannered midwesterner to McGuire's Yankee eminence. Or, as UNC alum Curry Kirkpatrick would eulogize Smith on the *Sports Illustrated* website a few days after his passing in 2015, Smith was "this plain little guy with the needle nose and the twangy voice and the charisma of the Kansas plains (which is to say none)."[15]

At the press conference ushering out McGuire and introducing Smith, the "fighting Irishman" regaled writers in one corner while glancing at his successor and saying: "Poor kid. He's got a tough road ahead."[16] Smith, with his back literally against the wall, answered questions in a matter-of-fact fashion. "Am I the youngest major college basketball coach in the country?" he repeated. "I believe there's a fellow at Iowa just a little younger. I'm actually 30, you know, not 29 like some of the stories said. I guess they picked that figure out of last year's brochure."[17]

Smith said he was "delighted with the opportunity," and while claiming "no one can replace Coach McGuire" called the UNC position "one of the choice coaching jobs in the country for two reasons . . . we have an outstanding academic reputation and Frank McGuire has established an incomparable basketball program as a foundation . . . [but] I realize I have some big shoes to fill."[18]

Despite the praise for his former boss, Smith hinted that McGuire's stand-around zone defense was a thing of the past at Carolina. "A coach can over-coach offense, causing a player to be tight," he said. "You can't over-coach defense."[19]

As would become his modus operandi, Smith revealed little else about himself, but he was prepared for the job more than any outsider could have known. An avid reader since childhood, when his parents left Chip Hilton books on his bedside table, Smith was always learning. His father noticed his imagination and creativity when Dean drew up football plays from an early age. Smith was a born leader, playing quarterback in football, point guard in basketball, and catcher in baseball. He felt compassion as a youngster when his best friend died suddenly from polio. And Spear sold McGuire on Smith's aggressive approach to coaching and recruiting. But Smith had quiet confidence and knew how to keep his mouth shut. Although it was perhaps unapparent at the time, he was extremely competitive in everything he did.

In the days and weeks to come, UNC Sports Information Director Jake Wade mentioned McGuire occasionally in his local notes column. Smith, on the other hand, was pretty much ignored by the North Carolina newspapers. Not once did his name appear in the *Chapel Hill Weekly*, which gave all of its sports ink to Jim Hickey's football team that was coming off a 3–7 season and had not had a winning record since 1958. *Weekly* reporter J. A. C. Dunn had a column entitled "A Talk With . . ." in every issue, with subjects ranging from newsmakers in town to athletic personnel such as assistant athletic director Joe Hilton and Hickey. There was no talk with Dean Smith, however—nary a word or follow-up story on the new head basketball coach.

The snub may have actually given Smith the peace and quiet to reorganize his office and get ready for his trial under fire, which would include escaping his predecessor's considerable shadow. McGuire kept his home in Chapel Hill and commuted to Philadelphia to prepare for coaching Wilt Chamberlain and the Warriors, ducking back into town to have lunch or dinner with friends like local veterinarian Lou Vine and his wife, Florence. In contrast, many considered

Smith the poor sucker left to take over a basketball program that was irreparably damaged by scandal and President Friday's subsequent sanctions.

On December 2, 1961, UNC opened the season under its new basketball coach against Virginia in Woollen Gym, when Smith infamously forgot to bring out the game ball and famously implemented the long-held innovation for Tar Heels, the raised fist as a tired signal. The 80–46 win was the first of what would be his 879 career victories over 36 years.

McGuire eventually moved his family back to New York and then resurfaced at the University of South Carolina. He would be close enough to watch Smith attempt to keep his own job, restore UNC's prowess on the court, and navigate the racial integration of athletics at a school Smith felt was ready for change.

CHAPTER

2

The Truth about Chapel Hill

The University of North Carolina's reputation as a progressive institution origi-nated in many places and was closely linked to Chapel Hill's standing as a liberal college town. Much of this had to do with its leader, Frank Porter Graham, who rose to the university's presidency in 1930 and served for an eventful nineteen years. In 1946, Graham agreed to serve on President Harry Truman's Committee on Civil Rights; later, "Dr. Frank" refused to disavow ties with the Communist Party when his affiliations were questioned by the House Un-American Activities Committee. Although Graham was a regis-tered Republican, his short appointment as a Democratic U.S. Senator during an era of contentious politics (Graham lost his 1950 senatorial race to Willis Smith, backed by supporters including a young political director named Jesse Helms) further branded him as a "flaming liberal."

Graham's own lifestyle offered a lens into the realities of UNC at the time. Hubert Samuel Robinson served as a butler, chauffeur, and gardener in the Graham household for more than fifteen years. Robinson later worked as a custodian at UNC; with Graham's encouragement, he grew active in commu-nity politics and eventually served as the first African American on the Chapel Hill Board of Aldermen from 1953 to 1965. He and his wife, Addie Bell Palmer, raised five children and bequeathed their scrapbooks about their life to the Southern Historical Collection.

The truth is that UNC wasn't making much of an effort to integrate, despite the rumblings of some faculty members. "I remember a conversation I had in the late 40s or early 50s with a fellow member of the physics department," UNC professor Joe Straley said in the 2007 documentary *The Town before Brown*, "and he was going on and on about what a liberal-spirited university this was. And I said, 'But, George, if this is such a liberal place, where are the blacks that might be here?'"

The documentary was produced by UNC education professor Gerald Unks after many of his students expressed disbelief about his description of Chapel Hill in the 1950s. It contends that the effects of segregation in Chapel Hill were softened by the presence of the university and its racially enlightened faculty. That said, while Chapel Hill might have been less hostile toward African Americans than many other southern communities, in reality Jim Crow segregation was a fact of life in the college town. Into the 1950s, most businesses, including nineteen restaurants, allowed no black customers or patrons. "White" and "colored" water fountains and bathrooms were a fixture in town, just as in Mississippi and Alabama, as were segregated waiting rooms at the bus station and doctors' offices. The first two theaters in Chapel Hill were "whites only," forcing blacks to go to movie houses in neighboring Durham, many miles away. In 1952, there were five barbershops, eight beauty shops, two funeral parlors, two cemeteries, four public schools, a bowling alley, one university, and one hospital. All were segregated to one degree or another.[1]

So at its core, exactly what was so "liberal" about Chapel Hill, other than many residents who talked a good game but did not walk the walk, standing on the sidelines and watching mostly blacks and a smattering of white supporters march in the civil rights protests of the early 1960s? Despite widespread debate on desegregation, including dozens of committee meetings and demonstrations that went on through mid-1964, only one Public Accommodations Ordinance ever made it to the six-person Board of Aldermen, which tabled it in June of 1963.

Chapel Hill blacks who bought food in white restaurants had to go around to the back door to pick it up or eat in the kitchen. They could order lemonade at Sutton's Drug on East Franklin Street or a Big "O" at Colonial Drug on West Franklin, two of a half-dozen downtown drugstores, but had to leave the premises after their purchases. Many Chapel Hill clothing stores had segregated dressing areas, and some would not allow blacks to try on clothes in the store before purchase at all. Meanwhile, some business owners who had to earn a living and feed their families feared that serving blacks could drive away their white clientele. They favored local laws that would force their own hand and save their customer base.

"Chapel Hill had an image of being very liberal, outwardly," longtime African American resident, teacher, and former town council member Reginald (R. D.) Smith said in 2007. "But underneath it, it was different."

Much of the liberal image was a fraud because little of what was being argued and proposed about ending segregation resulted in voluntary action. Thus, Graham's most famous quote likened Chapel Hill to a lighthouse that sent its strongest beam into the far distance, but at the base, can be very dark.

During his tenure, "Dr. Frank" had been trapped between his own more progressive beliefs, some of them supported by his faculty, and the state legislature that controlled the purse strings. Although he managed to eliminate segregated water fountains on campus and allowed UNC to be the first southern college to schedule football teams with black players, he was more powerless in a town that hid behind trespass and obstruction laws and ignored blatant racism. "We obeyed the law as it was. I couldn't, as president, lawfully admit Negroes to the university," Graham told UNC Public Television in 1962, long after he had left UNC and North Carolina politics for a position with the United Nations. (Three years later, Graham agreed that a local elementary school could bear his name only if it accepted children of all races and religions. And what became the Frank Porter Graham Bilingüe School in Chapel Hill celebrated its fiftieth anniversary in 2015.) Graham understood that the conservative North Carolina legislature could have cut off funds had the university violated state segregation laws by voluntarily admitting black students.

Fred Battle, a former local high school football star who turned civil rights demonstrator at North Carolina A&T College and later served on the Chapel Hill school board, bit his lip in *The Town before Brown* when he recalled UNC as an "active segregator that didn't live up to its creed and did nothing to help." Battle said he worked an hourly construction job during the summer to stay in shape for football and brought home a bigger weekly paycheck than his father, a janitor at UNC.

Blacks could attend UNC football games as long as they sat in a segregated section behind one of the goalposts. They weren't allowed into Carolina basketball or baseball games since the number of seats was limited. And, of course, all Tar Heels teams were still all white.

Forced integration of UNC began in 1951 when three law students transferred from North Carolina College for Negroes in Durham, which the Supreme Court ruled did not offer the same educational opportunities as the UNC law school.[2] Harvey Beech, the first African American to graduate from UNC, finished law school in 1952 and no white student would walk side by side with him at commencement until the editor of the *Law Review* volunteered.[3] Another graduate was Floyd McKissick, who went on to become a prominent civil rights attorney deeply involved in the Chapel Hill demonstrations that jailed nearly two thousand protestors. McKissick and his fellow black law students lived in a four-bedroom suite in Steele Hall, with the other two rooms left vacant despite a waiting list to get into that dorm.[4]

"There was an honor system in existence then," McKissick said. "No doors were locked, and I didn't lock my doors. I stayed in a cubicle in Steele where the other black students were supposed to stay [but] didn't want to stay at night. So I was alone there. And they (white students) would come in and put a black snake in my drawer, a dead black snake, in my drawer on my shirts. They would put water on your clothes, put a bucket of water over your door to trick you. When you came in, you opened the door, a bucket of water would fall. They had a lot of fun with you. They thought they were having fun. You'd get a letter every day from the Ku Klux Klan telling you that you're at the wrong place and what's going to happen to you."[5]

In 1954, three black male undergraduates from Durham joined the UNC freshman class after a federal court ordered the university to process all applications without regard to race. LeRoy Frasier enrolled with his brother Ralph and John Brandon, and commuted from their homes in Durham; subsequently, they spent one year on the segregated floor of Steele dorm. LeRoy Frasier found the all-white campus somewhat welcoming. He played pickup games at Woollen Gym, which often included members of the UNC basketball team, most of whom were from New York and spent their youth on multiracial playgrounds. Ralph Frasier had a more negative experience, recalling, "the attitude ranged from hostility to what we in modern times call 'benign neglect'—just ignore you, and maybe you'll go away. Well, we didn't."[6] The Frasier brothers did play at the university's Finley Golf Course with black friends from Durham, believed to be the first time the course was integrated.

They all had mostly solo racial experiences before transferring to North Carolina Central and earning their degrees there. Nevertheless, just as Charlie Scott did with scholarship athletes ten years later, they opened the campus to a slow but steady trickle of African American undergraduates. In 1961, David Dansby was the first African American male to earn an undergraduate degree at UNC.[7]

Segregation laws existed in every state of the old Confederacy, including North Carolina, but segregation by social norms was even more of a problem, even at UNC. "Every black employed by the university had either a broom or a shovel," said Dan Pollitt, a liberal law school professor who joined the UNC faculty in 1957. "They were not allowed to be electricians or anything that paid (well). Serfdom is what it looked like and what it was."[8]

When Dean Smith arrived in 1958, as he later described in his 1999 autobiography, he viewed Chapel Hill as "widely recognized as a major liberal voice in the South," perhaps because of Dr. Graham's reputation. It did not take long for Smith to learn that this was not exactly the case under the veneer of his new employer and hometown.

A facade of civility was one reason Chapel Hill's residents liked to differentiate between the town's racial attitudes and those in a more dangerous Deep South, where the 1955 murder of Emmett Till was an especially public example of the brutal violence blacks faced in the region. Some citizens who had not grown up in the South had "open" businesses. Ted Danziger, the son of Jewish immigrants who had escaped Nazi-occupied Austria, served both blacks and whites at his Rathskeller on East Franklin Street and Ranch House on Airport Road. Fewer blacks than whites came in, perhaps because both restaurants had all-black waiters and became wildly popular among white patrons.

Such surface signs of racial harmony or progress may have given Dean Smith some sense of similarity between where he now lived and the Kansas towns where he was born and raised. Smith had played on an integrated football team at Topeka High and complained to Principal Buck Weaver about having segregated basketball teams, with students separated because the school wanted them to hold separate parties after night games. Smith later said he regretted not organizing a boycott of both teams; Topeka integrated its basketball program the year after Smith graduated. (In 2014, on the sixtieth anniversary of *Brown v. Board of Education*, his high school alma mater honored Smith with a plaque for his dedication to civil rights.)

It is easy to see where Smith came by his convictions. His father, Alfred, coached the first integrated high school team in Kansas in 1934 when he refused to cut from his Emporia squad African American Paul Terry, the son of a janitor who swept floors at the local bank. Alfred Smith held firm despite requests from his principal, Rice Brown, and threats from the state's high school athletic association to banish Emporia to independent status. "They drop us and we'll find other schools to play," Alfred Smith told Brown. "Or I'll quit and you can have someone else put Terry off the team." One opponent, Chanute High School, sent a telegram to Brown warning his basketball coach to "leave the Negro boy at home or don't come." Paul Terry made the trip, played, and helped Emporia win a very tough game. Terry played the entire season until the state tournament, when the Kansas High School Athletic Association (KHSAA) ruled it would disqualify Emporia if he suited up with the team.

Sadly, Alfred Smith left Terry home but wrote his name down on the roster given to the scorer before the first game. His highly motivated Emporia team won the 1934 state title, and the elder Smith was still thrown out of the KHSAA at season's end. When Dean was old enough to process that incident, as well as others he witnessed firsthand, it seemed that his father, who was his hero and role model, had won the battle if not the war. The entire Smith family remained close with Terry for the rest of their lives.

Alfred Smith coached several other black athletes in Kansas after Paul Terry, and his son applied some life lessons learned to his own career, especially when he recruited minority athletes. While becoming legendary for treating all of his players equally, young Dean also took something from his mother, Vesta, during one of the dinners she hosted for the players' parents. Vesta made sure Dean's sister Joan sat at the table next to the mother of the only black player on that team, Chick Taylor. "We want to be nice to all the mothers," Vesta Smith said, "but we want to make a special effort to make Mrs. Taylor feel at home."[9] Smith credited such experiences as foundational for his ideas about what a "Carolina family" should mean, and how it should be inclusive.

Smith remained proud that the 1954 landmark Supreme Court ruling to desegregate all public schools began after a black, blue-collar family in Topeka named Brown sued the local Board of Education. Yet he also knew that many states, cities, and towns in the United States were not integrating their public schools with "all deliberate speed" as ordered by the court—or much else, for that matter, when it came to the South.

As Smith acquainted himself with his new hometown, he also found discomfort with the all-white Southern Baptist congregations he and Ann sampled while "shopping around" for a church. Most Southern Baptists shared the conservative identity of the national Southern Baptist Convention. "We were American Baptists," Ann recalled quite clearly, "and we made sure we weren't going to a Southern Baptist Church. We wanted to be around people who felt the same as we did about segregation." Looking back years later, Smith displayed gallows humor to friends when he wondered whether some of the middle-aged white men in the next pews might have traded their Sunday suits for the white robes of the Ku Klux Klan (KKK) the night before. North Carolina had the largest KKK membership of any state in the country by the mid-1960s, although not nearly the highest record of murder and mayhem wielded by Klans of the Deep South.[10]

In those early days, however, Smith had too much work to do to see very far beyond the image of a placid town and rigid university that treated segregation as a way of life and ignored it. Smith took his family to Gerrard Hall in April 1959, the morning First Minister Robert Seymour preached his initial sermon to what would officially become the Olin T. Binkley Memorial Baptist Church a few years later. Binkley was a renowned progressive Baptist preacher who as a young man had taught at UNC while serving as pastor of the Chapel Hill Baptist Church. Seymour welcomed parishioners of all ages, occupations, and races, following the lead of fellow progressives such as the Presbyterian Reverend Charlie Jones, whose liberal leadership of his church extended to informal 11 A.M. services that did not serve communion and featured Jones's preaching on issues affecting the community, including racial ones. Jones also started a discussion group over Sunday morning breakfast between services; some of the students who attended brought friends from neighboring Durham and North Carolina College for Negroes (now North Carolina Central University).

Jones was elected chairman of the Chapel Hill Interracial Committee in 1942 and held membership in the Fellowship of Southern Churchmen, an interdenominational network of black and white Christians across the South. He first drew the town's ire when he invited musicians from the all-black Navy band to bunk in the manse, and the police had to disperse protestors who had gathered outside the church. When Jones bailed out black activist Bayard Rustin and his colleagues on their Journey of Reconciliation to test enforcement of the Supreme Court's ban on segregated bus travel, white cab drivers and residents threatened to burn down the Joneses' house until the police intervened and allowed the demonstrators to get out of town.

On Sunday, July 2, 1944, twenty years to the day before the Civil Rights Act would be signed into law, an incident "crystallized the fears of many in the community that Jones was increasingly oblivious to the sensitivities in the town and treating blacks a little too much like equals."[11] The event in question was a low-key, two-hour picnic at Battle Park between East Franklin Street and Gimghoul Road. It was organized by a group of students who were ardent supporters of the Reverend Jones and believed in his progressive views on social issues, including race. These students had invited four black members of the Navy flight school band. Jones's wife, Dorcas, and their two daughters, Bettie and Virginia, were at the park, while the white and black students met at the church in the mid-afternoon. Joined by two black females and one black male from North Carolina College, the group of twelve walked down Franklin Street. Once they got to the park, they had supper by 6:30 P.M., talked, sang songs, and played charades. Then the bandsmen were driven home to their quarters at what was then referred to as the Negro Community Center in Carrboro.

However, an elderly woman had complained to the university after seeing the integrated group on Franklin Street, and word circulated throughout the town and university. The *Daily Tar Heel* (*DTH*)denounced the "juvenility" of those spreading the "vicious rumors that have run rampant about Chapel Hill during the past two weeks."[12] The incident, regardless of how exaggerated it may have been, further alienated the progressives from the proponents of the status quo. In response, Jones and three other like-minded ministers wrote a letter to the *Chapel Hill Weekly*: "In view of the misunderstood intentions and erroneous reports of Christian inter-racial activities in our community, we . . . desire to make the following statement: It is a fundamental principle of Christian progress that the spiritual growth and the social well-being of a community are the result of group co-operation and individual initiative. The following statement is the reasoned opinion of the ministers whose names appear below, with the understanding that each in his own way is free to carry out the spirit and intent of the declaration."[13]

After ten years of infighting within the Orange Presbytery between those who questioned Jones's interpretations of Christ and the Bible and those who agreed with his belief that Jesus wanted all races and religions to have their place in society, Jones was ousted in 1952. He served for ten years as pastor at the Chapel Hill Community Church, after which he and his family returned to his childhood home in the mountains of Tennessee.

Nearly twenty years later, the racial divide remained pronounced in Chapel Hill. Black neighborhoods were clustered at the "West End" of town from Cameron Avenue to "Tin Tops" (because all those roofs were made of tin). Northside was perhaps the closest-knit community, according to Velma Louise Perry, who grew up there and became a civil rights activist during her four decades of working as a maid at the Carolina Inn. "We had a neighborhood," Perry recalled in 2010. "Every child was answerable to the other adults. Neighbors looked after you and told your mom. Families looked after you, and if you were sick, they helped you."[14] The neighborhoods were within walking distance of the all-black First Baptist and St. Joseph C.M.E. churches and the Hargraves recreation center on Roberson Street, off West Rosemary. These buildings became the primary locations for civil rights meetings and starting points for marches and sit-ins.

Some black families might have seemed content with their rundown rental houses and apartments, owned mostly by white slumlords, and low-wage jobs

as domestics in private homes, janitors at the university, cooks at local restaurants and Greek houses on campus, and laborers at Carr Mill and sawmill
plants outside of town. Descendants say they merely "settled" for their lot—a
place to live and work and play around family and friends. That was not the
case with Mildred Council, however, who first cooked at the Carolina Inn
and several fraternity and sorority houses and became well known by whites
all over town and campus. Years later, she worked in a restaurant that was
eventually given to her by the owner. Council turned it into the original Mama
Dip's Country Kitchen. Hers was also the first fully integrated business in
Chapel Hill because so many black and white people had already eaten Mildred's fried chicken, mashed potatoes, and collard greens, and flocked there.
She recognized almost every face that walked in the door and welcomed
everybody.

"We were very poor, but it doesn't mean we weren't happy," DeLayne
Burnett Ingram, who was raised with seven siblings in "Tin Tops," recalled in
2014. "When you are born into this situation, you just settle. We didn't dream
that it could be any different . . . until Martin Luther King woke us up."

Dr. King spoke in Chapel Hill on May 9, 1960, to standing-room-only
audiences at the responsive Hargraves Center and later Hill Hall on campus,
where some of the students came to jeer a man they regarded as a trouble-
maker bent on ending the status quo of segregation. King's visit had been
approved by Chancellor Bill Aycock as the civil rights movement was just getting started, and according to Seymour, "before the evening was over (King)
had everyone listening intently and succeeded in disarming even the most
belligerent questioners."[15]

North Carolina's "separate but equal" statute 115-2 remained long after the
Brown v. Board decision, and the desegregation of Chapel Hill public schools
did not start in earnest until 1964, ten years later. "You could be separate but, if
so, had to be equal, and that became a myth," Pollitt said. "They were always
separate but never equal." Lincoln, the black high school on Merritt Mill Road,
had hard-working teachers who relied on their PTA to help buy sorely needed
supplies and equipment. Lincoln offered a mediocre education, fielded great
athletic teams, and played remarkable music first inspired by the all-black
Navy band living in the recreation building on Roberson Street off West
Rosemary in the 1940s. Chapel Hill High was on West Franklin on the site
of what became University Square and Granville Towers and was among the
most prestigious schools in the state, attended by hundreds of white UNC

faculty children who almost all qualified for college. It also offered technical courses for students who wanted to learn a trade and go right to work.

"I lived on Hillsborough Street, near Bette Smith and the Danzigers, in a somewhat integrated neighborhood," Fred Battle said, "and it was nothing for whites and blacks to play together. The worst part about it, for me, was every day I had to walk past Chapel Hill High School on my way to Lincoln at the other end of town."

Segregation was still very much the mind-set of the Chapel Hill that Dean Smith and Bob Seymour now called home. At his first visit to Seymour's congregation, Smith noticed a black student, UNC freshman George Grigsby, one of thirty-one African American undergraduates at Carolina in 1959.[16] Grigsby had just joined the church and sat with several white students who Seymour said seemed happy, if not proud, to be there. Seymour called the *Durham Morning Herald* when five months later it ran a story under the head-line "Negro Joins White Church." Seymour asked the editor if he usually gave dated news such prominent exposure.

Keen on sizing up people, Smith saw something in Seymour's congrega-tion that he hadn't seen in any other churches he had visited. A southerner, reared in Greenwood, South Carolina, Seymour had served in the Navy, earned a divinity degree from Duke (after three years at Yale), and a Ph.D. from the University of Edinburgh, after which he and two classmates took a three-month road trip to Jerusalem, following the route of the Apostle Fathers.

Seymour knew nothing about the young man who had entered his make-shift parish with his wife and three small children. "I had no idea who Dean Smith was," Seymour recalled. "No one did. But he became very active in our church ministry and agreed to be the chairperson of our student affairs com-mittee." In one of their many conversations that almost never included basket-ball, the kindred spirits learned about childhood mottos taught in each of their families. Smith grew up hearing that he should "never be proud of doing right, just do it." Seymour's parents raised him to "do right because it is right, not because you are afraid to do wrong."

Seymour's stunning wife, Pearl, played the organ and turned into much more of a basketball fan than her husband did. Bob Seymour had met and married Pearl Francis at Mars Hill, where she was a college music teacher while he built a reputation over his four years there as a liberal pastor, and they had two children. In the summer of 1958, at the urging of Jim Cansler, three men and a woman from what was then called the Chapel Hill Baptist Church had traveled to Mars Hill to recruit the Seymours for a new inclusionary congregation in the home of the nation's first state university.

"We were looking for a minister and everywhere we turned—from the church in Charlotte to the seminary to everybody we asked—the name Robert Seymour kept surfacing," said Bill Moffitt, one of the three in the pulpit committee. "So we went to hear him preach, and then we asked him to come to Chapel Hill. He did and we not only got him, but we got Pearl in the bargain, too. She was the icing on the cake. We got two tremendously talented, devoted people, and we never looked back."[17]

Seymour knew it would be challenging, but he jumped at the offer to take over "a fledgling fellowship of just over forty persons who had pooled their limited resources to purchase a parsonage and a piano."[18] "For me it was a unique and wonderful opportunity to be the first pastor at a new Baptist church in a university town," Seymour said in a 2014 interview. "So we could move in new directions for Baptists. And exercise one of the tenets of Baptist ecclesiology; that is, fulfill its autonomy as a local church to do as it chooses."

So many UNC faculty and students were going to Gerrard Hall that the nearby Chapel Hill Baptist Church held an emergency meeting and changed its name to University Baptist Church. "They were afraid we were going to take that name," Seymour recounted repeatedly over the years, usually with a smile.

By the spring of 1959, Smith was teaching a Sunday school class at Binkley and Seymour was well aware of the influence basketball played on the town of Chapel Hill and across the state, for that matter. The story of how Seymour, Smith, and a young theology student integrated The Pines restaurant has been recounted many times, often inaccurately and, in retrospect, in a way that was somewhat overblown. Some published reports have the episode occurring after Smith had become head coach. One story said the black theology student was James Forbes, who went on to become a minister at the prestigious Riverside Church in New York City. Forbes, then a senior seminary student, did visit Chapel Hill in 1962 as part of the controversial Summer Interracial Ministry. While a *Fayetteville Observer* story reported that Forbes was the first black customer to eat at The Pines, Forbes himself says in the article he has no memory of it. That's because it actually took place in 1959 when Smith was still an assistant coach to Frank McGuire and a theology summer school student, not Forbes, joined Seymour and Smith. Seymour felt it was long overdue in Chapel Hill, and bringing Smith along checkmated The Pines' managers,

Agnes and Leroy Merritt, since they knew Smith as McGuire's assistant and did not want to lose the business of the basketball team, which ate most of its pregame meals there. "If you come with us, I am certain they will serve us," Seymour told Smith.

Smith remained embarrassed that people made so much of what was a one-time demonstration. "Years afterwards, some reports have made it sound like I personally integrated every restaurant in Chapel Hill!" Smith wrote in his autobiography, *A Coach's Life.* "The truth is, I was just an assistant coach, and hardly the most influential person in town. . . . But Bob knew that I knew the management and that they valued the business of the basketball team."[19]

That may have been the reason Seymour's group was served, and while it was a bold gesture intended to open up other segregated businesses, it failed in that regard. At least three incidents have been documented of demonstrations in 1963 and early 1964 at The Pines when the restaurant remained segregated.[20] After one sit-in there in December of 1963, a black visitor from New York, David McReynolds, spent the night in jail and went home to write an article in *The Village Voice* entitled "A New Kind of Christmas in Chapel Hill." In the account, he called the town "smug and self-righteous and so proud of the past that it . . . is now fearfully close to being morally bankrupt."[21]

Nevertheless, the pieces were forming to help push Chapel Hill away from that past and toward compliance with the forthcoming Civil Rights Act, federal public accommodations laws, and eventually, full desegregation of the public schools and the University of North Carolina. And soon enough would come an attempt to break down the color barrier on its highest-profile athletic team. As a young coach who did not want to lose his job, Smith often let Seymour do his talking from the liberal pulpit and to the man on the street. However, integrating the UNC basketball program and UNC athletics—that was where Smith could make a difference.

Before Smith's first season as head coach (1961–62), UNC president Bill Friday had discontinued the Dixie Classic and limited UNC's schedule to sixteen games before the ACC Tournament. The loss of York Larese and Doug Moe, and several players who did not return after McGuire resigned, plus injuries, resulted in an 8–8 overall record that was the first indication of Smith's coaching ability, according to his junior point guard Larry Brown. "We were awful, but he kept us in every game," Brown said. "He kept working and never quit." The Tar Heels lost their opening game of the ACC Tournament to South Carolina, 57–55, ending Smith's only losing season.

With spectacular freshman forward Billy Cunningham, who was recruited by McGuire but chose to stay, moving up to the varsity to join Brown, Smith's second team figured to be stronger. His parallel path remained to add a black player to the program. "On the very day I was named head coach," Smith wrote in *A Coach's Life*, "Bob Seymour called me. His first question was about recruiting a black player."[22] This had not been their first such conversation, as Seymour considered it to be part of Smith's church ministry work. Smith had even discussed it with McGuire, who coached black players at St. John's and said during his first year in Chapel Hill that he tried to recruit Wilt Chamberlain out of Overbrook High School in Philadelphia. Chamberlain did not have the grades and test scores to be admitted among UNC's very few applications from black students and instead went to Kansas.

During the 1962 season, Smith had received two phone calls from acquaintances who believed they had identified the first black basketball player for Carolina. Frank McDuffie, the headmaster and coach at Laurinburg Institute who would be a key figure in the recruitment of Charlie Scott, claimed he had three players who were already better than anyone on the UNC varsity team. One of them was Jimmy Walker, whom Scott had watched on the playgrounds of New York. After seeing their transcripts and test scores, Smith notified McDuffie that none could qualify for UNC. Walker went on to be an All-American at Providence College, an NBA star, and eventually the estranged father of Michigan Fab Fiver Jalen Rose.

Later in the 1962 season, Greensboro attorney Willie Holderness, a member of the founding family of Jefferson Standard Life Insurance Co., called Smith and said he and his brother, Chick, an executive with the insurance company, wanted to send a senior at black Dudley High School to UNC on a Jefferson Standard Scholarship. The young man's name was Lou Hudson, the star of Dudley's team and ranked third in a class of more than three hundred students. The Holderness brothers aimed to circumvent the ACC's required SAT score for an athletic scholarship by paying for his college education.

Smith had heard of the six foot five Hudson and was convinced he could play for the Tar Heels, if admitted to UNC. And he knew Hudson had made the ACC minimum of 750 on his SATs, but apparently that was not high enough to meet UNC's requirements. As a first-year head coach, Smith had little influence with the admissions office. In the spring of 1962, UNC had fifty-four black undergraduates, according to the enrollment statistics in the UNC Archives. "He (Hudson) seemed like the perfect student-athlete for

Carolina, exactly what we were looking for. That was just one of the many instances over the years when I would disagree with standardized tests as a measure of classroom aptitude," Smith wrote in his book, calling such tests culturally, as well as racially, biased against students who tested poorly due to inferior elementary and secondary educations. Hudson instead went to Minnesota in the already integrated Big 10, where he was an All-American and graduated. Hudson was the fourth pick in the 1966 NBA draft; he was selected by the St. Louis Hawks and was a six-time All-Star after the team moved to Atlanta.

Through Frank McDuffie, Smith got to know Harvey Reid, the coach at Elm City High School in Eastern North Carolina. McDuffie and Reid attended Carolina games and loved the fast-paced play of the Tar Heels under Smith. Frustrated over not being able to get Hudson, Smith called Reid and asked him to "be on the lookout for a good student and good player, because we want to do something."[23] After watching eight-millimeter film of Elm City junior Willie Cooper and seeing his academic record, and eventually his SAT score, Smith decided to invite Cooper out for the freshman team if he gained admittance.

UNC accepted Cooper the following year, and he played for the 1965 freshmen with Larry Miller, Smith's marquee recruit whom he had taken away from Duke. Miller dominated the ball and the play, but Cooper was talented and unselfish enough that Smith and Assistant Coach Ken Rosemond asked him to walk on to the varsity team the next season. During the first week of practice for the 1965–66 season, Cooper dropped off the team because he wanted to major in business administration and had failed an accounting exam. "Had he remained, he would have been the first black athlete ever in the Deep South at a predominantly white university," Smith wrote. Cooper graduated, became an officer in the Army, and years later sent his two children to UNC; his son Brent played on the 1992 jayvee squad and his daughter Tonya on the Carolina women's team that won the 1994 NCAA championship.

In 1965, Smith took notice of a black player from Winston-Salem named Herm Gilliam, who wanted badly to attend Wake Forest but did not get in. The six foot three guard went to Purdue, made All–Big 10, and was selected in the first round of the NBA draft, the eighth pick by the old Cincinnati Royals. After being traded and playing four seasons with Hudson in Atlanta, he won an NBA ring with the 1977 Portland Trail Blazers. Gilliam had been hotly pursued by former Wake Forest star and assistant coach Billy Packer and head coach Bones McKinney, who caused a stir in Winston-Salem when Gilliam was not invited to play in the state high school all-star game. "He was the best player in the state of North Carolina, bar none," Packer told Joe Menzer in the book *Four Corners*.[24] "He was the Michael Jordan of his day."

A furious Packer called the North Carolina High School Athletic Association to complain that Gilliam was not invited. "Don't you understand? He's a Negro," he was told.

"That's crazy," Packer said.

"Yeah, well, that's your opinion. That's the way it is."[25]

That's the way it was all over the South, with certain basketball coaches at predominantly white colleges trying to figure out how to keep African American stars from leaving their state and staying home to play college basketball. Making it even more difficult, before the 1965–66 school year, the ACC *raised* its minimum SAT score for athletic scholarships to 800 from the 750 implemented in 1962. Football and basketball coaches, including Smith, criticized the change, because it kept even more African Americans from playing in the ACC. The rule lasted until two Clemson soccer recruits threatened a lawsuit against the ACC in 1972. Before then, Joe Namath, from Beaver Falls, Pennsylvania, committed to Maryland but did not make 750 on his SATs and went on to become an All-American quarterback at Alabama. Pete Maravich, who starred for Raleigh Broughton High School, was set to play basketball for his father, Press, at N.C. State until he failed to make the new 800 minimum; father and son then moved on to LSU (Louisiana State University), where "Pistol Pete" averaged more than forty points a game. The ACC thus missed on having those two legendary white athletes.

Western Carolina's Henry Logan (1965–66) was the first African American at a mostly white university in North Carolina and later played briefly in the pros with Charlie Scott. Billy Jones (1966) and Pete Johnson (1967) made the test scores and broke the ACC color barrier at Maryland for teams that finished in the lower half of the league for their three years and went out in their first ACC Tournament game each season. Jones was team captain and Johnson led the Terrapins in scoring as a junior, but according to Barry Jacobs's book *Across the Line*,[26] which chronicled dozens of accounts of pioneering black athletes in the South, both endured verbal abuse and were denied service at hotels and restaurants on Tobacco Road and in South Carolina during their college careers.

Duke's C. B. Claiborne was the first African American to play on Tobacco Road and came off the bench for most of his career during which he clashed with Coach Vic Bubas over, among other things, the height of his "Afro" haircut.[27] Claiborne was among the first black students at Duke, a private school that integrated even more slowly than the state universities in the ACC. He later called it the "worst mistake of my life" and did not have much to do with Duke basketball for the forty years after he returned for an alumni game and "they spelled my name wrong on the jersey. That's a statement in and of itself."[28] When Scott visited Duke, Claiborne discouraged him from going there, and they both spent a lot of time socializing at North Carolina Central. Claiborne never has been truly celebrated by Duke as the barrier breaker. It was more than ten years before the Blue Devils signed their first black star, Gene Banks, in 1976.

In 1966, Perry Wallace was the first black athlete at Vanderbilt in the segregated Southeastern Conference (SEC). He made All-SEC as a senior and was voted SEC Sportsman of the Year for enduring horrific racial hazing on the road, especially in Oxford, Mississippi, where, as in many Southern schools, the band played "Dixie" and students waved the Confederate flag. Wallace was considered the perfect choice to break the barrier in the SEC because he played hard, studied, and stayed out of trouble in Nashville, a place somewhat like Chapel Hill in that it was racially divided but also dominated by a prestigious university (as well as by the country music scene, which was all white at the time). Wallace, who waited until his career ended before criticizing Vanderbilt for misleading him during recruiting and cheering him on the court but shunning him in social circles,[29] went on to Columbia Law School, was a trial lawyer for the U.S. Justice Department, and still teaches law at American University.

Smith began his second season in the fall of 1962 bitterly disappointed that Lou Hudson was not playing on the UNC freshman team. From that experience, Smith made standardized testing one of his causes because he knew Hudson had been a good student at Dudley, which offered college prep courses. He had met Hudson and knew he was a youngster of high intelligence and character—"the perfect fit" for Carolina. Smith had yet to become an iconic coach; in fact, he was still under heavy pressure from a university faction that opposed his getting the job, so he had little leverage.

"I became certain that the SATs were culturally and economically biased—a suspicion that was confirmed not long ago by the Supreme Court," Smith wrote in his book. "I knew too many absolutely brilliant young men whose scores were low and then excelled in college. By the same token, I knew plenty of young men with high test scores who did not perform well in the classroom. I specifically remember one player who scored more than 1200 on his SATs, yet struggled to graduate. I knew another young man from a rural southern background who scored only 690, but excelled in his classes, graduated easily, and went on to get a master's degree."

Smith briefly escaped the pressure on his own job in 1963, when senior Larry Brown and sophomore Billy Cunningham both made first-team All-ACC and Cunningham easily led the conference in rebounding with a 16.1 average. The Tar Heels finished third in the ACC at 10–4 and 15–6 overall. They lost by one point to Wake Forest in the ACC Tournament semifinals, missing a chance to play for the conference championship—and an NCAA Tournament berth—against Duke. Led by All-American Art Heyman, who had originally committed to Frank McGuire and UNC, nationally second-ranked Duke went on to reach the first Final Four in school history before losing badly to No. 3 Loyola of Chicago in the 1963 national semifinals at Louisville's ironically named Freedom Hall. Loyola started four black players against the all-white Blue Devils and won easily, 94–75.

Back in New York City, Charlie Scott watched the game on television while in the midst of his second ninth-grade term at Stuyvesant High School. He was anxiously awaiting word from Laurinburg Institute after sending his transcripts and letters of recommendation to Frank McDuffie. The four black Loyola starters, who would be hailed as trailblazers in the college game, especially after dethroning two-time defending NCAA champion Cincinnati the next night in overtime, made an indelible impression on Scott, who was nine months from his fifteenth birthday.

That spring, with his father terminally ill from liver cancer that left the already self-sufficient youngster almost homeless, Scott had all the more reason to leave New York and begin blazing his own trail somewhere else. Meanwhile, Dean Smith had decided his first black player would not only have to be smart enough to get into UNC and make it through, but good enough to help the team win and not be regarded as a token; he would also have to possess the mental toughness to endure the racist treatment he would likely face on the road.

CHAPTER

3

Brave New World

Late in the summer of 1963, Charlie Scott took the subway from Harlem to the Greyhound station at the Port Authority on 42nd Street in midtown Manhattan. His one suitcase carried four pairs of pants, one jacket, and a pair of black shoes. Aside from some underwear and socks, he was wearing everything else he owned.[1] Scott boarded the bus southbound, and after six stops along the way, he got off in Laurinburg, North Carolina. Greyhound had made the sleepy Southern town twenty-five miles past Pinehurst and five miles from the South Carolina border a regular stop; over the last fifteen years, the bus line had been carrying dozens of teenage basketball players from New York to attend Laurinburg Institute, known at the time as a private high school for Negroes.

Still only fourteen, Scott wasn't scared at all; in fact, he was excited to be heading for his brave new world. After all, making the decision to apply and securing admission had been all his own doing—from the ninth-grade Stuyvesant transcript to the letters of recommendation he had mailed himself to Frank McDuffie, the school's headmaster and basketball coach, right through the phone call he had received saying he had been accepted with a partial scholarship (supplemented by some financial aid from New York City).[2]

It was a heady time in the rest of the country, too, as the nation basked in the presidency of John F. Kennedy following a decade of unparalleled middle-class prosperity. Challenging young Americans to think about how this affluence could be used, Kennedy had created the Peace Corps for college graduates who believed in service to their country. And on the home front, he also signaled a new beginning for black Americans with civil rights legislation, introduced that summer. While racism remained a problem everywhere, the fight to end Jim Crow gained momentum like never before. Kennedy's inaugural summons to "pay any price, bear any burden, and meet any hardship"

had given new support to African Americans and their multiracial sympathizers who marched and used civil disobedience in rising opposition to white
supremacy.

Scott's bus had stopped in Philadelphia, Baltimore, and Washington, D.C.,
crossed the Mason-Dixon Line, and passed by tobacco fields in Virginia and
North Carolina where descendants of slaves still toiled for low wages. One of
his last stops was in Durham, North Carolina, where Laurinburg native and
graduate Sam Jones went to North Carolina College for Negroes, and later on
to stardom with the NBA's Boston Celtics. Jones's journey, and those of Earl
Manigault, Jimmy Walker, Dexter Westbrook, and other legends of the New
York schoolyards, gave Scott his own road map for getting a scholarship and
joining the list of Laurinburg royalty.

McDuffie met Scott's bus in Laurinburg's small downtown for the five-
minute drive to what was the oldest all-black boarding school in the United
States, established in 1904 by family matriarch Tinny McDuffie at the request
of Booker T. Washington, the prominent African American educator who
started Tuskegee Institute in Alabama. Washington had sent Tinny McDuffie
and her husband, Emmanuel, to Laurinburg to help reduce illiteracy in North
Carolina. The cluster of one-story buildings in a tree-lined neighborhood on
McGirts Bridge Road off Highway 501 was built with the bricks from the original Laurinburg schoolhouse. The campus now included a new gymnasium
and adjacent football and baseball fields.

Scott would be living in Moore Hall, a dormitory beyond the tennis
courts on Laurinburg's otherwise grassy thirty acres. The newest enrollee had
been an A and B student at Stuyvesant, so his academic adjustments seemed
manageable. Scott's immediate focus was more on basketball. Nervous and more
talkative than usual, he asked about the gym and the team. Now almost six
foot four with wiry arms and legs, he wanted to check out the indoor court
with its parquet floor (like the one Sam Jones played on at the Boston Garden),
meticulously resurfaced every summer by assistant coach Gilbert Reynolds.
Did the court have glass backboards, he wondered? How many people came
to the games?

After only a few weeks at Laurinburg, Scott received word that his father
had died from liver cancer. He took the bus back to New York for the funeral
but returned soon thereafter to what would be his new family for three years.
McDuffie told him he never had to worry about going home again unless he
wanted to, and that seemed strangely comforting to Scott. "Mr. McDuffie
made it possible for me to stay there, even though I had no idea where it would

lead," Scott said. "But I knew I had a chance to go to college and get an education."

McDuffie, who had already sent about twenty graduates on to college scholarships, was surprised at how unpolished Scott was when he first saw him scrimmage. "To be honest, he was a problem," McDuffie told the *Greensboro Daily News* in 1969 after Scott had developed into a dynamic college All-American. "He was fresh from the streets of Harlem and he never had played real organized basketball. But all he wanted to do was play. He had no interest in his studies or his surroundings. He was a loner—a typical New York kid who didn't seem to like what he heard about the South. He hated white people, for instance, probably because he hadn't been around many for most of his life."[3]

In explaining the culture shock of landing at a black school in a Southern white community, where he could not move around freely, Scott called his upbringing in New York "segregation by diplomacy. You didn't know it but you were still segregated. Nothing had really changed; it's just that it wasn't talked about in the North. It was just a matter of where you lived."[4]

There was little spending money coming from his mother in New York, and Scott was too proud to say he needed more than the three squares Laurinburg provided. "We learned that before arriving, he hadn't had a real meal in about two months," McDuffie said. "About that time, my wife began to take a special interest. She could see promise in him that others couldn't."

McDuffie and his wife, Sammie, the school's math and science teacher, agreed that tough love was the best recipe for Scott. They felt he was as good a prospect for an academic scholarship as an athletic grant-in-aid. They decided there would be no sliding by on his natural ability either in the classroom or on the basketball court. As his tenth-grade algebra teacher, Sammie figured Scott "had been a typical underachiever in New York." She changed his routine, and Scott didn't balk. "He would head right to his dormitory when classes were over and worked until everything was done," she recalled in a 1986 story for *Carolina Court* magazine.[5] "Then, in the evening, he was more happy-go-lucky."

On one of those evenings, however, Scott had his first lesson about the hazards of being a young black man in the rural South. And it might have been his last. Scott and two friends from school were walking to a small commercial area in Laurinburg called First Town when flashing lights and sirens startled them from behind. The sheriff put them in the back seat of his cruiser. A white woman in town had reported a sexual assault by three black men, and Scott and his classmates were in the wrong place at the wrong time. The sheriff drove to the house of the alleged assault victim. At gunpoint, he brought the three black youngsters inside and gave the victim the opportunity to identify her assailants. But the woman said none of them was her attacker. Hearts pounding, Scott and his classmates were permitted to leave, quickly walking back to the safety of school grounds.

"The sheriff had a shotgun, people in the crowd had shotguns and were standing outside of the house," Scott recalled vividly years later. "If she had said it was us, I have no doubt I would not be here . . . today."[6] Suddenly, Scott knew how different his new home was from the city where on the playgrounds nobody's life ever seemed in danger. "It was like culture shock," Scott said. "Here it was, definitely right in front of you."

Despite doing so well in school that he eventually became valedictorian of his small graduating class, Scott grew more determined that basketball was his ticket from bigotry and limited opportunity to the big-time. He wasn't the star of the Laurinburg team as a sophomore. Instead, Scott and his teammates deferred to nineteen-year-old, fifth-year senior Earl Manigault's thirty points per game. Scott did catch the eye of Davidson coach Charles "Lefty" Driesell, however, who was about two hours away and actively looking to recruit the first black player for his burgeoning program. Davidson had senior Terry Holland (who led the nation in field goal percentage), junior Fred Hetzel, and sophomore Dick Snyder on the 1964 team that would win the first of three straight Southern Conference regular-season championships.

Driesell stayed in contact with McDuffie and every school year asked about any players who could qualify academically for Davidson. In 1963, before Scott had turned fifteen, McDuffie recommended junior Skip Hayes and also mentioned his new sophomore, who he thought would make the grades and test scores to warrant consideration. Not long after, Driesell invited McDuffie, Hayes, and Scott to a game at the old Charlotte Coliseum. After learning Hayes would be going back to New York for the summer, Driesell offered Scott a job at his camp to work with some of the biggest high school stars in the country, including Pete Maravich from Raleigh and Dave Cowens from Newport, Kentucky. At night that summer, the counselors played games in front of the campers against Davidson players, including Holland, Hetzel, and Snyder. Scott figured his ability was being measured.

Scott was invited back following his junior year, when he led Laurinburg in scoring with a twenty-point average. By then, he and Driesell had become good friends; Lefty offered him a scholarship and wanted Scott to meet all the other players he was recruiting from the same high school class. Charismatic and energetic, the thirty-three-year-old Driesell had Scott believing Davidson was his next home, especially after the Wildcats had climbed into the national rankings during the 1965 season behind forward Hetzel, an All-American and eventual NBA first-round draft pick, and Snyder, an All–Southern Conference guard and another future pro.

Driesell saw Scott as the player who could lead Davidson to its first-ever NCAA Tournament, in part because his grades and SAT scores (1200 out of a possible 1600) allowed him to apply for early admission and almost assured his acceptance by the start of his senior year at Laurinburg. Holland, who had joined Driesell's staff right out of school, was blown away by what he described as a rare talent. "I thought, 'This guy is really good. God, I can't believe how fast he is . . . the court's too small for this guy. The court needs to be bigger so he can take advantage of his speed. He's going to run off the court.' "[7]

Scott soon became Davidson's regular guest every time the Wildcats played a weekend game in Charlotte. Driesell put him up at a motel across the street from an integrated movie theater where the *Sound of Music* was having a prolonged run. Scott recalled watching the 1965 Academy Award–winning film more times than he could count, making Julie Andrews his favorite actress (he listed her as such in his basketball profile all the way through his senior year at UNC). Her performance even inspired him to join the Laurinburg choir.

"After I told Lefty I was coming, he said I could pick the other four guys," Scott recalled in 2014. "Every time a guy would visit, I went up there because Davidson was about two hours from Laurinburg. Someone drove me so I could see who he had recruited. Lefty asked me, did I want to play with these guys—what did I think of them? So, basically, I picked the other guys who ended up going to Davidson."

When Scott began his senior year, he believed he would play his college ball alongside fellow Driesell recruits Mike Maloy, also from New York City, Jerry Kroll, and Doug Cook. They thought another teammate might be high school All-American Geoff Petrie, from Darby, Pennsylvania, who showed interest in Davidson before signing with Princeton, where he made All–Ivy League, All-American, and became a first-round NBA draft choice.

In the days before athletes could sign NCAA grants-in-aid in the fall, non-binding letters-of-intent were no better than verbal commitments to Division I colleges and universities. McDuffie stopped Scott from signing anything, however, asking him to wait until he had visited other schools he liked. Scott confessed years later that he did not know McDuffie's motives, but they turned out to be that his coach, teacher, mentor, and surrogate father had another place in mind. Since Laurinburg was the oldest black prep school in North Carolina, with two generations of the same family having run it for sixty years, McDuffie knew the impact of sending the first African American athlete to the flagship state university. He believed that the large stage and the right player would force other colleges in the state, if not throughout the South, to follow his lead.

Early in his third season as head coach at UNC, almost three years before he would meet Charlie Scott, Dean Smith was building a new home in the Morgan Creek area of Chapel Hill, but he was afraid his family might never have the opportunity to live there. "I remember one of the neighbors walking by and asking if we weren't moving a little too fast," Ann Smith said, recalling the opinion "that maybe Dean wasn't going to keep his job even though we did beat Kentucky."

Smith had entered what he later described as "one of the darkest periods of my professional life,"[8] and it coincided with one of the darkest periods in UNC's history. Smith's second team had won fifteen games and placed third in the ACC, but some critics who thought he should never have had the job were unmoved. Larry Brown and Billy Cunningham, the stars of that 1963 team, were "(Frank) McGuire's players," and the upset of unranked Kentucky and All-American Cotton Nash in Lexington on December 17 hadn't convinced skeptics beyond making believers out of the players. Junior guard Charlie Shaffer, a Morehead Scholar, called it "the most perfect basketball game anyone has ever coached." The seminal Kentucky win was the first of hundreds of victories in hostile arenas that would give Smith the best road record of any coach in the history of college basketball at the time of his retirement: 201–116, not including his neutral site record of 331–93.

Smith's 1963 starting backcourt, Brown and Yogi Poteet, were among five seniors and eight total players who were gone the next season. Cunningham, at six foot five and already nicknamed the "Kangaroo Kid," was the best rebounder and highest returning scorer in the ACC, but Smith often tried to make him the best point guard as well. "I played Shaffer, an excellent athlete, at point guard and should have kept him at big guard. Then I started junior walk-on Bill Brown for a while and also tried sophomores Ray Respess and Johnny Yokely there," Smith said. "It was Billy do this, Billy do that, Billy bring it up against the press. It was also the only time I ever told a player he could rest at half-court on the fast break if he had gotten the defensive rebound. It all revolved around Billy."

Smith opened the 1963–64 season still mourning President Kennedy with the rest of the campus and country. JFK's assassination on November 22, 1963, hit some members of the Chapel Hill community particularly hard, especially with racial tensions at a peak. "I feel like the Negro has lost a savior," Karen Parker, the first African American female to attend and graduate from UNC in 1965, wrote in her acclaimed diaries. "I admired Kennedy. He was a person one could look up to. . . . I feel insecure, unsafe. The future looks quite uncertain. I hate to think about it."[9]

Kennedy had been in Chapel Hill two years earlier, on University Day, giving a moving fourteen-minute speech at Kenan Stadium that was repeatedly interrupted by standing ovations and wild cheering. Gary Blanchard, editor of the *DTH*, wrote the day after the assassination: "They loved him. Thirty-two thousand of them loved him. Children, students, housewives, working men with the morning off loved him. Yesterday, they loved him more. But yesterday it was different. John Fitzgerald Kennedy was gone."

The national tragedy gave Smith an opportunity as a head coach to show his compassion to his players while also keeping his commitment to the task at hand and asking the same of his young team. The experience would shape how he handled many other personal and professional distractions that waited in the future. Smith had heard Kennedy speak and embraced his ideology of helping the downtrodden and less fortunate, which solidified his lifelong support of the Democratic Party.

At the time of Kennedy's death, UNC students and faculty were enraged over the speaker ban law that had passed the North Carolina General Assembly (in fewer than five minutes by the House and almost as quickly in the Senate) on June 26, 1963, as "The Act to Regulate Visiting Speakers." The law limited public speech at all state-supported colleges but was squarely aimed at UNC. Since the 1930s, Chapel Hill had been home to enough noted Communists, such as Junius Scales, who was arrested and convicted under the Smith Act in 1954,[10] and others who espoused some form of socialism, to cause what was referred to as the "Red Scare." The speaker ban mirrored the Smith Act and was primarily meant to muzzle anyone who advocated the "overthrow of the Constitution" or had pleaded the Fifth Amendment in response to questions about their national loyalty. It also had far-reaching implications for those who believed in freedom of speech.

Dean Smith was a believer in freedom of speech, but he was hardly in a position to say much publicly, given his tenuous professional standing. He surely supported Chancellor Bill Aycock and President Bill Friday when they issued a joint statement that UNC opposed the speaker ban and would try to have it overturned, if for no other reason than the way lawmakers had rushed the bill through the legislature without the required number of readings and without giving the university a chance to be present and respond.

The law was drawn up by North Carolina Secretary of State Thad Eure "at the request of a tiny group of lawmakers and passed in irritation, in haste, under suspension of the rules and without debate," according to Bob Smith, associate editor of the Charlotte *News*.[11] In explaining the discord between UNC and the General Assembly, a *Chapel Hill Weekly* editorial called "communism a vastly overrated issue" and opined that the speaker ban was more "a reaction against civil rights militancy and demonstrations in Chapel Hill that had made the University's liberalism seem particularly abrasive to the legislators."[12]

The law kept most civil rights activity off campus and relegated regular protests that had begun two years earlier to the west end of Franklin Street. As Parker feared in her diary, Kennedy's murder also cast doubts about the passage of civil rights legislation he had asked for "giving all Americans the right to be served in facilities which are open to the public—hotels, restaurants, theaters, retail stores, and similar establishments" plus "greater protection for the right to vote."

Smith discussed the issue often with Bob Seymour, but as head coach, he kept a low profile and used his position to support the civil rights movement through back channels. For example, Smith allowed Braxton Foushee's African American Boy Scout troop to watch the Tar Heels practice on several occasions, each time taking a few minutes afterward to encourage the excited youngsters to stay in school and study if they wanted to go to college and maybe play basketball. Smith was doing the same with his all-white former players. Handled confidentially, he made it a habit to help them (and sometimes their friends) with job references, charitable favors, or occasional small loans, which created a sort of secret society that wasn't openly talked about.

Meanwhile, during games his team was not helping Smith's job security. "I did the worst coaching job of my career," he said of how the 1964 season unfolded, starting a long tradition of protecting his players by taking the heat himself. "We wound up relying on Billy and hope, and that was my fault." The year was otherwise profitable; letting Cunningham lag back after an outlet pass helped birth the renowned Carolina "secondary break" and the need to practice stalling tactics contributed to Smith accidentally discovering the Four Corners offense one day.

Hardly outspoken, Smith had nevertheless learned toughness from his father and the coaches for whom he had worked. Athletic director Chuck Erickson, who was still unhappy about Aycock leaving him out of the decision after Frank McGuire resigned, criticized Smith for spending too much money replacing the carpet in his office and a phone bill that "is higher than mine and the chancellor's." Smith countered sharply, "I should hope so; you and the chancellor are not trying to recruit basketball players."[13]

Smith's 1964 team opened with a home win over South Carolina. (Before long, the Gamecocks fired their head coach, Chuck Noe, and eventually replaced him with McGuire, who quit the NBA when the Philadelphia Warriors were sold and moved to San Francisco.) But then at Clemson, the Tar Heels lost their second game of the season for the first time in twenty-four years. It was the first of three double overtime games that Carolina lost in 1964. Smith's team looked solid in winning five of its next six after the heartbreaker at Clemson, losing only at revenge-minded and ninth-ranked Kentucky, and stood 6–2 when the ACC schedule resumed in January.

Smith got carried away after an impressive win over Notre Dame in Greensboro, and he was caught overselling his team when the students returned for the spring semester. In the first edition of the *DTH*, published in 1964, Smith made what seemed like an outlandish statement when he said, "We are one of the best teams in the country, I think we have proved that. Now we must continue to prove it, especially this week.[14] The quote was buried on page 6 of a newspaper that compiled all the news from over the semester break—front-page stories on racial violence in Chapel Hill, a graduate student charged with murdering his wife, a coed who died in a car crash, and *DTH* sportswriter Curry Kirkpatrick winning the top prize from the William Randolph Hearst journalism foundation. Inside was a reprint of David McReynolds's piece in *The Village Voice* about being jailed during a protest in Chapel Hill and a full-page spread on UNC's 35–0 victory over Air Force in the Gator Bowl. With better play, Smith's bold assessment of his third Tar Heel team might have been more ridiculed after the coming week resulted in lopsided losses at Wake Forest and ninth-ranked Duke. Disappointed in the road defeats, Smith said he was confident his players could rebound.

However, the rest of the season was a 6–10 washout that had some fans leaving Woollen Gym early. Why not, when the main attraction had become watching the preliminary games featuring Carolina's freshman team and high-flying first-year player Bob Lewis, who averaged more than thirty-five points per game?

One game that season, a 69–68 loss to NYU at Madison Square Garden, made an indelible impression on a high school sophomore named Dick Grubar, who had driven down from Schenectady with his coach. Billy Cunningham almost single-handedly beat the Violets, who had All-Americans Happy Hairston and Barry Kramer, before fouling out midway through the second half with twenty-three points and eleven rebounds. "After that, I always followed Carolina," said Grubar, who started for the Tar Heels three years later.

The prospect of Lewis, who found a recruiting letter from Smith with others in a shoebox under his bed after watching UNC defeat Notre Dame on television, moving up to join Cunningham the next season still did not give Smith much leeway with some alumni who had their minds made up. However, it began to quiet some of the students who wanted Smith out. Back in 1962, the *DTH* had printed a letter taking that view signed by three critics at the Zeta Psi house. Smith always remembered that letter, kept the clipping, and did invite one of the three Zetes to his office for a discussion about loyalty.

"He wasn't referring to loyalty *to him* necessarily, but loyalty as a concept that might come in handy as life moved on," 1965 UNC graduate Alfred Hamilton recalled. "He did, however, ask for a better chance to win basketball games than he'd been given by me and a few fraternity boys. Frankly, I had never thought much about loyalty up to then, but I gave it plenty of thought during a long walk back across campus. After all, Smith wasn't talking to me about *absolute* loyalty; he was only urging that people always consider loyalty as a first option." This was one of many teaching moments for Smith with a student who became one of his most loyal supporters from that point on.

Luckily for Smith, Aycock was still the chancellor in 1964 and stood behind the struggling coach. "No one could have gotten rid of Dean Smith unless they fired me first," Aycock said time and again over the years. After Aycock had announced his intention to step down the following summer, Smith sent him a heartfelt, hand-written note dated August 18, 1963, praising him for "tremendous leadership . . . these past six years . . . (finding) an adequate replacement will be a near impossible task." Smith continued in long hand, "On speaking for our basketball program in general, and myself in particular, a simple thank you would not be adequate. . . . After you gave me this opportunity as your basketball coach, you did everything possible to help me succeed."[15]

As the basketball season unfolded, storms around Chapel Hill over civil rights continued growing. Most of the local protests remained on the West End of Franklin Street that marked the edge of the black community, but they occasionally spread toward a campus where much of the student body and faculty were largely apathetic about what was called the Chapel Hill Freedom Movement. Karen Parker was among the black students who joined the marches as soon as she arrived in Chapel Hill from UNC-Greensboro, and was surprised that her white roommates went with her. South Building had several sit-ins after Aycock received a message from the police that "a group of demonstrators, mostly black, with some children, was marching across the campus, and we told them they couldn't." Aycock responded, "You'll have to go back, find 'em and tell them they certainly can. And they're welcome here at South Building."[16]

On February 8, 1964, after Smith's team had defeated Wake Forest for its tenth victory, the crowd dispersing from Woollen Gym found all exits in surrounding parking lots blocked by demonstrators either sitting or lying in the roads. Stretching all the way to Franklin Street and every road out of town, it was the largest, most organized local protest and the first to fully engage UNC campus police and Chief Arthur Beaumont, a huge man with a thick New York accent who had been brought to Chapel Hill by Frank McGuire.

The town police department had purchased a used bread truck and turned it into a paddy wagon that officers could repeatedly fill, shuttling demonstrators to the jail. Smith only learned of this after talking to his team and reporters about the victory over Wake Forest, in what turned out to be the last high point of the season; Carolina would win only two more games before the 12–12 dud came to an end. "I remember Dean being upset about a lot of things that were happening in town and on campus," Ann said, "and we discussed some of them when he got home. But most of the time, he just wanted to protect the family by not involving us."

After getting blown out by Duke, 104–69, at home and losing again to the nearby rival in the semifinals of the ACC Tournament, Smith's saving grace might have been out-recruiting the Blue Devils for left-handed high school All-American Larry Miller that spring, a decision Duke assistant coach Bucky Waters said "may have been the death knell as far as head coach Vic Bubas's zest for recruiting." If not the crucial turning point for Smith, Miller turned out to be an extraordinary member of the basketball program. Recruited by hundreds of schools with Duke the clear-cut favorite, Miller had the self-confidence to say no to the reigning king of the ACC and say yes to struggling Carolina and its embattled coach. Miller explained that he "just fell in love with Chapel Hill" on his official visit. Smith first believed he had a chance to sign the handsome six foot four recruit when he sent Miller off with the Tar Heels underclassmen while he and Ann entertained Miller's parents at a small gathering in the basement of their new home. He invited UNC alumni and close friends Tassie and Jimmy Dempsey and Mary Frances and Guy Andrews because they were closer to the Millers' age and, Smith surmised, might have more in common with them.

This group of "recruiting hosts" would expand to meet the demographics and interests of prospects, including African American friends Howard and Lillian Lee and professors from any academic department in which the recruits expressed interest. Thanks to the Dempseys and the Andrews, the entire Miller family greatly enjoyed the weekend and finally took to heart what assistant coach Ken Rosemond had told Miller during one visit to his home in Catasauqua, Pennsylvania. "You know, Larry, the saddest thing is if you went from here down to Duke, you'd be going all that way and you'd still be five minutes from heaven," Rosemond said.

Long before Miller became a two-time All-American, two-time ACC Player of the Year and two-time MVP of the ACC Tournament, he was one of three Tar Heels who made Charlie Scott feel accepted on his official visit to Chapel Hill. Growing up in the 96 percent white industrial Lehigh Valley, where he averaged thirty-five points for Catasauqua High School with a single-game high of sixty-five (two fewer than the sixty-seven he scored in 1972 to break the old American Basketball Association [ABA] single-game record), Miller wanted to win beyond any personal goals. And when he found out what Scott could do on a basketball court, Miller was totally committed to helping a youngster from Harlem feel welcome on a campus that was more than 98 percent white at that time.

Before Miller ever heard of Scott, he had played a freshman season with Willie Cooper, the Elm City youngster whom Smith had hoped to make the first black scholarship athlete at UNC. But all eyes were on Miller, who tore up the schedule of prep schools and other freshman teams in Rosemond's last season before he took the head-coaching job at Georgia. If freshmen had been eligible for varsity play back then, Miller would have joined Lewis and Cunningham on the 1965 varsity team, which had a very strange season without him. For one, Carmichael Auditorium was being built, attached to the Woollen Gym building, as UNC made an architectural step into big-time college basketball. Smith, meanwhile, continued to face pressure to win.

In fact, Smith was under the most intense heat of his career, and Aycock had lost the unilateral power to save him by stepping down before the 1964–65 Tar Heels opened as the thirteenth-ranked team in the nation, the first time that had happened since McGuire's heyday. However, they promptly lost their place in the polls by again dropping their second game, this time at Georgia. Not even another big win over No. 11 Kentucky at the old Charlotte Coliseum could restore Carolina's ranking for a season that very much looked like Smith's last at UNC.

With gangly six foot five senior Cunningham and the lithe Lewis among the top four scorers in the ACC and top ten rebounders, Carolina was almost unbeatable on certain nights. An upset of third-ranked Vanderbilt in Greensboro proved that, but then came a four-game losing streak away from home that prompted a group of students to hang the legendary effigy of Smith from a tree outside Woollen as the Tar Heels bused back from a twenty-two-point shellacking at Wake Forest. The story has been told in so many forms that the only consistent report has Cunningham seeing the dummy first and jumping off the team bus to pull it down and scare off the small mob with language he learned in Brooklyn. One story said Smith knew something was going on but never found out exactly what until later; another had Smith offering to talk to the complicit students as he left the bus.

Cunningham, an All-American who never played in the NCAA Tournament, felt like the team had let Smith down. "All the papers were on Dean, every day, all the time. Vicious stuff," Cunningham recalled more than fifteen years later. "It upset all of us because it wasn't his fault, it was ours. We weren't very good."

In his autobiography, Smith wrote that Rosemond first pointed out the dummy to Smith, who said, "I could tell it was me because of the long nose."[17] For sure, he was affected by what had happened. Later that night, Smith spent a few hours at the home of Lou and Florence Vine, the friends he had inherited from McGuire, having a drink of Scotch, and contemplated quitting. This wasn't because he lacked confidence in what he was doing, but the constant criticism was becoming too difficult for his family to endure. He even said it wouldn't be so bad to go back to Kansas and teach and coach in high school as his father had. The Vines encouraged him to at least stick it out for the rest of the season. After returning home, Smith called his sister, Joan, who lived in

St. Louis, and he spent most of the night talking with the Reverend Seymour. "I remember him searching," Joan recalled exactly forty years later, "asking himself if he was doing the right thing with his life."

"You don't forget a thing like that, ever," Smith said in 1981. And he pointed out that wasn't the only time he was hanged in effigy. It occurred again after the loss to N.C. State at home on January 13, 1965, when he learned that a small crowd had gathered and one student played "Taps" on his trumpet. Fortunately, Carolina had upset eighth-ranked Duke in Durham 65–62 between the two hangings for Smith's first victory after seven straight defeats at the hands of Vic Bubas's Blue Devils. By spreading out against a slower Duke team, the Tar Heels worked the ball until they got the shots they wanted and hit 51 percent. Cunningham and Lewis combined for forty-three of Carolina's sixty-five points while an intense man-to-man defense that would help define Smith's coaching career held Duke's All-ACC trio of Jack Marin, Steve Vacendak, and Bob Verga to a total eight for thirty-one from the floor. When the team bus returned to campus, another small group of students had gathered, not to hang the coach this time but to praise him. When they chanted "Dean! Dean!" for him to say something, he showed the dry wit and sarcasm for which he became known. "I'd like to but I can't speak," Smith said, "I have something around my throat."[18]

The Tar Heels upset the fifth-ranked Blue Devils again in their final game at Woollen Gym, but the second lopsided loss of the season to Wake Forest in the ACC Tournament completed a 15–9 campaign that saw Cunningham finally win Player of the Year and Smith stay in hot water with the alumni and fans. With Miller moving up to the varsity team the next season, Smith probably saved his job again when he and his new assistant coaches, Larry Brown and John Lotz, landed the signature high school recruiting class of 1965—Grubar, Rusty Clark, Bill Bunting, Joe Brown, and Gerald Tuttle. They, too, would have to play one year of freshman ball, but even the biggest critic could see what was coming the next season. And few people knew anything about who else might be coming.

It's good that Charlie Scott wasn't born three years earlier. Chapel Hill was far less ready for him in the early 1960s. Over the course of the decade, it went from a town clearly divided by race, through sixteen months of dangerous demonstrations before the Civil Rights Act passed, to eventually electing (and twice reelecting by overwhelming margins) Howard Lee as the first black mayor in a predominantly white municipality in the South.

Even before Martin Luther King Jr.'s visit in May 1960 when he campaigned for peaceful protest because "there must be no violence in the struggle for racial equality," the first major act of civil disobedience stunned the town. Five students from all-black Lincoln High School entered Colonial Drug on West Franklin Street through the front door (usually black customers went in the back), ordered food, and sat down in two booths. They never got served, and eventually owner John Carswell called the police and had them arrested for trespassing.

The high school students had been inspired by the "Greensboro Four"—four black freshmen at North Carolina A&T College who took seats at the segregated lunch counter of F. W. Woolworth's on February 1, 1960. The "Chapel Hill Five" staged their own sit-in symbolically four weeks later to the day. The act by courageous teenagers James Brittain, William Cureton, Harold Foster, Earl Greer, and Thomas Mason touched off a four-year crusade on the streets, in the local newspapers, and occasionally on Raleigh television stations. Brittain even tried again at Colonial and was carried out of the drugstore by Carswell and his teenage son.[19] The actions of the five Lincoln students awoke the town from its long-standing apathy on segregation.

Chapel Hill finally lived up to its reputation as North Carolina's most radical community. Citizens from respected black families, such as university employee Braxton Foushee and high school guidance counselor Hilliard Caldwell, stepped up and kept things under control as Mayor Sandy McClamroch and the Board of Aldermen debated how to stave off demonstrations that were beginning to boil all over the South.

Caldwell said he had no choice but to embrace protest, recalling with distaste having to ride in the back of the bus to Durham and drinking from "colored" water fountains. As codirector of the local movement with Foster, one of the Lincoln students in the Colonial Drug protest, Caldwell took to heart King's nonviolent pronouncement and helped Police Chief W. D. Blake keep the sit-ins mostly peaceful and without bloodshed. Caldwell's role helped him eventually win a seat on the Carrboro Board of Aldermen. "I was older (than Foster), a mature adult versus a young high school kid," Caldwell reflected years later. "And probably my middle of the road stance on this thing kept a lot of turmoil from happening."[20] Encouraging the expanding group to stage the sit-ins peacefully, Caldwell hoped that stopping short of further civil disobedience would break down the opposition rather than anger them into retaliation. He considered a mass sit-in on East Franklin Street on a football Saturday, hoping "the legislators who attended the game would go home, call up Mayor McClamroch and say you need to do something."[21]

Foushee called himself "more of an in-your-face" protestor who confronted both black and white leaders and said, "In your positions, you aren't doing enough." Elected four times to the Carrboro Board of Aldermen, Foushee opposed civil disobedience; rather, he wanted to work to change the system. "I always believed you had to be at the table to make things happen," Foushee said.

In his 1965 book *The Free Men*, John Ehle wrote that the first street marches in 1962 had the benign feeling of "we would like you to join us so we can improve the community"[22] as opposed to far more confrontational demonstrations in Raleigh. The town could not avoid its share of threatening incidents, however, such as Caldwell waking up one night to a Klan-planted cross burning in his yard and bar owner Clarence Grey, who hung Confederate flags all over his joint, turning a high-powered water hose on protestors. They were blocking entrance to Clarence's Bar & Grill, which along with the College Café, Tar Heel Sandwich Shop, Brady's, and the Watts Grill, faced regular demonstrations. The most popular target, of course, was Carswell's Colonial Drug, where he eventually tore out all the booths and left everyone standing in what he termed "vertical integration."

John Carswell, a 1943 UNC graduate, reportedly took money from black customers, gave them smaller portions than whites, and then chased them out of his store. He alienated the steady weekly business that came from the nearby First Baptist Church and Sunday school. Some people, who had their prescriptions filled at Colonial and were scared by the escalating protests, moved their accounts to other drugstores that had integrated staffs and customer bases.

"Carswell was a horse's ass," the late mayor McClamroch, who died in 2016, said years later in an interview. "He irritated everyone, and he was stupid because the blacks were his trade."

When the town passed an ordinance allowing picketing in 1963, demonstrators blocked the entrance to Carswell's business with signs such as "The Customer is Always WHITE at Colonial Drugs." His family and friends countered with their own signs, one reading, "2-4-6-8, who in the hell wants to integrate." Carswell filed a simple assault complaint against protestor Robert Brown, a leader on the Chapel Hill Committee for Open Business, whose sign grazed the head of Carswell's son. Brown was found not guilty after being defended by Durham NAACP (National Association for the Advancement of

Colored People) lawyer Floyd McKissick, one of the first three black law students to attend Carolina in 1951.

UNC continued to admit a dribble of African Americans into the 1960s. A small number of white students joined the Chapel Hill Freedom Movement to fight what they regarded as racial oppression in their chosen college town. John Dunne, a Morehead Scholar from Choate prep school in Connecticut, formed the UNC chapter of the Student Peace Union (SPU) in the spring of 1962 and initially organized sit-ins at segregated Memorial Hospital. His closest ally was Pat Cusick, a cherubic junior from Alabama who was reportedly embarrassed about being the great-grandson of a KKK leader. Both Dunne and Cusick received stern warnings from the Student Affairs Office that the university would not defend their actions if they broke the law.

When he heard about the SPU, the Reverend Charlie Jones from the non-denominational Community Church contacted the NAACP, which sent the leader of its North Carolina chapter, Quinton Baker, a student at North Carolina College in Durham. Dunne, Cusick, and the intense Baker, who was referred to as a "ramrod" by the local solicitor, were arrested and jailed repeatedly but gave the movement front-page headlines in almost every issue of the *DTH* and *Chapel Hill Weekly* for a solid year.

DTH photographer Jim Wallace, who later worked for the Smithsonian Institution and published the riveting and revealing picture book, *Courage in the Moment*,[23] captured much of what occurred on the streets in the early 1960s on camera. David Ethridge and Gary Blanchard were the coeditors of the *DTH*, which covered the controversy more closely and objectively than any other newspaper, with unvarnished accounts of the chaotic street scenes. "Holy adrenaline!" Blanchard said in 2006 when recalling those days. "We would get up in the morning and I would say, 'I have no idea what is going to happen today, but I know something will, and it will be surprising as hell.'"[24] The *DTH* had no faculty advisor or censorship and attracted talented students clamoring to join its staff and cover the news aggressively almost around the clock. This resulted in access to the protestors and police that even the *Weekly*, and certainly the Durham and Raleigh papers, did not have, or even try to get. *DTH* civil rights reporter Joel Bulkley drove a recognizable yellow convertible and was frequently tailed by Chapel Hill police, thinking he might lead them to some action somewhere. Still, the *DTH* was a campus publication discredited by many conservative adults, so the word did not spread very far.

Dunne, Cusick, and Baker held many of their planning sessions for protests at Harry's Deli, one of the first integrated restaurants on East Franklin

Street. It was owned by a Jewish couple from Durham, Harry and Sybil Macklin. After a large meeting of many clergy and protest leaders, what seemed inevitable occurred: pressure for a vote on a local public accommodations ordinance by the town's Board of Aldermen that would force the hand of segregated businesses. Mayor McClamroch, backed by an advisory opinion from the state Attorney General's office,[25] believed the town lacked authority to pass such a law and knew that most similar ordinances in other states wound up in their respective Supreme Courts. After attempting to influence the approximately thirty segregated businesses to voluntarily change their policies, McClamroch left integration up to the individual owners. He recalled in 2014 that he planned to use his required tie-breaker vote against the ordinance if the six aldermen were deadlocked at three to three.

The Merchants Association and Jaycees, two of the most conservative organizations in town, released strongly worded statements against forced desegregation, "despite its policy of urging all businesses to adopt non-discrimination."[26] Sit-ins and demonstrations increased, however, and became nightmares for Blake's police force, which had to press "cadets" or interns into service. By December of 1963, officers were to file for more than four hundred hours of overtime with the town and arrested seventy-five demonstrators.

The most intense period began the day after James Farmer from CORE led one hundred seventy protestors on a thirteen-mile "Walk for Freedom" in the rain on the two-lane highway from Durham to the First Baptist Church in Chapel Hill. The next evening, June 13, 1963, before an impassioned and overflow crowd in the Town Hall courtroom, the Chapel Hill Board of Aldermen, according to the *Weekly*, "sidestepped" passing the Public Accommodations Ordinance by approving a motion to negotiate further. This was seen by many, especially the nearly two thousand people who put their names on a two-page newspaper spread endorsing the local legislation,[27] as cowardice by the aldermen.

The marches, which had been suspended pending the vote, resumed the next day with far greater intensity and tested the resolve of local movement leaders to avoid a large-scale civil disobedience campaign. The largest sit-in to date took place on July 29, 1963, when police arrested thirty-four people at the Merchants Association after Chief Blake could not convince the protestors camped out in the main lobby to leave. The escalation continued over the next eight months, as protestors from as far away as Danville, Virginia, and Wilmington arrived to join hundreds of blacks and whites now shouting and singing "We Shall Overcome" all over town. CORE gave Chapel Hill a February 1,

1964, deadline to integrate, triggering a response from Governor Terry San-ford, who said, "[I] will not be coerced," and pledged "every resource" to keep the demonstrations from turning violent.[28]

"Chapel Hill was definitely a powder keg," said Lindy Pendergrass, who was a sergeant on Blake's police force and later served thirty-two years as the elected sheriff of Orange County. "If Chief Blake hadn't kept a lid on it, who knows what would have happened?"

Blake, an imposing figure who retired in 1975 and consulted with the police department until his death in 1978, was what Pendergrass called a "Renais-sance man of the time, far different from hard-ass cops of that era." He read about Gandhi's peaceful insurgence against British rule in India and embraced King's philosophy of nonviolent protest. He demanded that his officers and detectives not retaliate, threatening them with termination if they did, and showed them how to pick up the limp bodies of demonstrators and carry them safely to the police cars and paddy wagon rather than dragging them by their limbs. Blake was well aware of Wallace and other cameramen and how their photos might depict Chapel Hill. When he could not persuade marchers to disperse, he more or less treated the marches like parades and arrested no one. A calm figure among divergent personalities, Blake talked constantly with both sides—protestors and still-segregated businesses—and worked with McClamroch to keep the frustrated and conflicted townsfolk informed. McClamroch owned the local radio station, WCHL, but said he purposely did not feed any infor-mation to the station because he felt it would be a conflict of interest, leaving reporters to chase down the stories.

The late Gary Blanchard, who had covered the protests as coeditor of the *DTH*, went to work for WCHL his senior year at UNC. "He was an aggressive student reporter for us and was all over it," recalled Jim Heavner, the WCHL general manager at the time. "Gary seemed to know all the key local people planning the demonstrations. And he was seen as something of a thorn in the side of downtown business guys, but I had no trouble defending his reporting. What we did not do was editorialize. I thought that was beyond our capabili-ties. But we sure covered it."

Since the demonstrations rarely moved close to campus, Chief Blake received little or no help from UNC. Much of the student body, which had fewer than fifty black students, paid little heed to what was happening on the West End and lower East Franklin Street, happily spending their time in the dorms, library, student union, fraternity houses, and East Franklin Street bars. Seemingly, more students complained about how badly Dean Smith's third team was doing during the 1963–64 season than worried about civil rights. Robert Reddick, an African American who earned three degrees from UNC, said he and other black students such as Karen Parker participated in the protests, but most white students could not have cared less. "They were there to get an education, not to change the social atmosphere," Reddick said.[29]

"To actually go out and actively participate and march was not something the mainstream student did," said Phil Baddour, a student legislator at that time who went on to serve nine years as a Democrat in the North Carolina House of Representatives. "I applaud those who at the time had the courage to participate; in hindsight, I wish I had been part of the group, but I wasn't."[30]

Pat Cusick ruminated years later, "Our biggest tactical mistake was not putting more of a burden on the university . . . as obviously the university has leverage on the town." Dan Pollitt, a liberal UNC law professor, called the university a "grizzly bear, and it can do what it wants to do. It let the merchants and the students fight it out."

In retrospect, memories are flavored by individual points of view. "Lots of sleepless nights," Lindy Pendergrass said in 2014, "but every time we needed to be somewhere, Chief Blake was right there with us, talking to both sides." However, in his 1991 book, *Whites Only*, Bob Seymour had a very different recollection. "All hell broke loose in Chapel Hill," Seymour wrote. "The tension was at a point of potential violence; it was rather frightening."[31] Yet if you asked students who were around campus at the time, most would say they were waiting around for the next episode of *The Fugitive* or grabbing a cheap hamburger at The Goody Shop.

Some especially violent episodes did occur. One of the worst took place on December 28, 1963, the same night Carolina's football team blanked Air Force in the Gator Bowl in Jacksonville, Florida. Carlton's Rock Pile, owned by Carlton Mize, was a segregated convenience store and gas station literally built from a pile of large rocks on East Franklin Street next to Brady's restaurant, another segregated establishment. Carlton Mize and Brady McLendon both displayed large "WHITES ONLY" signs in their front windows.

By then Dunne, Cusick, and Baker had their strategy down to a science, including instructing protestors to meet at the all-black First Baptist and St. Joseph churches in Chapel Hill and Carrboro, keeping their destinations secret until the cars loaded up and departed. They informed the police when and where they were going, hoping to protect themselves from serious injury. Sit-ins sometimes attracted more than a hundred people, joined by Duke divinity students and faculty as well as blacks from North Carolina Central.

Charles Thompson, a fuzzy-faced UNC freshman from Greensboro, showed up the night they all sat in at the Rock Pile, where Mize had a different plan than simply refusing to serve black customers and telling part of the mob to get out of his small shop. "Instead, he went to the front door and locked it and then did the same at the back door," Thompson wrote in the March/April 2006 Carolina *Alumni Review*. "Then he brought out bottles of Clorox and ammonia and poured the bottles over our (black) friends' heads. When they gasped for air, streams of ammonia and bleach ran into their mouths. All of us who went out on the sit-ins had vowed not to offer more than passive resistance. So they neither moved or fought him but shut their eyes tight and twisted back and forth trying to keep the chemicals out of their eyes and mouths."

Fortunately, the police arrived and saw what was happening through the windows. Forcing Mize to open up, they took those who had been burned to the hospital for treatment. Then they brought them to the magistrate, charged them with trespassing, and locked them up with those who had already been arrested. Mize, by contrast, escaped prosecution, claiming "they tore my screen door off by the hinges."[32] None of the protestors pressed charges, and Blake said his officers got there too late to actually witness Mize in the act. Thompson remembered as many as thirty people in one sixteen-person holding cell and how he and others took the thick yellow ointment and tongue depressors the hospital had provided and treated the burns on their bodies. Thompson recalled the poignancy of the interracial moment. "My friend James Foushee, a local black fellow who was a little older than most of us and whom we all revered, put the ointment on a white demonstrator sitting on the floor in front of him," Thompson wrote. "I smoothed it on the back of another fellow I didn't know well . . . but had been in jail with several times. It was the first time I had ever touched a black person's skin that intimately. I was very careful; the skin on his back had darkened where the burns were worst."

James Foushee, a Chapel Hill native (and Braxton Foushee's brother) who once remained locked up for three months, went back to jail a few weeks later after another especially tense episode. Foushee entered Colonial Drug and sat down at the counter. Carswell pulled out a double-barrel shotgun, pointed it at Foushee's head and cocked one hammer, saying he would kill him if he didn't leave. "I reckon you are just going to have to kill me then," Foushee said.[33] Carswell called the police, who arrested Foushee for trespassing.

Jim Shumaker, editor of the *Weekly*, which flip-flopped between prointegration and antidemonstration, condemned the Rock Pile violence in a scathing editorial, calling it an "animal act" and wrote, "A man who deliberately inflicts bodily harm (like that) deserves the fullest punishment under the law and utter contempt of the community."[34]

Shumaker, who helped Blake and the town draft various statements, crafted a formal proposal for the Human Relations Committee to pass a public accommodations ordinance that the Board of Aldermen ducked six months earlier. The statement said the committee could not condone violation of the trespass law during sit-ins, obviously trying to spare the protestors from more incidents like the one at the Rock Pile. The Inter-Faith Council (IFC) for Social Service, championed by Bob Seymour, also urged passage, while dozens of people continued to be arrested at picket lines obstructing traffic and sit-ins that created constant chaos in Chapel Hill.

On Sunday, December 29, the day after the Rock Pile arrests, Seymour moderated a tense panel discussion between town leaders and protest organizers sponsored by the IFC. Dunne and Baker sat across from Chief Blake and Mayor McClamroch on one side of the U-shaped table and Joe Augustine from the Merchants Association and Alderman Roland Giduz sat on the other side. The only point they all agreed on was that racial discrimination existed in Chapel Hill despite strenuous efforts to eliminate it. More than two hundred people crowded into the Episcopal Chapel of the Cross sanctuary to watch and hear the sometimes emotional exchanges.

Dunne emphasized the "deep-seated" nature of the problem by pointing out that no black member sat on the town side of the panel. The failed public accommodations ordinance was at the heart of the discussion, which was closer to a debate. "How can you expect a person to prepare for a job when the job is not open to him?" Baker said. "How can you expect a Negro to prepare himself when all around people are saying, 'You are different'? Also, is it not the American tradition that when a law is being used unjustly, you make the most effective protest you can?"[35] Dunne, the white preppy, added that sit-in demonstrators were not resisting arrest for trespassing when going limp. "We are refusing to *assist* arrest, and I am not playing word games," he said.[36]

However, further episodes went on unabated.

Two incidents featured in memories of the Chapel Hill movement occurred on consecutive nights early the next year at the steadfastly segregated Watts Grill on U.S. 15-501 South, which was outside the town limits. On January 2, 1964, Lou Calhoun, a white UNC senior and member of the Wesley

Methodist Foundation, joined the two-mile-long march that included faculty and divinity students from Duke. Upon arriving and entering the grill adjacent to the Watts Motel, several demonstrators sat down at empty booths and were refused service. Others, including Calhoun, went to the floor and assumed the prone position they had been taught by Dunne, Cusick, and Baker. Calhoun, who was considered a "subleader" of the Freedom Movement, was almost dragged out the front door by two employees. At that point, Jeppie Watts, who owned the grill with her husband, Austin, stepped over Calhoun, hiked up her skirt and urinated on his head. Many of the customers clapped and shouted their approval.[37] Jeppie Watts further derided "anybody that'd let somebody piss on him."[38]

On the next night, Friday, January 3, a faculty group marched back to the Watts Grill. UNC psychology professor Albert Amon, who regularly accompanied evening protestors to segregated businesses, was grabbed by Austin Watts and kicked and severely beaten by white employees and customers. Amon died from a brain aneurysm several months later, although it was never proven to be medically related to his beating. German-born Duke zoology professor Peter Klopfer, who did not enter the grill, was still charged with trespassing. When his case was repeatedly continued through a legal procedure called "nolle prosequi with leave," he fought his right to a speedy trial all the way to the North Carolina and United States Supreme Courts. U.S. Chief Justice Earl Warren wrote the ruling in favor of Klopfer in 1967 and forced the case back to Orange County, where the charge was eventually dropped.

After the February 1, 1964, deadline passed, CORE threatened to bring in more volunteers and hold more demonstrations. This implied possible aggression that Blake could not stop even with the help of police and fire fighters from the county and neighboring cities and towns. The pot kept boiling, particularly the mass blockade after the Wake Forest-UNC basketball game, but reports from Washington that Kennedy's civil rights legislation was being navigated through Congress by President Lyndon Johnson seemed to quell the controversy. It could not come soon enough for most of Chapel Hill, which had grown more bitterly divided over the protests than the segregation it had lived with peacefully. The last major event before Easter Sunday in March was an eight-day Holy Week Fast on the front lawn of the downtown post office. It was chronicled daily by the *New York Times*, one of the few times the national press took notice. While the KKK held rallies north of town, the fast supported those of the more than 1,500 people arrested who were still jailed and charged with trespassing, obstruction, or both. A few citizens showed up daily at the courthouse to pay the $150 bail per arrest, sometimes leaving multiples of $450, $750, $900 to others who could not afford it. Some professors' wives brought meals and fresh clothing for the incarcerated, a mixture of black and white, young and old.

Most of them received additional $250 fines and suspended sentences, which were eventually commuted (but not pardoned) by Sanford. The leaders of the SPU and Chapel Hill Freedom Movement, including Baker, Cusick, and Dunne, got no mercy from stern Superior Court Judge Raymond Mallard, considered a "hanging judge" from Tabor City, North Carolina, who sentenced them to state prison for up to two years, although none of them served a full term. At the same hearing, Joseph "Buddy" Tieger, a Durham native and former Angier B. Duke Scholar, faced twenty-three counts of trespassing and obstruction, and was accused by Mallard of serving the cause of "an international conspiracy that would destroy this country."

After one year in prison, Dunne was paroled to Connecticut. He had already dropped out and lost his Morehead scholarship when he joined CORE. He transferred to Harvard and then went to law school at Yale. He practiced law in Boston before dying from cancer in his late thirties. Cusick never went back to school and worked for antipoverty groups in Boston before losing his lifetime battle with diabetes in 2004. (Their Student Peace Union stayed active and led campus protests against the invasion of Cambodia and after the fatal shootings at Kent State in 1970.) Baker, who dropped out of North Carolina College after his arrests, left the NAACP and transferred to the University of Wisconsin, did community work throughout the country for years, and finally returned to North Carolina to start a consulting firm in Hillsborough, where he retired. And when the darkest period in Chapel Hill history finally brightened, the debate continued over what exactly had been achieved, if anything besides fracturing a college town.

"The real issue that emerged was the belief that Chapel Hill could be the first community in the South . . . to voluntarily pass local legislation," said the Reverend Seymour, whose Binkley Baptist congregation was active in the protests. He added, "And we failed. Not until the federal government passed the public accommodation law was Chapel Hill able to say we have an open community."

Looking back some thirty years later, Seymour said, "It must be very hard for those of this generation to understand what it was like back then. The resistance to integration was very stubborn. It was a difficult time for a lot of people. The church came into being with a commitment to move in a new direction, and it was committed to civil rights from the word go."

Charles Thompson, the UNC freshman protestor, commented, "During the several months that we sat and demonstrated, we accomplished nothing locally. Not a single restaurant desegregated voluntarily. Nor any country store. No supermarket began hiring blacks. No mass support for desegregation arose, either from the town or from within the university. Not among the students, nor among the faculty, nor among the other local residents. Some local liberals said we had done both the town and university a disservice by moving too fast. People were not yet ready for desegregation."[39]

Still, law student Phil Baddour said he and others were watching from the university. "It helped the people who were on campus at the time to see the injustice of the customs and the laws that were part of our society," he said. "I think a lot of people learned from all of that how wrong it was."[40]

CHAPTER

4

The Right Timing

Far from the tumult of Chapel Hill's strife over desegregation, Charlie Scott had reached a pivotal crossroads. All his hard work, coupled with the support he received at Laurinburg, had brought him to the moment he dreamed would be his escape from the streets of Harlem: acceptance of a major college scholarship. And it looked for all the world like Davidson would win the prize as Scott's choice.

"Lefty was the first guy to recruit me," Scott remembered of the Davidson coach in the 1960s. "If there was no Lefty, there would be no Charlie Scott."

When word got around that Charles "Lefty" Driesell had a black recruit all lined up and that he had good enough grades and SAT scores to get into Davidson, the rest of the college basketball world, at least in the South, quickly discovered Charles Thomas Scott.

"At the end of my junior year at Laurinburg, I made a high enough score on my SAT to apply for early admission to Davidson," Scott explained. "That let coaches know I was open to going to school in the South. The ACC only required 800 on the SAT, but Davidson was the tough one. Once I got into Davidson, all the other schools started recruiting me."

Dean Smith first found out about Scott through UNC radio announcer Bill Currie, the famed "Mouth of the South" who worked for a station in Charlotte when he wasn't calling Carolina games. Smith was on the bus on the way back to Chapel Hill, stewing over a 70–69 loss at Virginia to a Cavaliers team that would finish the 1966 season with a 4–10 record in the ACC and 7–15 overall. With sophomore Larry Miller and junior Bobby Lewis, the Tar Heels had two of the best players in the league. They also had a sterling freshman team that had defeated the varsity in a serious preseason scrimmage. Smith later regretted holding that game, which was open to the public, because it created unhealthy competition within the program, something Smith abhorred.

The still-besieged UNC head coach, in his fifth season, had just lost to a school that didn't take basketball seriously. Virginia had an assistant on the bench who was also Virginia's lacrosse coach in the spring and whose best player, Jim Connelly, did not even make second team All-ACC. Smith sat gloomily in the back of the bus when Currie stopped by his seat. "Ol' Lefty's got himself a black player coming in next year," Currie told Smith. "He's visiting Duke this weekend." Smith looked up from the notes he was taking and said, "If he's going to visit Duke, he must not be all set for Davidson."[1]

Currie reported that Scott was tearing up opponents at Laurinburg Institute, whose headmaster and basketball coach, Frank McDuffie, had been coming to Carolina games for several years with Harvey Reid, the Elm City High School whom Smith had asked to be on the lookout for a quality and qualified African American player. Upon returning to Chapel Hill, Smith called McDuffie and learned that a couple of times he had left two tickets for him at the box office, Scott used the other seat. McDuffie told Smith that, yes, Scott was visiting Duke that weekend, and West Virginia the following week. McDuffie confirmed that Charlie hadn't signed anywhere yet.

A quirk in the schedule gave Carolina two weeks off before its next game against Wake Forest, and Smith planned to work his team hard in practice while assistants Larry Brown and John Lotz hit the recruiting trail. McDuffie encouraged Smith to attend Laurinburg's next game and scout Scott, who was averaging almost thirty points and twelve assists, and led the team in rebounding as a senior. Not long before, in front of a beaming Driesell, Scott had also poured in thirty-seven points against Davidson's freshman squad. Smith did not want to miss any practice but said he might send one of his assistants.

Larry Brown was already scheduled to fly to Indiana to see Lebanon High School All-American Rick Mount, who was having his picture taken for the cover of *Sports Illustrated* before his game. Dozens of college coaches were attending the spectacle, although the six foot four, blond-haired, blue-eyed gunner in the mold of other Hoosier hotshots was pretty much locked up to play for his uncle, George King, the coach at Purdue. So Smith assigned Lotz to make the short trip to Laurinburg.

Brown called the basketball office the next day, and Lotz answered the phone. "Hey, the guy I saw last night is better than the guy you saw," Lotz needled. Brown said he doubted it and asked Lotz to put Smith on the phone. Smith always liked to get a second opinion on players he had not seen and instructed Brown to fly back through Charlotte not far from Laurinburg; first, though, he told Brown to drive to Greensboro to check out a six foot two guard named Jim Folds, who played for Coach John Morris at Page High School. Subsequently, his lieutenant was to go down to Laurinburg to see Scott's next game the following night. A few days later, after leaving the tiny Laurinburg gym, Brown could not wait until the next morning to tell Smith what he had seen. He pulled into a gas station and used a pay phone to call his boss at home.

"Coach," Brown said, "I saw Rick Mount this week and I saw Charlie Scott tonight. Charlie is better." When Smith expressed some doubt, Brown insisted, describing Scott's bullet speed and slashing style that would later enthrall Tar Heels fans. "Better athlete, jumps out of the gym and shoots it from outside. You have to come down here and see how fast he is. And the people sitting around me said he was also ranked No. 1 in his class."

Smith had already heard the same from McDuffie. They had a longer phone conversation the next day, during which Smith learned more about Laurinburg's rich history and began to understand why McDuffie might want his latest star to play for the state university. McDuffie was born and reared in North Carolina, and before sending dozens of kids off with football and basketball scholarships, had serious interest in preparing them to graduate from college. He was a forward thinker, much like Smith, and had devised a formula of attracting black athletes with the lure of earning an athletic scholarship but also fulfilling the academic mission before they left Laurinburg.

Throughout his career, Smith recruited high school coaches as much as he did their star players. The McDuffies were devout Christians, and Lotz and his brother, Danny, a UNC player under Frank McGuire, were trying to start a North Carolina chapter of the Fellowship of Christian Athletes (FCA). Smith certainly did not mind that the Lotz brothers and former Tar Heel four-sport athlete Albert Long made regular trips to Laurinburg to enlist the McDuffies in the FCA. "We went down there three or four times and, I think, only saw Charlie once," Long recalled in 2016. "Dean was cunning as a fox, we all know that, and it was part of the process. When it came to recruiting the player, Dean handled that. But all of it helped, I'm sure. I got very close to the McDuffies, who were absolutely wonderful people, and eventually to Charlie."

McDuffie told Smith that Scott had talked about maybe becoming a lawyer or a doctor, and he invited the Carolina head coach down for their game the following week. "We had a rule that I had to see a player play before offering a scholarship," Smith wrote in his autobiography, "so I drove down to watch a game and brought along some friends to help recruit when meeting with the McDuffies and Charles after the game. Accompanying me were Frank Klingberg, a Carolina history professor, Thal Elliott, an African American member of Binkley Baptist and a medical student at the university, and Dan Pollitt, a Carolina law professor who at the time had just been featured in *U.S. News & World Report* as one of Lyndon Johnson's 'idea men.' "[2]

They watched Scott play, and Smith concurred with Brown and Lotz on his athletic ability, if not his court discipline. At this point in recruiting, Smith liked to call kids "prospects" because he was never sure how they would adapt to a freshman year and college basketball. The combination of Scott's athleticism and academics, however, made him by far the best current candidate to become the first black scholarship athlete at UNC. After the game, Smith met Scott for the first time.

"Frank and Mrs. McDuffie welcomed us to their home and were most hospitable," Smith later wrote of the conversation. "Coach McDuffie said that while Charlie had made an initial commitment to Lefty Driesell at Davidson in September, he had since backed away from it and was open to recruitment. Mrs. McDuffie, who was the dean of students, covered the academic situation while Coach McDuffie talked basketball. Still, most of the ninety minutes were spent discussing black-white relations at the university and in the town of Chapel Hill."[3]

Smith eventually learned the story of what happened at Davidson. At the time, Scott was still very close to Driesell as a recruit and planned to go there. However, an incident near campus had made the McDuffies, if not Scott himself, question the decision.

"Early in my senior season," Scott recounted during an interview before the 2014 game between UNC and Ohio State, where his youngest son, Shannon, played point guard for the Buckeyes:

> We had gone to Charlotte for a press conference before we played
> West Charlotte, one of the top black schools in North Carolina.
> Everyone knew I had committed to play at Davidson, so there was a
> lot of publicity. After that, Coach McDuffie said let's go up and see
> Lefty because Davidson was only thirty miles away. We went to the
> basketball office and (assistant coach) Terry Holland said Lefty was
> down at this restaurant eating, and he would take us over there. We got
> there, went in, and Lefty was eating black-eyed peas and rice, and
> Mrs. McDuffie said, "those black-eye peas look good." Lefty said to sit

down and order something to eat. So we sat down, and the waitress took the order. Five or ten minutes later, the owner of the restaurant [named the Coffee Cup] came over and said to Lefty, "Coach, I'm sorry, but my wife and I don't serve niggers on this side of the restaurant." Lefty was really embarrassed, and the McDuffies [were] very angry.

Although Driesell began a campaign that eventually shut down the Coffee Cup, Scott insisted the incident didn't sour him on Davidson as much as it upset the McDuffies. "I knew about that restaurant because I had been up there in the summer and Lefty always had some black friend take me around, and when we went there they made us eat in the back," Scott recalled.

Of course, none of this could have been known to Smith when he visited Laurinburg. At the end of the time in the McDuffie home, Smith asked if Scott could come to Chapel Hill for the annual spring Jubilee weekend in late April. They all agreed, and McDuffie said he would drive Scott up on Friday if someone could bring him back on Sunday. Smith said that could be arranged and mentioned to Scott, almost as an aside, "The Temptations and Smokey Robinson and the Miracles are performing that weekend. You like them, Charlie?" Scott lit up. After learning all the songs from *The Sound of Music* and joining the Laurinburg choir, he thought he was a pretty good singer himself.

In the intervening weeks, Scott finished his senior prep season, leading the team to a 23–3 record (he played in eighty total wins over three years). Meanwhile, he had to decide on Davidson or another of the schools chasing him. He visited UCLA, Villanova, Purdue, N.C. State, and Wake Forest during March and April.

"At that time, Davidson was really the No. 4 team in the country with Fred Hetzel," Scott recalled during the 2014 interview, "and I wasn't that much into the ACC. I just knew the rankings of the schools. I had seen Duke lose to UCLA on television, and I had visited there, so I knew a little about Duke, but I didn't know much about the ACC. North Carolina wasn't winning much back then. It was about Davidson being the No. 4 team in the country and this coach wanting to recruit me to play basketball there. That was something I never dreamed would happen, and I felt very fortunate that I was going to have that opportunity."

Still, McDuffie told Scott that he could not sign until he completed his visits, some of which were scheduled when he got back from the weekend in Chapel Hill. That only made Scott surer he would end up at Davidson, where he already felt special through the few relationships he had formed during his weekends there and the two summers working at Driesell's camp. "Because if you asked me which coach I loved the most, it was Lefty, by far, wasn't even close," Scott said. "With Lefty, I was his friend. Lefty did anything I wanted. Of course, I was a seventeen-year-old kid who never had anything. He would give me anything I wanted. Plus, a doctor in Laurinburg, a Dr. Richardson, was a Davidson grad. I wrecked his car; he gave me a car to drive and I tore it up, and he said that's okay and don't worry about it."

Scott wanted to be part of a college community and not seen as merely a basketball player. "When I went up to Davidson, Lefty got some black kid who lived in the city to take me around," Scott said. "And I had a girlfriend up there. That was my whole circumstance with Davidson, which at that time was very small, just a school. I had met some people in West Charlotte, and I figured that when I wanted to go out, I would have to go to Charlotte."

None of the other schools he had visited so far seemed to have anything different from Davidson to offer. Visiting more schools meant just seeing another campus—briefly—and meeting more basketball players. "At Duke, I went out to the Stallion Club and saw Otis Redding," Scott said. "But I didn't talk to alumni and meet any other people. At Wake Forest, I went out with Billy Packer," who was an assistant coach and former Deacons star.

Looking back, Scott believed those schools weren't ready for a black basketball star and perceived they may have been shielding him from meeting other students, faculty, and alumni—anyone outside the basketball program. Unlike most of the African American kids who went off to colleges that had already integrated, such as those in the old Pac-8 (Pacific-8 Conference) and Big 10, Scott still liked the idea of being the first African American athlete at the southern college of his choice, despite having seen segregation and bigotry up close.

"It was the only time I had felt wanted in my life," he said. "Subliminally, it was the admiration. The way I was recruited by Davidson and North Carolina was different from the way I was recruited by UCLA and Purdue. I loved Purdue, but the coach was talking about how great Rick Mount was going to be. At North Carolina State, I'll never forget Press Maravich saying he was going to give me the biggest thrill of my life by playing with his son Pete."

Scott and McDuffie drove to Chapel Hill after Laurinburg's 1966 season ended to start the recruiting process. Although Smith would never have done it later in his career, he tipped off a *DTH* photographer that Scott was coming and posed for a picture with him in front of a chalk board alongside former

UNC All-American and NBA player Lee Shaffer and rising All-ACC star Larry Miller; as a sophomore, Miller had averaged twenty-one points and made second team all-conference. The caption in the *DTH* read in part, "Scott, who has medical school aspirations, is a fine young man the University is anxious to have become part of its family."[4] The photo was Smith's way of forewarning alumni that he was seriously pursuing a *black* player.

Smith received one threat from a Rams Club donor that it would cost UNC $1 million in endowment money if he signed Scott or any other African American. Smith called Ernie Williamson, who ran the Educational Foundation (aka the Rams Club), and found out that this particular donor had never given more than $10 a year. At about the same time, Smith showed that this was more about civil liberties than recruiting by refusing to join the Chapel Hill Country Club, with the best golf course in town, until it admitted blacks.[5]

On Friday, April 29, 1966, McDuffie drove Scott back to Chapel Hill for the Jubilee weekend and his player's official recruiting visit. He dropped Scott in front of brand-new Carmichael Auditorium, where Bobby Lewis had set UNC's single-game scoring record with forty-nine points the previous December against Florida State. Even before the first visit with McDuffie, Scott had already been in that building for two games, after which he and McDuffie drove right back to Laurinburg. Carolina was the only other school McDuffie ever took him to see a college game besides Davidson.

Scott said he would see McDuffie back at Laurinburg on Sunday afternoon and walked through the glass doors of Carmichael. A trophy case sat against the wall in the main lobby with the hardware from the 1957 ACC and NCAA championships, the only major titles UNC had won in basketball to that point. The young recruit ambled around the concourse until he found the basketball office. Entering the small suite, which had Carolina blue carpeting and pictures of the Old Well and Bell Tower campus landmarks on the wall, Scott was greeted by Betsy Terrell, the secretary whom Smith considered a "third assistant," both for her sports savvy and her indispensable ability to handle every situation that arose when the coaches were away. (Terrell's husband, Simon, was then executive director of the North Carolina High School Athletic Association and a regular member of Smith's golf foursome.) Terrell greeted Scott with her warm smile and said Smith was on a long-distance phone call. She handed Scott two tickets to the Temptations concert that night at Carmichael and gave him information on where to meet his campus host for the weekend, who turned out to be senior James Womack, the first black male cheerleader at UNC. Comparing that to hearing a racial slur at an eatery in Davidson, Scott's weekend in Chapel Hill had gotten off to a considerably different start.

"Coach Smith would like you to come by at ten o'clock in the morning," Terrell said with her best Southern charm. "You can meet some of the players and have a tour of campus."

Later in his career, Smith began copying several recruiting methods from Duke coach Vic Bubas that Frank McGuire never needed because he knew so many people in New York, his almost exclusive talent base. Bubas started the process earlier than most coaches, split the country up by regions and assigned one to each of his assistants, and was a master at staying in touch with prospects and their families through phone calls and handwritten notes. Smith copied that and throughout his career was known as a serial letter writer to his future, current, and former players. He even wrote to favorite recruits who went elsewhere, wishing them good luck and then happy holidays.

After five seasons, Smith had his own secrets that many coaches would learn from him. He knew, mainly from talking to prospects and their families, that other schools tried to impress highly rated recruits by having them spend time with the established stars on their teams, hoping to send them home bragging about who they hung out with on their official visit. Smith was more interested in recruits getting to know the members of the team they might actually *play with* if they came. His current freshmen and sophomores were therefore his chief recruiters.

Thus, Scott's basketball host for Jubilee weekend was Dick Grubar, whose freshman team had gone 15–1, the only blemish coming when seven-foot center Rusty Clark missed a game. Grubar was also from upstate New York, had seen the Tar Heels play in that 1964 loss at the Garden when Billy Cunningham was a one-man team, and was excited about Scott taking the open position after Lewis graduated following the 1967 season.

"We knew Charlie was a great player and I was anxious to have him on the team, especially since he wasn't going to take my position as point guard," Grubar said in 2015. "We were going to need another 'two guard' and I wanted to play. By the time Charlie got to the varsity, Bobby would be gone. And while Bobby was a good player, Coach Smith had told us how good Charlie was."

On Saturday morning, Smith, Brown, and Lotz asked Scott about the concert, inquiring whether he had enjoyed the Temptations, and gave him the schedule for the rest of the weekend. Smith had set up a meeting with his friend and assistant dean of the medical school, Chris Fordham. Scott and Fordham spent several hours together, part of the time donning surgical masks and viewing an actual operation. Back at the basketball office, Smith asked Scott the question he asked many recruits: what name would he like to be called. Scott said everyone knew him as "Charlie" or "Scotty," but that he preferred the name his mother had given him at birth, Charles. From that point on, it was Charles, at least for Smith, who would be regularly needled by the media and fans for steadfastly using the formal name—and perhaps force-feeding dignity and respect upon a black athlete—instead of the much more common "Charlie." Smith then invited Scott to attend church with him the next morning. Scott agreed and it turned out to be a key piece of the weekend, as he said later, "No other coach ever asked me to go to church with him."

After this, it was off with Grubar and fellow freshman Joe Brown; they walked around the campus on a perfect spring day in Chapel Hill. Live music blared from fraternities, including the local Carrboro band Doug Clark and the Hot Nuts. Grubar had tipped off a couple of his friends at the Kappa Alpha (KA) house that he might stop by with a star basketball recruit who was black. "KA was one of the most Southern houses on campus, but everyone there was great to Charlie," Grubar said. "They knew he was a basketball star we wanted, and we all had a blast. They might have been all white and Southern, but they were also big basketball fans."

Before going to hear Smokey Robinson and the Miracles that night, they met up with Miller, already the star of the team. The group went to dinner at the Ranch House on Airport Road, one of the most expensive restaurants in town, and all ordered chateaubriand. Lotz, who had clicked immediately with Scott and offered to drive him back to Laurinburg with Larry Brown on Sunday, told Grubar to go anywhere and order anything. This was their one shot at Scott, so they were to make it good. "The concert in Carmichael was great," Grubar said. "It was a mostly white crowd, but Charlie seemed completely comfortable. We were up singing and dancing in the aisles. And afterward we went by the St. A house, which was the most Northern fraternity on campus, and they loved Charlie, too. We had a pretty late night."

Scott said years later, "What turned it around for me was going out with Dickie Grubar, Joe Brown, and Larry Miller." He added, "At other schools, I went around with guys I would never be playing with. Like at Duke, I went out with Steve Vacendak and Bob Verga. They would be gone after the next season. Coach Smith said, 'These are the guys you will be playing with.' That was the way he did things. It was smart."

It may seem obvious today, but Smith bringing two professors and a black medical student with him to Laurinburg and inviting him to a mixed-congregation church service were cutting-edge tactics back then. It should be noted as well that those tactics might not have worked at other schools because Chapel Hill was still considerably more progressive than anywhere else in the South. At Duke, for example, the savvy Bubas probably knew to keep Scott away from a campus that was even whiter than UNC, with mostly Northerners from very wealthy families.

At Binkley Baptist Church the next morning, Scott heard the Reverend Seymour deliver a sermon that touched on racial equality. He also met Howard and Lillian Lee, who would be his good friends during his four years at UNC. And he renewed his acquaintance with ex-pro Lee Shaffer, at the time in an executive position with a company owned by millionaire alumnus Frank Kenan in Chapel Hill. In addition, he also met Charlie Shaffer (no relation), a Morehead Scholar and two-sport athlete at Carolina who was in law school there. Smith's strategy was working well, and he hoped to ask Scott directly before he departed whether he would like to play for the Tar Heels.

After church, Lotz took Scott to lunch at the Rathskeller, a favorite restaurant of the coaches and many of the players, where most of the waiters were black. Scott told Lotz he would meet him at the basketball office at two o'clock for the drive back to Laurinburg, but rather than walking across campus, Scott went up and down Franklin Street a few times. It turned out to be one of the most consequential strolls in UNC basketball history. Scott returned to Carmichael around 2:30, and for the punctually obsessed Smith that would normally have been a red flag. Of all the people he was with over the weekend, Scott had only seen Smith for a couple of hours and at church. And he knew from what the players said that Smith was no "buddy-buddy" coach like Driesell.

"Back then, everyone was a little scared of Coach Smith," Scott said. "I related much more to Coach Lotz and Coach Brown because they were from New York and we told each other a lot of stories. When I got to the office, I apologized and said I enjoyed lunch with Coach Lotz at the Rathskeller because all the guys who worked there were very friendly to me. Then, I walked up Franklin Street by myself just to see how it would be when most people didn't know who I was."

Smith, sensing that Scott might have helped with his own recruitment, asked how the walk went and learned that a non-negative could be as important as a positive. "It was more that I didn't feel ostracized, I didn't feel strained,"

Scott recalled of his answer to Smith. "The atmosphere was one where I wasn't intimidated if they didn't know I was a basketball player, so I felt comfortable." Since Scott was already late leaving for Laurinburg, Smith left the shakedown to Lotz and Brown, with whom Scott had already bonded. On the ride back, the coaches asked him what he liked most about the weekend and how relaxed he felt with the players, in Chapel Hill and on campus. And then the big question: Would he come to Carolina?

Scott was direct, saying that he liked everything about the weekend and, yes, he could see himself playing for UNC. But he said that didn't matter since McDuffie wasn't letting him sign anywhere until he finished all of his recruiting visits. "I didn't think my answer would be (considered) the definitive answer because Coach McDuffie already told me I couldn't sign to go anywhere," Scott said. "So I told them, 'Yeah, I'd like to come here' but didn't think it would go any further than that. I pretty much thought that would be the end of it and I would still go to Davidson."

When the group pulled into the parking lot at Laurinburg, right in front of the red brick wall with the school name in big letters, McDuffie was there to greet them. Brown was never shy, and Lotz was already a great recruiting salesman. They confronted McDuffie with what Scott had told them in the car. "Larry and John told Coach McDuffie that I would like to go to Carolina, but he said I couldn't sign anywhere yet," Scott recalled in 2014. "And Coach McDuffie said, 'No, he can sign to go there.' So I was caught in that conundrum. I thought he would tell them I couldn't sign yet. That's why, looking back, Carolina was always where he wanted me to go. He was steering me in that direction. I thought he would tell them no and that would keep it (recruiting) going. I was stuck because I told them I wanted to go there."

Bishop McDuffie, who took over running Laurinburg after his father died in 1994, confirmed in 2014 that his parents knew the importance of Scott being the first black scholarship athlete at the state university as compared to a small, private school such as Davidson. "My father had great wisdom and had lived the history of Laurinburg," Bishop said. "He coached the basketball team, was the headmaster, and also directed the school band and the choir. He was like a Renaissance man. For Charlie to go to Carolina would be much bigger than anywhere else in this state. He would become part of history, part of the story, of both Carolina and Laurinburg."

After Brown and Lotz departed, Scott and McDuffie spent Sunday afternoon together going over the respective pluses and minuses of Davidson and UNC because, among the ninety schools that had contacted them, there were only two real choices. Scott knew the social life at Davidson was limited and he would have to travel the twenty miles to Charlotte to find another black community. At UNC, it was only ten miles to North Carolina Central in Durham. They broke down the respective basketball programs and their immediate futures. Although Davidson was nationally ranked in 1966, Fred Hetzel was already gone and Dick Snyder was graduating that spring. And what did they really know about Mike Maloy, Jerry Kroll, and Doug Cook? Neither had ever seen them play against good competition. "I had seen Rusty Clark play in Fayetteville, which was a half hour from Laurinburg," Scott said. "And I had watched the North Carolina high school all-star game the year before and saw Rusty, Bill Bunting, and Joe Brown play. So I knew they were all good. I figured Dickie (Grubar) could play, and Larry Miller had averaged twenty points as a sophomore and made All-ACC. Carolina hadn't won yet, but they were going to win. It was pretty clear to me after I thought about it."

Despite no championships to date, Smith had begun winning in the ACC with a 41–29 record over his first five seasons. Only the dominant Bubas (61–9) had done better from 1962 through 1966, and Scott already knew he wasn't going to Duke.

By late Sunday afternoon, Scott had decided on UNC over Davidson. The most difficult part was telling Driesell, and Scott dreaded that phone call. When he finally made it, Driesell's wife, Joyce, said Lefty was recruiting in Texas and would have to call him back. Scott knew the Driesells well; he knew they had been sweethearts since junior high school in Norfolk and eloped while Lefty was a student and basketball player at Duke. Scott was relieved to leave the message with Joyce, especially given how much he feared telling her husband directly. "I love Lefty the best, but Chapel Hill is just a better place for me to go to school," Scott said, and then hung up the phone.

McDuffie called Smith, who drove to Laurinburg on Sunday night with Lotz and Brown to get the news in person from Scott. They met at the McDuffie home, and after Scott went back to his dorm, sat at the kitchen table for a historic dinner, plotting how they were about to integrate college basketball in the South. While it is true that there were African American players at other ACC schools, and Vanderbilt had signed the first black player in the SEC, none of them would ever make the same impact as Charlie Scott at North Carolina. "It was a special time for our family and our school," related Bishop, who was only six years old at the time but heard the stories often growing up.

The actual signing occurred on Tuesday in Frank McDuffie's office because Scott wanted more time to personally talk to Driesell. When Smith and Sports Information Director Bob Quincy walked in the main door of the Laurinburg administration building, Driesell was waiting in the hallway. Lefty had flown back to Charlotte that morning and driven right to Laurinburg, hoping to change Scott's mind. Stories of a confrontation between the coaches were downplayed for years, and Scott has since said, "I don't remember any incident like that. But I don't really know because I was probably hiding some place. I didn't know how to tell Lefty I wasn't coming."

The task fell to McDuffie. He told Lefty he could not talk to Scott because the recruitment was over and he was signing with UNC. Despite the awkwardness of the day, Scott remained close with Driesell and visited him at least once a year after college. He pushes back tears when recalling the time Lefty pulled out a box of old letters from Scott and still had every one he had written to Driesell.

Bishop said his father was smiling when he told Quincy, "Charlie is a great ballplayer, but I often tell him he isn't as good as he thinks he is. He can do almost anything with a basketball, but his scoring average is misleading. It could actually be more. He passed up numerous shots to feed the ball last season. The boy has gone through a lot. He wants to please everyone, but he knows when a decision is reached some will not be happy."

According to Bishop, a couple of deals were on the table and he wished there had been two more. "Coach Smith told my dad that as long as he was at Carolina, Charlie's children would be able to follow him there." (Scott's daughter, Simone, and son Shaun graduated from Carolina forty years later; Shannon, a recruited point guard, opted for Ohio State when Roy Williams already had Kendall Marshall and was hoping to sign Marcus Paige.)

Bishop continued, "My father also wanted Coach Smith's help in making John Russell the first African American basketball official in the ACC. Russell, who was one of the lead officials in the CIAA [Central Intercollegiate Athletic Association], had lived with our family since Dad had rescued him from a situation when he might have gone to prison. And he turned out to be a very good ref." With Smith's recommendation, Russell wound up officiating in the ACC for almost twenty years. Bishop also recalled the two deals he later told his father they should have made in perpetuity. "Although he could go to any game he wanted, the Laurinburg headmaster should have had two season tickets to UNC football and basketball forever, but that never happened. And for our recruiting, we needed to play the UNC freshmen (and later junior varsity) every season in Chapel Hill. That stopped about ten years ago."

Scott's innocence that day was apparent when he told Quincy on the record, "The campus is beautiful, and I think I will fit in with the student body. I don't want to be just a basketball player. I want to be part of student life." He recounted what he had observed on Jubilee weekend. "Chapel Hill is cosmopolitan, at least from what I have seen. I saw a few Beatniks on the street. Now, I want no part of being a beatnik, but it does show there is a tolerance on the campus, and I think that is important."

Smith confirmed to the *DTH* that "the atmosphere for the Negro student" at UNC was a big part of Scott's decision.[6] In retrospect, it was somewhat naïve on Scott's part and a stretch for Smith, who had to believe he had found an African American player strong enough to endure what was ahead. Smith knew there were barely fifty undergraduate black students on campus in 1966.

That was the first and only time Smith talked extensively about signing a black player, emphasizing there were no restrictions on any high school students as long as they met UNC's entrance requirements. "We recruited Louis Hudson about five years ago," Smith told the *DTH*. "Carolina's policy has been in this direction. . . . Scott's the first one to have both the academic and athletic qualifications. He will fit our system of run and pressure defense perfectly. He's quick as a cat. Great reaction time. And Charles is a fine boy, and first-line student . . . not just a gladiator."[7]

The Davidson community and Driesell took Scott's defection very hard, and it continued to be a sore point for decades. In 1969, McDuffie spoke about Driesell in a fashion that did not seem to square with Scott's view. "I believe in letting my boys make their own decisions on where to go to college," McDuffie told the *Greensboro Daily News*. "In Charlie's case, he didn't think he would get along with a violent, demanding coach. He felt the Carolina coaches, Dean Smith and John Lotz, were real fine gentlemen. He also preferred the cosmopolitan atmosphere at Carolina."[8] Those were McDuffie's words, but Scott always got along with Lefty and never characterized him that way.

Although included with Charlotte, Greensboro, and Winston-Salem as among the first communities in North Carolina to desegregate schools, Chapel Hill's change did not come smoothly for the liberal college town. A full five years after the *Brown v. Board of Education* Supreme Court decision declared "separate but equal" unconstitutional, Chapel Hill had done exactly what the rest of the South had done to open up its schools—nothing. In 1959, in fact, there were fewer black students enrolled in North Carolina public schools than in

1957.[9] School systems denied hundreds of requests across the state for black students to attend white schools.[10]

The North Carolina legislature had passed the "Pearsall Plan" in 1956, which was designed to slow the pace of desegregation, some say, with the hope that it might not work and go away. Also referred to as the "Freedom of Choice" plan, it could be customized by individual school boards and required families that wanted their children to go to schools with the opposite race to apply for a transfer. The first Chapel Hill application was filed in 1957 by African American parent Preston R. Weaver, who favored a white elementary school for its superior facilities and art instruction. The school board denied the transfer, saying the reason for the request was inadequate.[11] Frustrated by that and other transfers being turned down for what he believed were racial reasons, school board member Harry Brandis, a professor at the UNC law school, resigned in 1959.

John R. Manley, pastor of the First Baptist Church, was the first black appointed to the school board, calling himself "respected but not accepted." Manley, who left rural Hertford County to graduate from Shaw University and get his master's at Duke, was ready for the ensuing battles, having previously threatened to sue the school board when it refused to build a gymnasium at Lincoln High (the board backed down and funds were found).

When board members were looking for a site for the new high school, they asked Manley to ride with them to a location on Piney Mountain Road, where a dozen or so black families lived in tumbledown housing. "They were looking for land that was owned by the blacks. And I asked, 'Would the blacks want to sell it?' I was told by a member of the school board, 'They don't have to sell it. We can condemn it,'" Manley said.[12]

Manley opposed condemning the land because it was zoned residential and could be further developed by other black families, with homes built there. As a compromise of sorts, he was asked to look for another location and found one hundred acres off Homestead Road, which was owned by a member of his congregation who was heir to a wealthy family. "We bought that land for $100 an acre undeveloped and we put the high school out there," Manley said. "There was tension because they had left me out of the loop on the first site, and when they knew I would not only vote against it, but was prepared to work to oppose it, they sort of gave me the respect and accepted that I found another solution."[13]

When the Vickers family of Chapel Hill was denied a transfer to a white school for their son Stanley, they sued the school board. At the federal court hearing, Manley refused to go along with the board's testimony as to why the transfer had been denied. He then tipped off the federal attorneys (who included Thurgood Marshall, soon to be the first African American Supreme Court justice) to ask school board members specific questions under oath about denying the Vickers' application. When asked those questions, board members could not lie, and consequently, Stanley Vickers won his right to transfer to a white school.

Manley found himself in the majority voting bloc in 1961 after Fred Ellis and Richard Peters, two white members of Bob Seymour's Binkley Baptist congregation who had young children in the school system, won seats on the board. Just as Dean Smith was "assigned" to find a black basketball player, Ellis and Peters were answering the call of their church ministry and won due to the strong support from the town's white liberal and black church coalition. Manley, Peters, and Ellis turned out to cast the deciding votes for school desegregation in the town.

Finally, in 1961, the school board ruled that first-graders who could walk to an opposite-race school could go there. Without rescheduling bus transportation for such moves, the "walking distance" stipulation passed. Three first-graders walked to Estes Hills Elementary School for the 1961–62 school year. Over the next two years, with the help of redistricting, eighty black and seventy white grade-schoolers crisscrossed over racial barriers. The junior highs and high schools remained segregated.

Despite what his own newspaper had trumpeted as a "Historic Integration Plan Adopted for Chapel Hill School District" because it came without a single court order, Jim Shumaker called out the plan in a *Chapel Hill Weekly* editorial as "token integration."

"In the nine years since the Supreme Court's desegregation ruling, Chapel Hill has accomplished no more than legal window dressing," Shumaker wrote. "Five formerly white schools have token desegregation; three Negro schools remain completely segregated. . . . The official policy has been one of legal compliance, while the School Board's official acts have served to perpetuate segregation."[14]

Being hailed as "best in the South" should not have been deemed good enough for Chapel Hill, according to Shumaker and other proponents of desegregation. Before the first day of school in the fall of 1962, Shumaker's paper printed the total projected enrollment and number of blacks registered at former all-white schools. The following day, the *Weekly* published the actual numbers—along with one other statistic: how many white students were at schools where blacks were now attending, almost as if those kids were having their educations compromised by integration. Why else would such a distinguishing figure be published?

Believing and afraid the conflict was tearing apart church congregations, Seymour formed the Fellowship for School Integration. With ground having been broken on the new Chapel Hill High School, "all deliberate speed" was not nearly fast enough to effect complete desegregation by the time it opened. "The Fellowship for School Integration pulled people from various places in the community who wanted to see this happen but were frustrated by an inability to get a handle on it," Seymour said. "This was a very liberal group that spared the churches from having internal conflicts over this issue."

Seymour saw the "school board dragging its feet" and many of the church congregations being fractured. "Chapel Hill was still a very Southern town," he said, "and those who wanted to see this happen could work through the Fellowship rather than their churches. History will show that this group had a very positive effect toward the integration goal."

The Pearsall Plan turned out beneficial by keeping cities and towns in North Carolina from integrating "en masse" and creating cultural, professional, and social conflicts that truly needed "deliberate speed." As it was, both races struggled over the loss of their respective school cultures. Some familiar teachers and administrators lost their jobs, and students were thrown into integrated classes, clubs, bands, and sports teams. To many, it was a strange new world.

Chapel Hill never passed its own Public Accommodations Ordinance, waiting until President Johnson signed the Civil Rights Act to into law on July 2, 1964. Not every segregated business complied right away, based on groups of "testers" the town sent out to restaurants that had not served blacks before. Leo's Grill, Brady's, The Pines, and the Tar Heel Sandwich Shop all opened for racially mixed groups of customers. "We're not going to disobey the law of the U.S. government," said Leroy Merritt, owner of The Pines, which was believed to have served one black customer over a five-year span—the theology student who went to dinner there with Dean Smith and Robert Seymour in 1959. "If colored people come in and behave themselves, they'll be treated just like everybody else," he continued. Even The Rock Pile, site of Carlton Mize's "animal act," began accepting black customers.

In what he read as an unfair attack on a town that had been through five years of ideological and racial warfare, Jim Shumaker reacted strongly to a nationally syndicated United Press International story that characterized Chapel Hill as "straining to keep up the liberal image long associated with this historic university town."

"The people in Chapel Hill at whom today's civil rights demonstrations are aimed do not respond to such appeals," Shumaker editorialized just before the Civil Rights Act passed. "They do not understand or even listen. We think it is more realistic than cynical to accept the fact that there will always be a certain number of these human blights on the face of Chapel Hill, and other places. Except by geographical accident, they do not represent Chapel Hill, its people or its spirit. Chapel Hill will try to continue to eliminate discrimination where it exists in whatever way seems best. We will not indulge in an orgy of self-flagellation because all is not right, nor will we try to pretend that nothing is wrong. But whatever we do or try to do will be done, not in the fond hope of trying to live up to some nebulous image, but simply because we believe it to be right."[15]

The university, for the most part, never engaged in the civil rights conflict. President Bill Friday and former Chancellor Bill Aycock had taken on the speaker ban by mounting what the *DTH* termed, upon Aycock's death in 2015, a "relentless campaign to promote free speech." When it was originally passed, Aycock had blistered the so-called "gag law" before the Greensboro Bar Association, charging its creators in Raleigh with the "sloppiest and poorest-drafted legislation I have ever seen. This law is so full of ambiguities that even the author couldn't possibly say what it really means." Some critics of the UNC administration wondered why the leadership fought so hard against the speaker ban while having little to say about segregation.

"The idea was—and we never varied in this—do whatever is necessary to get rid of it," Friday said. "And we kept that right on through. Sometimes underground and sometimes out visible. Always negotiating but never compromising. Because there are not many things left in this country that you can stand on without any fear. And one of them is the right to say what you think. . . . And most of all, universities are places where freedom should be spoken."[16]

President Friday, who might have been advising behind the scenes, said he had good reasons why the liberal-labeled flagship university had stayed out of the desegregation fray. "It was not our jurisdiction, and in those days everybody was super-sensitive about who was responsible for what," he said. "That was an issue in the town government, and I was caught up (in the speaker ban) 24 hours a day almost."[17]

Ironically, UNC brought in former Mississippi governor and acknowledged racist Ross Barnett to speak at Memorial Hall to a mixed crowd of 1,200 students and faculty, and more than a hundred blacks and whites walked out when Barnett used the word "nigger" in answering a question; they then stood outside singing freedom songs.[18]

In 1965, following more than a year of vigorous protests from students and faculty, the General Assembly amended the speaker ban, returning such control to the campus boards of trustees, some of which were still in favor of the law and bounced it back to their respective administrations. Dissatisfied UNC student leaders were determined to get the law repealed or amended and had their chance when Chancellor Paul F. Sharp turned down a request from student body president Paul Dickson to have Communist Party member Herbert Aptheker and sympathizer Frank Wilkinson speak on campus. They were invited anyway and spoke to a small group of faculty and students at McCorkle Place from the sidewalk on East Franklin Street. Students held up a banner proclaiming that "Governor Dan Moore's (Chapel Hill) Stone Wall" separated the university from free speech.

Jock Lauterer, a *DTH* photographer who covered the protest, said "it was an homage in a way and a reference—not too veiled—to the Berlin Wall, which, of course, to us at the time meant this barrier between black and white, good and evil, practically."[19]

Aside from the speaker ban controversy, the town and campus calmed considerably over the next year, with Mayor Sandy McClamroch disbanding all the local committees that had fought segregation so passionately. The new Chapel Hill High School was nearing completion, planning to open with integrated grades 10 through 12 in the fall of 1966, ironically, the same time Charlie Scott would be enrolling at UNC. It was a sad day for the African American community, which had taken great pride in Lincoln's undefeated 1961 state football championship team and its decorated marching band. Eventually, the Lincoln building headquartered the Chapel Hill–Carrboro school system and retained its gymnasium and playing fields for local recreation leagues.

The 1965–66 UNC basketball team turned out to be the last over the next thirty years that would have the word "mediocre" associated with it. Despite junior Bob Lewis, who led the ACC with 27.4 points per game, and sophomore Larry Miller, who averaged 21 points and 10.3 rebounds, the Tar Heels had only one player (senior Bob Bennett) as tall as six foot eight. Their overall record was 16–11, but with an 8–6 mark, they were the second of what would be thirty-six consecutive Carolina teams to finish in the top three of the ACC standings. Smith lost three more times to Duke and Vic Bubas, who would go on to their third Final Four in four years, but the third defeat was the epic slowdown in the semifinals of the last ACC Tournament played in Raleigh, when Smith called for Four Corners to try to pull the bigger Blue Devils out of their zone. They never came out and sweated through a 21–20 win in which the crowd went from booing the Tar Heels to cheering them and their gutsy coach as they left the court. Smith said, "We did not come over here to play a close game. We came over here to win." The victories would soon be piling up, thanks to a plethora of recruiting successes that would go on almost indefinitely.

On March 19, 1966, in College Park, Maryland, Texas Western (later UTEP) became the first team to win the NCAA Tournament championship with five black starters, defeating Kentucky and segregationist coach Adolph Rupp. That June, Smith spoke at Charlie Scott's Laurinburg graduation ceremony, as the senior class valedictorian completed the first step of a dream he once thought unreachable on the streets of Harlem. For five years, Smith had tried to find an African American who by other people's standards qualified to play for his team, and now the balance he had long sought in his program was beginning to form.

CHAPTER

5

Together Alone

Barely two years after the height of civil rights strife that had roiled Chapel Hill, no one knew for sure how Charlie Scott's enrollment at UNC would evolve. Resentment remained over the university's detached attitude toward the racial turbulence in town, and now Dean Smith was bringing in UNC's first black scholarship athlete. Scott had made a bold decision but could hardly know what to expect of his new surroundings and how he would react to them.

Smith believed that Scott being a star player would mitigate most outward prejudice. For example, the all-white, traditionally southern Kappa Alpha house that proudly flew a Confederate flag out front had greeted Scott without a murmur after Dick Grubar notified his frat friends that he was "bringing over a great recruit." The fraternity boys who didn't know about Scott's skin color still shook his hand and slapped his back. It was pretty much all an act for the sake of beating Duke and State.

Despite record enrollment of 13,000 students in the fall of 1966, when Scott began his freshman year, the *DTH* estimated there were "about 50 Negro undergraduates ... fewer than were enrolled last year,"[1] according to Juan Cofield, president of the campus NAACP. Perhaps due to growing criticism from some that UNC was not actively recruiting minority students, racial statistics were not readily available after the fall of 1963, when it listed 53 total African American enrollments, including 15 undergraduate students. The highest figure the year before had 110 graduate students among the total 182 blacks on campus. No numbers were easily accessible for more than 35 years, only percentages. (In the freshman class of 2014, the 3,974 enrollees were 11 percent black, which was approximately 437 students).[2]

It is difficult to know what might have led to a decline of African American students enrolling at this time, but their lack of social life on campus likely played a part. With North Carolina boasting more historically black colleges and universities than any other state, minority students capable of admission to UNC may have chosen to attend African American colleges because they were happier there—and UNC wasn't doing much to recruit minorities in 1966.

Cofield said the university "made some efforts as far as recruitment is concerned, but we know for a fact that the recruitment program as a whole has gone down."[3] In a letter to the *DTH* in the fall of 1967, a student named Charles Cherry said that UNC finding and recruiting black students who met the minimum freshman entry standards was "admirable and praiseworthy [but] many colored students, incapacitated by inadequate high school training, cannot meet SAT requirements; yet should this be a convenient excuse for negligence of any university's responsibility to educate? Relax requirements and admit such students on a provisional basis so that, given a healthier academic environment, they might best develop their potential.... It is a great shame that the ... long reputable, progressive institution, should not respond more positively to rectify the major education problems in our society."[4]

Cherry, a UNC senior at the time, might not have known Dean Smith but was certainly a young man after Smith's heart. Smith preached the same message throughout his life: find the potential in all people and give them an opportunity to grow. He considered Charles Scott smart enough to graduate, but would he last four years on a campus that had so few black students? Smith would do his best to give him every chance possible. It has been said that Smith treated all of his players the same, but it would be more accurate to say he treated them all *fairly*, a relative term that allowed for differences in individual circumstances.

Scott arrived in Chapel Hill from Laurinburg in June 1966 and went to work for a local poverty program that recruited students to work for North Carolina Outward Bound. He could earn money because he was not yet on scholarship, which would soon pay for his tuition, room, board, and books, plus fifteen dollars a month ("laundry money"), which most athletes usually spent on beer. Although Scott could not work at the Carolina basketball camp after his senior year in high school (an NCAA rule), he occasionally went to Carmichael at night and scrimmaged with the counselors, sometimes in front of the campers. While his athleticism was transcendent, he seemed like a pro playing with amateurs. It was difficult to imagine him as a member of the Tar Heels, who were all home for the summer, and Scott was generally the only black face in the gym. In those early days, he began to spend a considerable amount of time with coaches John Lotz and Larry Brown, his New York kindred spirits who could talk basketball and the city with him over long lunches and dinners at the Rat.

Smith had also signed freshmen Eddie Fogler, a ball-handling whiz from Queens, New York, and tough-nosed Jim Delany from South Orange, N.J., both barely six feet tall and seen as backup point guards for Grubar. Also joining the program were Al Armour, a six foot two shooting guard from suburban Chicago, and six foot five forward Gra Whitehead, whose family was among the wealthiest in the rural northeastern North Carolina farming town of Scotland Neck. The Whitehead estate had acres and acres of fields farmed by blacks who lived in rows of shacks connected by electricity lines.

"Dean came to Scotland Neck and saw the environment I was from," Whitehead said many years later. "He asked me, 'Is it going to bother you with Charlie on the team? We won't ask you to room with him.' I told him not one bit, that I had played with colored farming children all my life, and some of them were my best friends."

During his first summer in Chapel Hill, Scott must have earned enough money to purchase a round-trip airline ticket in August to fulfill one of his dreams and play in the Rucker Tournament in Harlem. He had not been back to New York in three years, and during that time, had virtually no communication with his mother. He found her peeved at him for changing his mind on Davidson. "I told her I was afraid to see Lefty the week I signed with Carolina; I felt very ashamed of that," Scott said years later. "She said I went back on my word. My family had visited Davidson the summer I committed (1965), and Lefty had taken them all out. They knew Lefty and they liked him. In fact, my mother slammed the door when Coach Smith went up to Harlem to see her. She wouldn't let him in because she felt like he made me go against my word."

Despite what must have a been a bittersweet homecoming, Scott burst onto the Rucker scene, driving the crowd crazy with his all-around game, especially his speed, crossover dribble, and leaping ability while dunking on fast breaks. Those who had not seen "Scotty" since he left Harlem for Laurinburg in 1963 were already comparing him to Jackie Robinson for his bravery in integrating an elite white university like North Carolina. Scott would soon soar to the basket at UNC, but had to drop the ball over the rim; perhaps timed to coincide with seven foot Lew Alcindor's junior year at UCLA in 1968, the dunk had been ruled out of the college game for what would be nine years.

Meanwhile, back in Chapel Hill, Smith and his staff worked on the tricky room assignments for the freshman suites on the first floor of Avery Hall, the dormitory next to UNC's baseball field, Boshamer Stadium. Delany, on the advice of his older brother, requested to not live with another scholarship athlete, hoping to make contacts in different corners of the campus. After Fogler and Whitehead met at Smith's summer camp the year before, they had agreed to room together as freshmen. That left Scott with Armour, a middle-class midwestern honor student; Smith hoped he would treat Scott without prejudice in any fashion.

"I didn't know who Charlie Scott was, but it didn't matter to me that he was black," Armour said in 2015. "I was there to play ball and get an education. We slept in the same room but didn't have much conversation. He was very quiet, into himself, and would look at you kind of sideways. He seemed intimidated by everything at Carolina except when he was on the basketball court. Considering what he was going through, that was probably a good way to be."

Smith could have found another black undergraduate or left Scott without a roommate, but that was too similar to what happened at Steele Hall in the 1950s, and he did not want to create a segregated environment within the team. He wished for a color-blind campus but also faced reality.

In early September, Lotz went to the Raleigh-Durham Airport to meet Scott's flight from LaGuardia. On the same plane was Rich Gersten, a skinny seventeen-year-old freshman whose father, Bob Gersten, had cocaptained the 1942 Tar Heels and remained connected to Carolina Basketball and athletics ever since. The younger Gersten had also worked at Smith's camp that summer and was already considered a part of the UNC basketball program because his father coached Larry Brown at Long Beach High School and sent the five foot ten guard to play for Frank McGuire. Bob Gersten knew the basketball players lived in Avery and told his son to request a room there with the idea that as a decent high school player, he had a chance to make the freshman team coached by Brown.

When the passengers deplaned, Lotz easily found the six foot five Scott but did not notice Gersten until he walked up to say hello. Lotz offered him a ride back to Chapel Hill with Scott, and on the twenty-five-minute drive down the two-lane country Highway 54 learned where Gersten was living and thought it could solve the problem of finding a nonscholarship roommate for Delany; after all, they both hailed from the New York area and should get along well. Having known Gersten since he starred for Long Beach High, Brown recalled that the coach's son, then a grade-schooler, was at almost every practice and game. The young Gersten had long idolized Brown for his wizardry on the court and kindness off, and would happily do anything Brown asked of him. Since Gersten did not know who his Avery roommate would be, he agreed to bunk with Delany.

They stopped at Brown's apartment in Glen Lennox just off campus, where Brown called the housing office and had Gersten switched to room with Delany in the same suite as Scott and Armour. In retrospect, Gersten, who was from an ultraliberal family, would have been better off with Scott, who said he did not have much of a relationship with Armour. "He never talked to me," Scott said of his freshman roommate. "I don't think we said more than two words to each other."

Armour remembered Avery as an antiquated dorm with an old steam heater next to Scott's bed. He said Scott liked to keep the temperature so high that Armour said he had to open the window or, after Scott went to sleep, turn the steam off. It became a running joke among the freshmen that lasted a lifetime, according to members of the team.

Wanting Scott to succeed in college and basketball, and perhaps struggling with how to handle his first black recruit, Smith was seen by some of the other players as favoring him, protecting him, and letting Scott play by his own set of rules. Seniority and separation existed between the varsity players secluded in Avery's basement suites and the first-floor freshmen, who, for example, weren't allowed to speak to the press; Scott didn't know or care, however, and often went downstairs to hang out with Grubar, whom he had befriended since their Jubilee weekend together. Smith got angry when teammates played practical jokes in the dorm at Scott's expense and asked Whitehead if he had thrown a firecracker into Scott's room on such a prank. He was not yet the Dean Smith who commanded universal respect of his players, mainly because he had not won any championships, and, still only in his thirties, his stern discipline rankled some of them.

Although the odds were long that Scott would seamlessly join the mostly white, in-state student body, Smith hoped the tall, lean freshman—a singular black face above the crowd passing between classes—would become a star athlete who could help the basketball team win. That was far better than Scott being viewed as a "one-off" outcast whose presence in Chapel Hill was little more than a curiosity, or the "token black" who never got off the bench.

At least outwardly, Scott's race was never a problem for the basketball program, but under the surface, there was an issue. In his teammates' minds, the hugely talented Scott did not need to be the "coaches' pet" he became. After classes his freshman year, Scott often went right to the basketball office and sat with Brown and Lotz, adults who had a greater appreciation for the extreme culture shock Scott was experiencing. Hanging out with Lotz and Brown was part of Scott's instinctual survival mode because in 1966 the relatively few black students could not easily form interracial friendships on a southern campus. Scott, especially, knew not to go places that might create a scene. "I wasn't dating white girls," he said, "and I am sure that made the coaches happy."

His teammates, likely consumed with their own adolescent angst, do not recall Scott having a tough time; rather, they noticed he had nicer clothes and many friends. They watched frequent visitors, mostly other black students, come and go from his suite—when he was there. Scott spent a lot of time out of the dorm, some with local families that provided homes away from the home he never really had, particularly Ed and Eva Caldwell of Church Street in Chapel Hill. Scott also helped one of his friends, fellow freshman Lee Upperman, get a manager's job on the freshman team in 1968 and the varsity team in 1970. The son of noted black physician Dr. Leroy Upperman in Wilmington, North Carolina, Lee Upperman went on to UNC law school, and in 1977, sought Smith's help in asking Governor Jim Hunt to pardon the Wilmington Ten who had been wrongly convicted of burning down a white-owned grocery store in 1971 during the height of racial tensions.

Scott had already been socializing at North Carolina Central in Durham when Larry Brown gave him a rental car to entertain the first black recruit for new football coach Bill Dooley. Scott needed the car to take quarterback Ricky Lanier, an honor student from Williamston, North Carolina, to Central and show him the larger black community only ten miles away. Late Sunday, after Scott had returned to the dorm and then went out, several of the players "borrowed" the keys for a joy ride. On the way back, they lost control of the car on winding Ridge Road between the law school and baseball stadium and slammed it into a telephone pole. Smith severely disciplined the guilty players, and for years, Scott kidded with his classmates at reunions about who "stole my car" that night.

By the time of Scott's arrival, the UNC program had morphed into a sort of three plus one: players who bought into Smith's team-first system and got most of the minutes; those just happy to be wearing Carolina Blue and liked being cheerleaders on the bench; and those who wanted to play more and thought they were not given the chance. The "plus one" represented superstars such as Larry Miller and Scott, who had more freedom because they were such great players, and because Smith could not risk losing them in the days when he was still fighting to keep his job. Miller, for example, challenged Smith's policy that his players had to attend some type of church service every Sunday morning and won an exemption because he said he never went to church at home.

The 1967 freshman team had an interesting makeup beyond Scott, who was by far the best player. On the court, particularly in practice, the integration of Carolina Basketball created a true dichotomy; compared to the other freshmen, Scott was an athletic freak. He was far quicker than anyone else in the program, including the varsity players, and Smith knew petty jealousies existed on most athletic teams. So, the theory goes, he sought to put together a roster that would be at least intellectually accepting of the superior athlete among them and, in retrospect, cherish the recognition and memories of them as historic trailblazers. And by the very nature of the other recruits signed alongside Scott—no one taller than he was—little doubt remained about the indispensable player on the team.

Fogler and Delany, the point guards from New York and New Jersey, respectively, started in the backcourt for what was Brown's second freshman team. Armour, at six foot two and acknowledged by Smith as the best shooter in the class, played out of position at small forward alongside Scott, who roamed the court and was the leading scorer, taking most of the shots, and rebounder. Whitehead was undersized, but an inside force who wound up leading the team in field goal percentage and averaged ten rebounds a game. All five scholarship players, four from the North, were high school hotshots in their own right, and freshman team manager Randy Forehand remembers they all brought a certain cynicism that spelled trouble almost from day one. "It was like some of them didn't respect the other players or thought they weren't getting the respect they deserved," said Forehand, now a physician in Virginia. "So there was friction, not on the court as much as off. It was almost always there." Forehand also noted that John Lotz was tantamount to Scott's guardian and constantly worried that this basketball commodity was underappreciated by his teammates. Lotz became Scott's best friend at UNC, served as best man at Scott's second wedding in 1986, and remained close to him until Lotz's death in 2001.

Ricky Webb, who had been a star athlete at Greenville (N.C.) Rose High School, came without a scholarship and got into every game, averaging 6.9 points. The six foot four Webb grew up a rabid Tar Heels fan who went to the Carolina Basketball School almost every summer. Smith also knew the other walk-ons from his summer camp and had met their families: Jim Folds from Greensboro and Burke Archer from Pilot Mountain, both of whom had played with or against blacks in high school; chemistry major Jeff Joyce from the affluent Pittsburgh suburb of Upper St. Clair; and Gersten, the last man picked and a second-generation UNC student who knew he made the team because of his father's connection with Brown and McGuire, as well as Smith.

The five other players were all Morehead Scholars; it was the first and only time so many recipients of the prestigious academic honor played on the same UNC athletic team. They were Bob Bode from Raleigh and Harold Pollard from Burlington, both future lawyers, and three who died between 2006 and 2010: Lynn Orr from Winston-Salem went on to medical school at East Carolina; Don Gowan from Bridgewater, Connecticut, later taught and coached at the prestigious Kent School in his home state; and Fred Rawlings from segregated Durham Jordan High School played UNC varsity tennis in the spring before turning pro. Rawlings recalled never before having been "in the same space with a black person."

Walk-on Archer recounted the funniest story from his "recruiting" visit to Chapel Hill on Jubilee weekend when Scott met his not-very-liberal mother. "She was introduced to Charlie, who extended his hand," Archer recalled, laughing, "and I said to myself, 'Oh, my God, she won't want to touch him.' But she grabbed his hand with both of hers and said, 'Charlie, you have to come to Carolina, it's a great school.' On the ride home to Pilot Mountain, I told my mother how impressed I was with her and she said, 'Don't you know who that is? He can turn the whole program around!'"

Webb, who also knew the coaches from camp, had his own story about meeting Scott their freshman year. He was hanging out in Carmichael with Larry Brown when Scott walked toward them, wearing khakis, a T-shirt, and sneakers with some books under one arm. Brown threw a basketball to him, and Scott caught it with one hand. Webb asked him to show them his best dunk. "It was a double tomahawk, and he might have bounced it off the backboard first," Webb said and remembered thinking, "Well, I guess I'll go to dental school."

None of the ten, except for Webb, played in every game, and only Pollard (2.5) and Folds (1.9) among the rest of the players averaged more than one point. They were essentially practice fodder handpicked by Smith and Brown after freshmen tryouts to help create the safest possible atmosphere for Scott. "The tryouts didn't seem like tryouts," Gersten said. "There were a lot of students in Carmichael playing basketball, but based on who was playing with who, you got the distinct feeling that the coaches knew who was going to be on the team. A lot of players were better than me, but I knew people in the program and had already met Charlie in Avery."

Bode, who also played tennis for UNC and turned down an appointment to West Point to accept the Morehead Scholarship, had attended private Cardinal Gibbons in Raleigh and had competed against good integrated teams since the sixth grade. "It was no big deal to me that UNC had a black basketball player," Bode said. "The big deal was how fantastic a player and person he was. Coach Smith was so far ahead of his time and such a sensitive man that he recognized there was much more to our team than just putting fourteen good players together with Charlie."

During one of Bode's Morehead interviews in the prior year, a committee member revealed how Smith had lobbied for him. After the interview, Bode received several letters from Smith, who was quoted by the Raleigh *News & Observer* as hoping Bode accepted the Morehead so he could play on the freshman team. It was not unusual for Smith, during his thirty-six years as UNC's head coach, to recommend outstanding students. There was something else at work in Bode's case, however: he was both bright and liberal when it came to race.

"I guess that confirmed I would be on the team even though I understood the tryouts were open," Bode said. "Many all-state players were on campus who did not have any word from the coaches about trying out. Most of those guys were very talented and did try out. None of them made the team. I always wondered how one got to the invited status that year."

After three days of tryouts, Brown posted the freshman team roster on the door of the basketball office. It had the perfect 5-5-5 symmetry Smith had stage-managed, hoping to control the tone around Scott and get through his training season without any incidents. No one on the team seemed to realize or care they were making history. "It didn't register with me, went right over my head,"

Folds said. "At eighteen years old I wasn't paying much attention; I was just excited to be there. For me, Charlie was one of the guys. But on the court, he was so much better than us."

Team manager Robert Crawford, whom Brown let suit up for three games when someone was injured, called Smith's plan "brilliant." Crawford said not only were the Moreheads most apt to be accepting of Scott; they were also preparing to major in a myriad of subjects, and were available to help Scott or any other teammate with tough classroom assignments.

Brown had them practice right through the Thanksgiving weekend, giving players Thursday off. Whitehead took Armour, Delany, and Fogler home for the holiday feast, but not Scott—and he heard about it from Smith when they returned. "He called me in and asked why I didn't invite Charlie," Whitehead remembered clearly. "I said I didn't really think about it. He had wanted to know if it bothered me that he had signed Charlie and told me I would never room with him. And now he was asking me why I didn't bring him home to my family."

Scott did go out with teammates on occasion, usually Forehand and the walk-ons. A bunch of them went to Dorton Arena in Raleigh, without tickets, hoping to see the Supremes. "It was sold out and we were about to leave," Folds said, "but Charlie knew someone who got us all in and then brought us right up to the front. Without Charlie, we were on our way back to Chapel Hill." Instead, they enjoyed a night together swaying to Diana Ross and the original dream girls.

Early in preseason practice, Scott came down on Folds's foot and broke a metatarsal bone that sidelined him for the first four games. Brown, a brutally competitive twenty-six-year-old coach, worked the team so hard that the players sometimes vomited after practice. Brown challenged them to make up for the star all his mates knew would dominate once he returned. However, the nicknamed Tar Babies had four recruited players who believed they did not need Scott. The now all-white, undersized lineup won those first four games, including at Duke, by at least eighteen points. Scott then rejoined a team convinced it would keep winning—with or without him. If they ever accepted that everything was going to revolve around Scott, they no longer did. Nevertheless, the freshman games were billed as the "Charlie Scott Show."

"The first four games without Charlie, nobody came," Webb said, "because he was already known as the star." And obviously, he was something of a novelty, as well.

In January of 1967, the new era began in earnest for UNC Basketball, and Smith and his assistants wondered how the Tar Babies would be greeted, home and away, when Scott finally took the court in Carolina Blue. In the days of freshman teams, the games could be as contentious as the varsity headliners, sometimes more if heralded recruits were on display for the first time. And on the road came the taunts, catcalls, and occasional racial slurs. Carmichael Auditorium and Duke Indoor Stadium were at or near capacity when the highly touted Carolina and Duke freshmen played. The local dailies advanced and covered the games, and the student newspapers blew them up with full box scores and photos. They were already big and Scott made them bigger.

With more than 5,000 fans at Carmichael to watch the preliminary before the nationally third-ranked varsity team lost to unranked Princeton, the first black scholarship athlete at UNC debuted with 22 points and 11 rebounds against North Greenville junior college. Whitehead was already averaging a double-double, including 34 points at Duke, and upstaged him with 26 and 19 in the 84–66 win. In his second game back, against Wake Forest in Winston-Salem, Scott stirred up the hissing crowd by making 10 of 12 shots on his way to 24 points. Fogler hit 11 of 13 for 23 points and Delany scored 16. The team shot 71 percent from the floor in the 83–67 blowout. As Scott almost always scored between 20 and 30 per game, his confident teammates wanted to stay involved, and the other four scholarship players went on to average between 12 and 14 points each. They also needed to pay attention when Scott had the ball, as he often went up for a shot and instead fired a pass to someone closer to the basket. Everyone on the team took at least one rocket ball to the back of the head at some point that season.

After winning their first ten games, the 1967 freshmen did not finish nearly as well, losing three of the last six for a 13–3 record. Just before the skid began, Armour and Scott, the two roomies who barely talked, had their best combined scoring game of the season, with 51 points in an otherwise error-prone 87–79 win over N.C. State. It was to be Armour's high-water mark in college, with 24 points.

Before the last game, a loss at Duke, according to members of the team, Brown excused Scott and the nonscholarship players from what he was about to say and took out his frustrations on Armour, Delany, Fogler, and White-head for having what he considered a selfish attitude throughout the season. Brown had coached the 1966 freshmen (the Rusty Clark–Bill Bunting–Grubar group) to a 15–1 record, after which he said, "It was like I died and went to heaven." Not so, the next year, with two scholarships players who eventually left the program, two more who almost left, and Scott, whom the coaches were desperately trying to keep happy.

Brown ran the undersized team unmercifully and emphasized defense to make up for its lack of height; he always seemed on edge. Brown often scrimmaged with the team and still wanted to play professionally. He got the chance in 1967 by signing with the New Orleans franchise of the new American Basketball Association and went on to a long playing and coaching career in the ABA, NBA, and college. Through 2015, Brown was the only coach to win both NBA (Detroit, 2004) and NCAA (Kansas, 1988) championships.

"It was kind of a rocky situation," Brown said thirty years later. "For example, Eddie (Fogler) was like a best friend during recruiting. Then you go from that to being his freshman coach. The same guy who was telling him he was the best point guard in the nation was now yelling at him." All eighteen-year-olds, four of them no longer basketball *stars*, the recruits not named Scott were already worried about their own futures. The ten walk-ons ended a dream come true and became ambassadors for Smith and the Tar Heels, eventually forgiving Brown for the brutal practices. Most believed that the hard season made them better men in the long run; it hatched the fabled Carolina Basketball Family, with Smith building a legion from those who had played, coached, or managed for him at any level. Freshmen walk-ons became statisticians and some eventually went into coaching, most notably Roy Williams. Loyalty was their bond, and Smith repaid numerous favors forward throughout most of their lives.

Not everyone automatically fell in line, however. Armour and Whitehead felt like Smith had wronged them for different reasons.

Armour was recruited primarily by Brown, and he claimed Brown promised him a chance to replace Bobby Lewis at shooting guard for the 1968 season. While playing forward on a freshman team that indeed "revolved around Scott," he watched the varsity system change into a high-percentage, get-the-ball inside game where he said the guards were all but banned from shooting. While it is true that Smith now had his two tallest players to date, six foot eleven Clark and six foot nine Bunting, wing players Scott and Miller both went on to make All-ACC and All-American, shooting whenever and from wherever they got open. For someone who averaged twenty-eight points in high school and was captain of the ten-man All-Illinois team, Armour said he knew his basketball career was dead. He was in all likelihood a casualty of playing the same positions as Scott and Miller.

"I worked my ass off and wasn't rewarded for it," Armour, who went on to law school in Denver and later retired to a lake in Wisconsin, still contended in 2015. "Dean told me I should be most proud of wearing the Tar Heel uniform. But I wasn't. He suspended me early in the (1967–68) season for what he called a bad attitude, because I didn't jump up and down on the bench while the other guys were playing. I went home for Thanksgiving and never went back to the team." Armour, who roomed with reserve Jim Frye as a sophomore, kept his scholarship and did not attend another basketball game during his last two and a half years at UNC. He let his hair grow out and joined protests against the escalating Vietnam War, helping with negotiations during the student strike of 1970 when final exams became optional in most courses. "I loved Chapel Hill and had a good experience in everything but basketball," he said. "As for basketball, I picked the wrong school." Armour has never returned to North Carolina and said he rooted against the Tar Heels, Smith, and especially Larry Brown ever since he left.

Whitehead played two years and went back to Scotland Neck after he graduated to operate the massive family farm until he retired. Then he dabbled in the specialty peanut business. The kid who drove to Chapel Hill in his new Mustang convertible with hopes of being a big-time basketball star for the state university has limped through the last half of life after three knee replacements. He was never as angry as Armour, but long considered himself Smith's "whipping boy" since not inviting Scott home for Thanksgiving their freshman year and being questioned about throwing the firecracker into Scott's dorm room. After Whitehead dropped off the team, Smith asked him whether he was keeping his scholarship. Whitehead, who did not need it, said yes but gave it back six months later. The scholarship went to Webb, a career reserve who loved jumping off the bench to celebrate someone else's good play and is still a proud member of the basketball family. Whitehead has since followed Carolina Basketball from afar and watched Smith mature from an edgy young coach to a deceased icon of the university, the state, and the sport. "He was different after he became a made man," Whitehead said.

The Yankee point guards, Fogler and Delany, played out their careers with moderate success, but both became staunch supporters of Smith.

Fogler wasn't allowed to shoot as much as he did while averaging thirty points as an all–New York City high school guard; this turned his outspoken father against Smith and he announced he was transferring to St. John's after playing a reserve role as a sophomore. He changed his mind that summer and returned to start as a junior when Grubar moved to big guard. Smith had something to do with keeping Fogler at UNC. In April 1968, he wrote a letter to Bob Gersten, the alum and former Tar Heel player who was still a high school teacher and coach in New York and owner of a summer camp in the Adirondacks. Smith thanked Gersten for visiting with the Fogler family and wrote that he hoped it worked out "for Eddie's best interest which, of course, would be to stay at North Carolina."[5] Fogler began his own college coaching career on the UNC staff and was one of "Dean's guys" through Smith's death in 2015. In the same letter, Smith recommended an African American graduate student named Ben Renwick as a counselor for Gersten's camp, tactfully acknowledging, "Ben is a Negro."[6] Smith later showed how calculating he could be by helping Renwick, who died in 2009, land a job in the UNC undergraduate admissions office, where he then had an ally in getting black recruits accepted after missing on Lou Hudson five years earlier.

Delany, who was not as highly recruited as Fogler but even more competitive, was also planning on leaving the team until he told his father, a high school teacher and coach. "I said I'm moving on. He said, 'No you're not. I sat in the living room when Coach Smith came up with the letter of intent. And he promised two things, no more than that. One, he would make sure you had an opportunity for a good education, and two, you would have an opportunity to compete to play. And you had both, so where are you going?'" Delany admits his anger about not playing might have gotten him kicked off the team. "I remember doing things, saying things, where Coach Smith could have closed the book," said the longtime commissioner of the Big Ten Conference who was voted by his peers in 2015 as the Most Influential Person in College Sports and a year later was a special-category nominee to the Naismith Basketball Hall of Fame. "He gave young people second chances, but he disciplined them and also told them the truth." Looking back on how Smith signposted a balance of social activism and personal responsibility, Delany said, "We were young people and Coach Smith was a young man, and there was a lot going on with civil rights and Vietnam; it seems to me he did a good job in allowing a certain amount of flexibility."

As for Charles Scott, his lonely first college basketball season ended and he continued toward varsity play and college and professional stardom. But it wouldn't happen without the help of his coaches and especially his older teammates who had already cut their teeth without him.

With Smith's Tar Heels on the way to their best season since 1957 and Scott moving up to the varsity team, Carolina Basketball had suddenly turned into the hottest ticket in town. Racial strains in the surrounding area remained, however, especially when the KKK and North Carolina grand dragon Robert Jones became visible antagonists opposing gains in desegregation. In addition, the first protests against U.S. involvement in the Vietnam War started popping up on campus. Nevertheless, the excitement over UNC hoops again brought Carolina and Chapel Hill together, as it had in the middle of the Frank McGuire era.

The 1967 varsity team relieved Scott from any savior role in 1968 by ripping off a 21–4 regular-season record and a late run of championships that began the day after the freshman team's last game. The Tar Heels defeated Duke at home to finish atop the ACC standings with a 12–2 record. It was Smith's first regular-season championship and took the heat off the sixth-year head coach, who admitted feeling personal pressure that winter.[7] He still lived in McGuire's shadow despite several great players and good teams. He had not been able to beat Vic Bubas's Blue Devils when it counted, however. The decisive 92–79 victory before a crazed Carmichael crowd ended that—at least until the ACC Tournament the following weekend in Greensboro. UNC welcomed moving the tournament from Reynolds Coliseum in Raleigh to the 8,766-seat Greensboro Coliseum. In the thirteen years the three-day event had been held on the N.C. State campus, the Wolfpack of Everett Case had won five championships; Duke, four; Wake Forest, two; and UNC only one in McGuire's undefeated season of 1957 (Maryland also won once). Since Smith took over, Carolina had clearly been the smallest of the Big Four.

Greensboro meant a fresh start for Smith, who had led the campaign among ACC coaches to take the tournament to a neutral site even if it meant less ticket revenue for the conference (Greensboro had 3,600 fewer seats than Raleigh). However, the city of Greensboro had made a commitment to expand the coliseum's capacity to more than 15,000 by raising the roof while the tournament moved to Charlotte (11,666) for three years after 1967. Smith had wisely scheduled nine games in Greensboro over the past six seasons, including three in 1967. Those games, plus playing seventeen times at the old Charlotte Coliseum on Independence Boulevard, including the North-South Doubleheaders every year, had given the Tar Heels two other de facto home courts while allowing thousands of people around the state to see them play. The built-in fan base was primed and ready to come out of the woodwork once Smith reached the ACC summit.

However, since only one conference team, that is, the ACC Tournament champion, could advance to the NCAA Tournament, what happened in the regular season meant little beyond seeding in the ACC tourney. In 1967, the Tar Heels squeaked by N.C. State, which had finished last in the standings with a 2–12 record under new coach Norman Sloan, in the first round and defeated Wake Forest by ten points in the semifinals. Duke clobbered Virginia and edged Frank McGuire's third South Carolina team 69–66, to give the Blue Devils a third crack at the Tar Heels, after being swept in the home-and-home games. Duke was the dominant program of the early 1960s, having been to three Final Fours, and the old adage about beating a good team thrice in the same season seemed in play. In fact, sports columnist Smith Barrier of the *Greensboro Daily News* had written that Duke would win the title for that very reason and the Blue Devils' tournament experience.[8]

Larry Miller, who with senior Bob Lewis made first-team All-ACC and eventually won ACC Player of the Year, tore out Barrier's column and kept it in his locker all week.

Only two years removed from being hanged in effigy twice and realizing that he might lose his job, the thirty-six-year-old Smith, still thin with slick black hair, had quietly built alliances on campus with faculty members and administrators who believed in him, even if many fans and some prominent alumni did not. One alumnus, a wealthy furniture manufacturer from High Point, had been in Smith's corner since UNC stayed in the Four Corners offense the entire game against Duke in the 1966 ACC Tournament before losing 21–20. On the following Monday morning, lifetime Carolina fan Jack Petty drove the eighty miles from his home west of High Point on old U.S. Route 64 to Chapel Hill and walked into the basketball office. Smith greeted Petty, who said he was sorry the team lost to Duke but regarded the strategy against the Blue Devils as the "finest piece of coaching I have seen in twenty-five years of watching basketball." Smith thanked Petty and said he would leave a ticket for him whenever he needed one. Jack Petty did not miss another Carolina game, home or away, until he grew ill and died in 1998.

When the Tar Heels bused to Greensboro, Miller still had Barrier's clipping with him. When they advanced to Saturday night's championship game, Miller folded it and put it in his left sneaker. Carolina led 40–34 at halftime and survived a Duke comeback late in the game to win 82–73. Miller scored 32 points and hit 13 of his 14 shots. Lewis had 26 points, 10 from the free throw line, as six Duke players fouled out chasing their quicker opponents. Several Tar Heels hoisted Smith on their shoulders and handed him scissors to begin cutting down the nets. At the post-game press conference, Smith personalized the accomplishment, something he rarely did as a veteran coach. He responded to a question by calling it "the greatest victory I've had as a coach. Yes, it has to be my greatest victory."[9] Meanwhile, in the raucous UNC locker room, a smiling Miller gave the sweat-soaked clipping to Barrier, who took it in good spirit. The Carolina program had reached a new turning point. Duke would not win another ACC Tournament for eleven years, while Smith won five more in that span.

The three grueling days in Greensboro gave the Tar Heels their first NCAA Tournament berth since 1959. Smith wanted to take his team's mind off basketball after Carolina drew a bye into the Sweet Sixteen and had five days before playing Princeton in College Park, Maryland. When the players arrived for practice on Monday, they found a volleyball net set up in Carmichael. Smith split up the fourteen players, three coaches, and one manager into nine-man teams. Of course, he chose the skyscraping Clark to play on his side of the net. Carolina avenged the regular-season loss to now fifth-ranked Princeton by winning a taut 78–70 game—the first of what would be Smith's sixty-five NCAA Tournament victories—and moved on to face No. 9 Boston College (BC), coached by Bob Cousy, in the Eastern Regional championship game.

With sophomores Clark and Bunting the first options in Smith's high-percentage offense, Lewis's league-leading scoring average as a junior dropped almost ten points as a senior. He had sacrificed more than any other player on the team had after being the go-to guy for most of his career. He scored when he had to, however, such as thirty-one points against BC to send UNC to its second NCAA Final Four after 1957 and the first of eleven for Smith. "I am glad that Bobby was the MVP in the Eastern Regional that year near his home," Grubar recalled, "because already people were talking about how much better we would be the next year with Charlie. With Miller back for his senior year, they were saying we would have the best team in the country."

While many believed that the heralded freshman class of 1966 had the task of lifting Lewis and Miller to the next level, Larry Brown thought the so-called L&M Boys allowed his first freshman team to play relaxed by joining the two superstars on the varsity team. "They were put in the best possible position because they had two fabulous players with them," Brown said of his former frosh dream team that he had helped recruit. "They didn't have to come in and be stars. When you look at Bobby and Larry, and how good they were, now they had Clark and Bunting, 6-6 (Joe) Brown and 6-4 point guard Grubar around them, so they could be even more spectacular."

Smith saw it the other way: "Our sophomores are good, but I have to give credit to Bob Lewis and Larry Miller for sacrificing to bring them along and give them confidence."[10]

When hundreds of cheering students formed a gauntlet outside Woollen Gym to bid the Tar Heels farewell for the 1967 Final Four in Louisville, it wasn't lost on Smith that the dummy accentuating his big nose went up in about the same place.

A year later, Charlie Scott would join a team that needed him to replace Lewis but had already won an NCAA regional and an ACC title. This would help reduce some of the pressure on Scott that still existed off the court.

A *New York Times* story dated February 26, 1967, carried the headline "Fraternity Pledges Negro at Carolina." With a Chapel Hill dateline, the five-paragraph article reported, "Charlie Scott, a freshman basketball player at the University of North Carolina, has been pledged by St. Anthony Hall fraternity. He is the first Negro pledged by a fraternity here."

Three days earlier, the *DTH* had published an analysis of the Greek system at UNC and its racial makeup with a somber tone. It reported that while Scott was the first of his race to receive a pledge invitation at Carolina, "at least two other Negroes in the last two years have been refused admittance into St. A." One of them, Eric Clay, "YMCA officer, sometime DTH letter writer, Carolina Political Union member...says he was candidly told that he was refused because he is a Negro."[11] Clay appealed to the Faculty Committee on Fraternities and Sororities, which censored the fraternity and asked the house to apologize to Clay but did not "impose any sanctions forcing Clay's admission into St. Anthony Hall." Clay considered legal action, and the article posited that St. Anthony Hall accepting Scott "might mitigate a successful suit against the University." Clay never filed suit, graduated, went to law school at Yale, and became a judge in Michigan.[12]

Scott first heard of St. Anthony Hall, commonly referred to as St. A, when he met newly appointed UNC Chancellor J. Carlyle Sitterson on his official recruiting visit in 1966. Sitterson's son, Joe, a Morehead Scholar and eventual Phi Beta Kappa, was just finishing his junior year and was a brother at the house on Pittsboro Street near the Carolina Inn. According to Dean Smith's biography, the chancellor told Scott he "should pledge the fraternity at St. Anthony Hall."[13]

The suggestion was a case of just trying to make Scott comfortable. However, the main difference between Scott and the St. A brotherhood remained, well, black and white. According to Barry Armour, who was the chapter president in 1967, the fraternity was packed with preppies from the Northeast. Armour was one of four in his pledge class alone from the prestigious Groton School, whose prominent alumni included thirty-second president Franklin Delano Roosevelt.

When he heard St. A was after Scott, freshman teammate Bob Bode enlisted fraternity brother Pete Wales at the Chi Psi lodge, who was also a "Grottie," to see whether he could get Scott to rush at their house on Cameron Avenue. But Bode said Scott never visited Chi Psi and later learned that St. A had indeed extended him a bid to pledge just before their freshman season ended.

St. A and Chi Psi were two frats that helped make up an elite white sector of the student body in the 1960s. If the university was not finding many qualified black students, it *was* attracting the wealthy private school element. Besides Groton, dozens of wealthy students also came down from Exeter, Andover, Choate, and other boarding schools, primarily in New England. Some had short hair, some long; some were athletes, some scholars, and some were politicos deeply involved in the local civil rights movement. Notable St. A alumni around Scott's time were Hall of Fame baseball writer Peter Gammons and Pulitzer Prize–winning cartoonist Jeff MacNelly. Chi Psi brothers of note included Taylor Branch, who won a Pulitzer writing about Martin Luther King Jr., and Wimbledon and U.S. Open champion Vic Sexias, who, as the story goes, got into the fraternity after ducking claims that he was Jewish.[14]

In the *Times* article, Barry Armour is credited with saying that Scott was chosen for his personality rather than his athletic ability.[15] Almost fifty years later, Armour does not recall being interviewed by the newspaper but said the article "certainly doesn't allude to the fact that we were well aware of being on the cutting edge of race relations at UNC and that Charlie's academic record, personality, and athletic ability, while considerable in their own right, were more like lubricants to let us slide past the fact that he was black. It was a pretty contentious pledging process even for a mostly Northern prep school set of brothers." He continued:

> Not everyone at the Hall that year was, shall I say, "comfortable" with the decision to offer a pledge to Charlie, but there were only two or maybe three members who spoke out against it and they were persuaded to acquiesce. I really can't say more than that about the pledge offer process. Charlie never actually accepted the offer to pledge, though, as I remember. If he did, then he dropped out pretty quickly because he was never really a presence at the Hall. It was disappointing at the time, but I think that was because of the principle and an interest among most of us at the Hall to do what we could to further the civil rights cause at Carolina rather than any disappointment in Charlie. It was clear he certainly had enough pressure on him just being there, and I doubt that we could have eased that burden even with our support. We really didn't have any ongoing relationship with him after the offer was declined.

Smith's explanation was that Scott said he "wasn't a fraternity type. Our team was my fraternity." With the issue still bubbling a year later, a letter to the *DTH* said Scott "chose to de-pledge after three weeks when he found basketball took up too much time."[16] It's not much of a stretch, however, to guess that Scott learned of Clay's ordeal, might have even met him, and grew too uneasy to continue with St. A. It is interesting to note that Scott's once-to-be black teammate Mike Maloy at Davidson, a school that was expected to be less accepting of African Americans than UNC, pledged Sigma Chi his freshman year. When the fraternity's national office said it would not recognize Maloy's membership, the Davidson chapter refused to rescind Maloy's pledge offer and disassociated itself with Sigma Chi national. Maloy, the first black scholarship athlete at Davidson, worked at Smith's camp for two summers and was one of the most popular counselors.

Scott regretted not forming any enduring friendships at UNC. "You did things with other people in college that you had lifelong relationships with," he said. "I was not able to do that; it was a choice I made and I understand that choice. But being sixty-seven years old now and looking back, I don't have friends from college and I regret that. It wasn't an experience I would wish upon my kids." Because of Scott and other trailblazers who followed him, his own children had what their father had missed at Chapel Hill. "My son and my daughter had a fantastic experience," Scott said. "They enjoyed everything about Carolina. Shaun goes back now and he sees a friend, that's great; I didn't have that opportunity."

Later that spring of 1967, after the varsity returned from the Final Four, where it lost to Dayton and Houston (in the meaningless consolation game Smith wanted dropped for more than twelve years), Scott spent several days at the UNC dental school. He got a new set of front teeth that were knocked out on the playground as a kid and a matching set of crowns that gave him an All-American smile. Smith also encouraged "Charles" to take some speech courses at Carolina, as he did for many of his players who would be talking often to the press. As it turned out, the animated and emotional Scott had a lot to say over the next three years, on and off the court.

After the season, Scott became a regular visitor in Durham, both playing ball and hanging out with students at N.C. Central. When word filtered back to Chapel Hill, many believed this was part of Smith's plan to ensure that Scott would not depart the Carolina campus for a more-integrated school up North. Such a theory angered Scott. "I remember people saying that Coach Smith did things for me," he said. "What business was it of his where I hung out? I don't understand that. Coach Smith didn't know where I was hanging out; he didn't know where I went. I went there because I had nowhere else to hang out on campus. I decided how I was going to survive."

Scott, who along with many fellow Tar Heels later referred to Smith as a mentor and "second father," recalled the days before his coach garnered ulti-mate respect and trust from his players, when some of them objected to his controlling nature and referred to him jokingly and somewhat disrespect-fully behind his back as "Smitty." Rusty Clark, the Morehead Scholar who had been on a track for medical school since his freshman year, came to resent the time that practices and meetings consumed. Before his senior season, rumors swirled that Clark was giving up basketball to make sure he got into medical school, although Clark denied ever seriously considering it because he "would have had to leave the state." The years, and hearing how other coaches treated their players, gave Clark perspective. "I never felt exploited or used," Clark said after he had become a successful surgeon. "He (Smith) went overboard to see I got a good education. He did that for anybody, and for those who weren't interested, he tried to get them interested."

Smith remained a disciplinarian coach until the day he retired, but by the 1970s, most of his teams believed in him so much that they came to dread letting him down more than they did losing. He kept a certain distance from his active players; then, after they left the program, Smith truly became their godfather figure for the rest of his life. Into middle age, most of them having become husbands and parents, they revered him even more by realizing how much he had always been looking out for their welfare. That was borne out by numerous disciples, including alumni and fans, naming their children after Smith. Scott's second son is Shannon Dean.

Dean Smith was a young coach under fire after taking over from Frank McGuire in August 1961. Here he meets with his team in Lexington, Kentucky, on December 17, 1962, before stunning Adolph Rupp's Wildcats and All-American Cotton Nash, 68–66, that night. (Courtesy of UNC Sports Information)

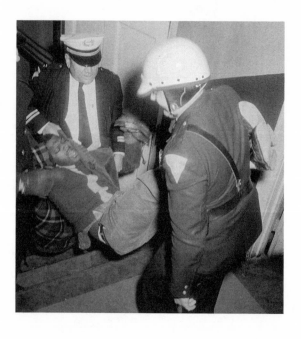

Meanwhile, in Chapel Hill, civil rights unrest had been boiling with sit-ins and demonstrations almost daily. In this photo from March 9, 1960, police officers Coy Durham and Lindy Pendergrass carry Chapel Hill resident Hilliard Caldwell down the stairs to jail. (Roland Giduz Photographic Collection, North Carolina Collection, Wilson Library, University of North Carolina at Chapel Hill)

UNC police chief Arthur Beaumont drags a protestor away from the entrance to the Woollen Gym parking lot after the Wake Forest–UNC basketball game on February 8, 1964. This marked the most widespread and best-organized "obstruction" demonstration of the Chapel Hill civil rights movement. (Photo © Jim Wallace)

John Dunne, the one-time Morehead Scholar at UNC and leader of the Student Peace Union, rejoices with choir and Golden Asro Frinks (seated) at the First Baptist Church on April 1, 1964. Frinks, a principal civil rights organizer in North Carolina during the 1960s known as "The Great Agitator," was jailed eighty-seven times during his lifetime. Frinks favored nonviolent protests and was a close colleague of Dr. Martin Luther King Jr. (Jock Lauterer Photographic Collection, North Carolina Collection, Wilson Library, University of North Carolina at Chapel Hill)

Opposite: Sit-in protestors sing and wave while blocking the front door to segregated Brady's Restaurant on East Franklin Street, as Chapel Hill police chief W. D. Blake looks at camera. Brady's was next to the Rock Pile on a site where the Siena Hotel is located today. (Photo © Jim Wallace)

The Reverend Robert Seymour preaches from the pulpit in the 1960s. His Binkley Baptist Church congregation was actively involved in the civil rights movement, the Vietnam War protests, and town politics. (Photo courtesy of Dr. Robert Seymour)

Sensational freshman Charlie Scott waited to join the varsity team while attending a Fellowship of Christian Athletes camp that summer with former four-sport UNC athlete Albert Long, assistant coach John Lotz, and incoming Tar Heel freshman Dave Chadwick. (Photo courtesy of Albert Long)

Opposite: Basketball became the rallying point in Chapel Hill in 1966, as the Tar Heels beat Duke to win their first ACC championship under Dean Smith and then advanced to the 1967 Final Four (Jock Lauterer Photographic Collection, North Carolina Collection, Wilson Library, University of North Carolina at Chapel Hill)

Opposite, top: As UNC's first African American scholarship athlete, Scott proved to be a transcendent talent and overcame racial taunts at several ACC arenas, especially in his first varsity game at N.C. State on January 10, 1968. Scott's fifteen points helped rally UNC to a 68–66 victory. (Reprinted with permission of *The News & Observer*, Raleigh, N.C.)

Opposite, bottom: Sophomore Charlie Scott joined senior All-American Larry Miller (far right) and three locked-in juniors—Bill Bunting, Dick Grubar, and Rusty Clark—as the Tar Heels readied to take on third-ranked and undefeated St. Bonaventure in the 1968 NCAA Sweet Sixteen in Raleigh. UNC won, 91–72, as Scott scored twenty-one points in his first NCAA Tournament game. (Courtesy of UNC Sports Information)

Smith leads the happy Tar Heels, including Ralph Fletcher, Dick Grubar (13), Joe Brown, Gerald Tuttle, Charlie Scott (33), NCAA Eastern Regional MVP Rusty Clark, and Gra Whitehead, off the court at Reynolds Coliseum after defeating Davidson, 70–66, to advance to their second straight Final Four. (Jock Lauterer Photographic Collection, North Carolina Collection, Wilson Library, University of North Carolina at Chapel Hill)

Heading for Los Angeles and a date with UCLA, the team poses with 1968 NCAA
Regional trophy. Front row: Jim Delany, Eddie Fogler, Charlie Scott, Larry Miller, Dick
Grubar, Dean Smith; middle row: Rusty Clark, Bill Bunting; back row: Gra Whitehead,
Jim Frye, Gerald Tuttle, coach Bill Guthridge, Joe Brown, trainer John Lacey, Ricky
Webb, coach John Lotz. (Hugh Morton Photographic Collection, North Carolina
Collection, Wilson Library, University of North Carolina at Chapel Hill)

In 1969, the ACC's first race controversy erupted over Charlie Scott not making unanimous All-ACC and eventually losing Player of the Year to South Carolina's John Roche. On Valentine's Day at the original Charlotte Coliseum, Roche thrust himself into the ACC Player of the Year debate by playing all forty minutes, scoring thirty-eight points, and engineering a 68–66 upset of the No. 2-ranked Tar Heels. UNC avenged the loss at South Carolina twelve days later. (Photo by Hugh Morton)

Howard Lee's family was threatened and almost stopped from buying their first home in a new white subdivision, Colony Woods, prompting Lee to seek an open-housing ordinance and run for mayor of Chapel Hill in 1969. With the help of Charlie Scott and backed by Dean Smith, Lee defeated Alderman Roland Giduz by four hundred votes on May 6, 1969, to become the first African American mayor in a predominantly white southern town since Reconstruction. (Photo by Billy Barnes)

In February of 1969, the Black Student Movement at UNC helped cafeteria workers stage
a strike for higher wages and better working conditions. It brought the Highway Patrol
to campus before mayoral candidate Howard Lee convinced Governor Bob Scott to
withdraw the troops. After a second strike in December, 1969, UNC president William
Friday and Mayor Lee negotiated a settlement with the workers' unions. (Photo by Ric
Spencer, Photographic Archives, North Carolina Collection, Wilson Library, University
of North Carolina at Chapel Hill)

6

Crosswinds of Change

Before Charles Scott played a minute for the UNC varsity team, Dean Smith called Major John Yesulaitis, director of the Marching Tar Heels band, and requested a meeting. "Major Y" greeted Smith in his office at Hill Hall, where they had met during Yesulaitis's first year at Carolina in 1964. Smith had asked him to put together a small pep band for basketball, and Major Y agreed to try it for a few home games at Woollen Gym. When Carmichael Auditorium opened the next season, Smith gave the pep band a permanent corner section above the runway to the home-team locker room. The band blaring out "Here Comes Carolina!" created a hair-raising welcome when the Tar Heels burst from the small door and took the court, most having to duck their heads under the low door casing.

The rest of the pep band's repertoire was largely drawn from its work at football games, featuring popular music of the day and old ditties. The regular tunes included other school songs like "Fight, Fight, Fight for the Blue and White" and "Carolina Victory." And, as was common for many football programs throughout the South, Major Y's band played "Dixie" before configuring into a "U-N-C" for the national anthem and the team taking the field.

"Dixie" was seen by some southerners as an anthem of the old South, not a racially charged reminder of slavery before the Civil War. Almost every state university in the Old Confederacy played it at football games and waved the Confederate flag while the bands belted out the tune and fans proudly sang the lyrics. The song held no special meaning for Major Y, the youngest son of a Lithuanian coal miner who grew up in Pennsylvania. Plus, he had spent thirty years in the military, finishing his career as the associate conductor of the Air Force Orchestra, which sometimes played at the Kennedy White House.

Smith, who viewed "Dixie" as derogatory to blacks, discussed his concerns with Major Y, who appreciated the basketball coach coming to him personally and not turning the decision into a debate on campus—the last thing Smith wanted. Yesulaitis agreed to take "Dixie" out of the pep band's songbook for basketball games, where a black star had joined a Carolina team. Although the song remained part of the marching band's performances at Kenan Stadium for one more year, Smith's advocacy with Major Y marked the beginning of the end for "Dixie" at UNC. After Ricky Lanier and two other black football players talked to coach Bill Dooley, "Dixie" was done for good.[1]

In the late 1960s, racism on campus remained a fact of life that could not be changed by a federal law, a meeting between campus figures, or the banishing of a controversial song. With African American enrollment slowly growing at UNC, Smith knew the Black Student Movement (BSM) had organized and was beginning to make noise about the all-white faculty and working conditions for nonacademic employees, most of whom were black. This was of ongoing concern to Smith because he knew that sooner or later, Scott's high profile and allegiance to his race would draw him into the campus conflict.

Behind sophomore leader Preston Dobbins, the BSM viewed the campus chapter of the NAACP as "antique" and banned it from their own activities. Despite the organization's proud history and involvement in everything from the *Brown v. Board of Education* decision in 1954 and the 1963 March on Washington, where Dr. Martin Luther King Jr. delivered his "I Have a Dream" speech, Dobbins and other black students at UNC saw the NAACP as ineffectual in dealing with their rights and those of black workers in Chapel Hill.

The campus, by numerical metrics, was far more segregated than the town of Chapel Hill, with its well-established black community of more than 1,200 people. The basketball team was a stark reminder of this fact. The loner Scott remembered sitting in his dorm room and hearing the players talk about where they were going on a given night: Rusty Clark would go to his Delta Kappa Epsilon (DKE) fraternity, Joe Brown and Dick Grubar to a party at the KA house, and Larry Miller to Ehringhaus dorm to hang out with the football team. Scott already knew, from his short experience with St. Anthony's Hall, that he was uncomfortable in such places. Besides practicing and playing at Carmichael Auditorium, he said he "never did anything on campus. . . . it would ostracize the people who were with me because it put them in a situation they might not want to be in, and there were no circumstances for me to have a good experience." When his teammates began hitting the fraternity parties in the fall of his sophomore year, Scott said he made a conscious decision to get away from Chapel Hill as much as possible. By contrast, other differences among white teammates were navigated far more easily. For example, Scott's fellow freshmen Eddie Fogler and Rich Gersten had joined the predominantly Jewish Tau Epsilon Phi (TEP) fraternity, which welcomed the Catholic-raised Jim Delany. Delany first became a social affiliate and then a full-fledged brother.

"At that time, no matter how comfortable I felt with my teammates, they still had to deal with the fact that they never had been around black people either," Scott said years later. "I still couldn't go anywhere with their friends because their friends were still brought up in a South that was very separate. There was a lot of loneliness on my part and a lot of times I questioned myself why I was there."[2]

Scott's routine included getting up early every morning and buying three or four local newspapers so he could follow the college and pro stars he admired. When he wasn't in class or in practice, he sat in the basketball office talking hoops with John Lotz until the coach finally sent him out so he could get some work done. Scott was almost always there when other players dropped by to pick up their mail or laundry money, the only reasons they ever went to the office in the 1960s.

Team manager Randy Forehand from Missouri thinks it was Lotz who asked him to room with Scott for the 1967–68 school year, but can't remember for sure. They got along well, having both moved up from the freshman team. But Scott was still disappointed not to have a teammate share a room.

"Charlie was an intellect; he took some hard courses and could talk about politics, race relations; he had thoughts on just about anything," Forehand said. "But he was really a basketball junkie. He could talk basketball all day long."

That was perhaps part of why Scott felt so insulted by the new room assignment, although Forehand said he often found his roommate happily dancing to the Temptations music blasting from his record player.

"They roomed me with the manager," Scott said years later. "Randy was a great guy, but how do you think I felt being a sophomore, everybody had a basketball player and they roomed me with the manager? I felt strange about that—I got the manager. It made me think that no one wanted to room with me. Randy was a great roommate, but he wasn't a basketball player."

There was no playbook to guide the complicated group dynamics on Carolina's first integrated team. Was Scott, with immense pride and little experience living among whites, expected to reach out for acceptance? Or were his teammates expected to include him in everything they did, which Scott already knew would not work in most situations? Against this backdrop and away from the team, Scott was forming his own circle of friends in Chapel Hill and Durham.

He was more independent than anyone else on the team because he *had* to be. And his teammates already had their own friends on campus. The court, where basketball was the common denominator, proved to be the safest place to get along.

When practice began on October 15, 1967, Dean Smith continued to designate a couple of days a week to let the public in to watch the Tar Heels scrimmage. He had begun closing practices on most days two years earlier because he wanted more privacy with his players. "When it is necessary to criticize, we won't have to go clear across the court to talk to the person," Smith said. "Having open sessions has possibly hurt us in the teaching aspect where you can't criticize in front of people for fear it would embarrass the players."[3]

The occasional open scrimmage continued until Scott joined the varsity team in the fall of 1967. He could do things the rest of the players could not do; he had a move thousands of fans loved—going to his left against a defense favoring the righty, stopping on a dime, and launching a jumper against his body. If trapped, he would pump fake, step through the double team, and either shoot or pass. Occasionally, even his varsity teammates had trouble catching the passes he threw even while he was traveling at high speed and high altitude. When he fired a bullet that was dropped or whistled through someone's hands, fans would cheer. That sort of thing ended open practices for good at Carolina; Smith had curtains installed at every portal and managers stationed to evict anyone who tried to come in. From that point on, visitors had to call the basketball office, get approval from Betsy Terrell, and stop by for a pass. Generally, professional scouts and high school coaches were allowed in, but they still had to sit above the yellow railings that separated the lower and upper arena. Smith did not want them hearing every word he said, especially when he yelled at a player. Early on, Scott was particularly sensitive to such criticism, even merely a long stare from the coach. Perhaps in the back of Scott's mind, he knew Frank McDuffie had warned Smith that "Charlie is good, but maybe not as good as he thinks he is."

When the 1967–68 basketball media guide came out, it featured the four returning starters on the cover, holding the net-draped 1967 ACC trophy and NCAA plaques, looking down at two admiring young boys with a basketball and a puppy under their arms. The cover reeked of family, and it was the first time Smith put a picture of his own family—his wife, Ann; daughters Sharon and Sandy; and son, Scott—on the inside of the publication. (Throughout his coaching career, Smith went out of his way to keep his personal life just that—personal.) The same year, new sports information director Jack Williams began his tradition of having coeds pictured with one of the players, but it would be two years—Scott's senior season—before Smith agreed to let Williams have their black star and a white teammate pose with a group of female students of different races.

With anticipation growing to see Scott play for the varsity team, a capacity, excited, and curious crowd gathered on November 24, 1967, for the annual Blue-White game, which had been watered down to a glorified scrimmage since the highly touted freshman class led by Clark, Grubar, and Bill Bunting had defeated the varsity in November of 1965. Scott played on the White team coached by John Lotz with Miller, Clark, and Grubar—four sure starters. The Blue team, coached by new assistant Bill Guthridge, had only one returning starter, Bunting. That left the fans to speculate over the lineup when the regular season opened on December 2 against Virginia Tech. Would Scott move into the shooting guard spot vacated by Bobby Lewis or would he unseat Bunting at power forward, with Grubar going to big guard and Fogler to the point? Rumors were rampant, but it was clear Scott would be one of the five starters, regardless of where he played.

However highly anticipated Scott's joining the Tar Heels was, it had not automatically started a stream of African Americans to the UNC basketball program. It would be another year before Bill Chamberlain signed, as other black recruits took more of a wait-and-see approach. Smith lost Austin Carr, a six foot six scorer from Washington, D.C., to Notre Dame, leaving Guthridge with a weak 1968 freshman team. Only six foot ten beanpole Lee Dedmon was projected to help the Tar Heels in the years to come. "Last spring's recruiting program was disappointing," Guthridge admitted to Rick Brewer of the *DTH*.[4]

Scott jumped to the varsity level without skipping a beat. He hit 9 of 15 shots, plus 4 free throws, to score a game-high of 22 points, with 7 rebounds. Clark had 16 points and 13 rebounds, while Miller missed 10 of his 13 shots and scored an uncharacteristic 8 points. But the White team barely hung on to win, 72–69, as Bunting and the Blue reserves shot 48 percent. Bunting led his teammates with 19 points and 15 rebounds, showing why he should remain a starter. Everyone on the team scored except Al Armour, already sulking because he believed he was beating out Grubar in practice and not being recognized for his hard work. It was Scott who would take the open position on the brochure cover and in the starting lineup.

Smith confirmed that when he told the *Daily Tar Heel*, "We will drill Charles at both big guard and small forward before we decide where to play him."[5] As it turned out, the barely six foot four Miller moved to guard and

Scott moved to small forward, positions that were basically interchangeable and depended on whom each man was assigned to guard and who was guarding them. They had different styles: Miller, the slightly better outside shooter and bullish driver, always drew more fouls than anyone on the team; Scott, lightning fast, was the first Carolina basketball star to truly play above the rim. Turning out to be a much quicker defender than Lewis, Scott ultimately made the 1968 Tar Heels better than the defending ACC champions.

Scott's stardom made it easier for him to move around in a town where, as Smith hoped, most white students saw him as a superstar and not a minority. He occasionally walked Franklin Street with other tall young men who were obviously his teammates. "Charlie definitely stood out in Chapel Hill," Ricky Webb said. "Everybody acted like they loved him because he was a star. I loved to go out to eat with him and watch how people treated him; plus, we usually didn't have to pay when we were with him."

Forehand often went to Lum's on West Rosemary Street with Scott and remembers early on that students gave him a standing ovation. "Charlie looked down, almost did not acknowledge them," Forehand said. "Some people took that like he was aloof, or arrogant. I think it was more that he was shy and not sure how to act around a lot of white people." How he expressed himself between the lines at Carmichael proved to be his true comfort zone.

Scott also demonstrated a comfort zone in relating to kids. Lillian Lee worked at the Carrington Hospital School for gravely ill children who faced long stays. When Scott came over with several teammates to visit them, she was moved by how they took to him as much as any of the white players. The Lees, who were drawn to Dean Smith for his parental nature, forged a friendship with Scott that grew throughout his career. They learned about his background on the streets of Harlem and helped to reinforce the discipline he had received from Frank and Sammie McDuffie at Laurinburg Institute. It was working, at least outwardly, and Scott seemed like a model student-athlete. Colorblind fans of all ages flocked to him for autographs when the team walked into coliseums in Charlotte and Greensboro.

Smith asked Scott to visit with African American high school recruits when they visited campus, like he had football player Ricky Lanier and then his second in basketball, Bill Chamberlain, who eventually turned down Princeton in the spring of 1968 in favor of UNC. Scott honestly wanted life to become easier for all his black brethren who he knew clustered together for moral support. They were typically not as enterprising as Scott, who was coping by living a dual existence between UNC and North Carolina Central.

Some administrators knew history was working against pioneers such as Scott. David Robinson, cochairman of UNC's Scholarship Information Center, said that "because of the long discriminatory policy of admission offices in the South, Negroes haven't been able to adjust" to predominantly white schools. Faculty and student groups were working to change that, but usually faced obstacles. The American Association of University Professors (AAUP) sought funds to recruit more black students, but student-driven proposals were shot down by the state legislature. Charles Morrow, the dean of Arts and Sciences, explained that a program to recruit more blacks was "something that the University would appreciate" but was not moving forward because "under the law" it could not pick out a certain group to recruit. Student body president Jed Dietz outlined three reasons his cabinet also backed off: the state legislature thought the proposal was discriminatory, recruiting wasn't the proper job for undergraduates, and student government at Carolina could not afford the cost of such a campaign.

Despite his team's preseason No. 4 national ranking, Smith prepared for a season opener against Virginia Tech with three major concerns. First, high expectations for the team created additional pressure. Second was the anticipation of Scott playing his first varsity game, marking the official integration of UNC athletics. And third, Virginia Tech was a dangerous team under coach Howie Shannon that had beaten Carolina in Chapel Hill in 1964 and 1966, and despite having been blown out in Carmichael by thirty-two points in 1967, Virginia Tech had rallied to reach the regional final of the 1967 NCAA Tournament, losing to the same Dayton team that a week later ousted UNC in the Final Four at Louisville. "Since I've been the head coach, this is the most difficult opener we have had," Smith said.

As the game approached, whether influenced by Smith or not, the university acted amazingly neutral about Scott's long-awaited debut, underscoring Smith's hope that a star black athlete could play in an atmosphere of normalcy. He had referred to "the first athletic scholarship Negro" in the *DTH* when Scott signed in May of 1966. However, race was not mentioned in any *DTH* sports story during Scott's freshman season or in previews for his varsity debut. "I just don't remember thinking anything of it," said 1968 *DTH* sports editor Larry Keith, who went on to work at *Sports Illustrated*. "I figured it was reported as a part of history when he enrolled, but all of us were excited to see him play ACC basketball." In stories and letters to the editor about the fraternity flap, skin color was the issue, but never in the context of basketball for his first two years at UNC. Meanwhile, Smith vigilantly controlled the wording of regular releases from the sports information office. The prospectus for the 1967–68 season listed Scott once on the second page among "best of the newcomers."

When Scott was introduced before the Virginia Tech game on his home court, those in attendance noted more of a "buzz" that could have meant a mixed reception compared with the more elevated cheers, clapping, and horn blowing for the other starters. Scott was clearly anxious or nervous, or both, to start his varsity career. During the national anthem, Keith wrote the next day, "He fidgeted . . . bit his lower lip, forced a glance at the flag strung on the side of the press box and shuffled his feet. When the team broke (the huddle) for the center jump circle, he seemed uncertain as to where he belonged."[6]

It took Scott only his first twenty minutes of big-time college basketball to confirm he belonged. "As it turned out," Keith wrote, "the stylish performer turned in anything but a sophomoric game."[7]

Scott deferred to Miller, who scored 19 points in the first half as Carolina led 44–37. But while Miller finished with 30 points, Scott took only one fewer shot than the captain and matched him with 9 rebounds (Clark led all with 17). And it was Scott who ignited a 13–0 run in the second half that brought the Tar Heels from 11 points down to 2 ahead in the 89–76 victory. His 18 points would eventually be close to his season average. The *DTH* reported that the home fans finished the game cheering him wildly. Bill Dooley was in the stands that night and was so amazed by Scott's athleticism that he told the *DTH* he would love to have Scott as a defensive back. A perturbed Smith put a stop to that speculation immediately.

The 1968 Tar Heels, ranked third behind UCLA and Houston most of the season, won twenty-two of their first twenty-three games, including Smith's first milestone 100th career victory. The only loss came on December 9 at eighth-ranked Vanderbilt, where Scott played against the SEC's first black scholarship athlete, Perry Wallace. Before the game in Nashville, Scott drove with Wallace across town to Tennessee State, the all-black school where they both knew several players and students. Scott was still socializing when Wallace left, and no taxi would come to that side of town to get him. Smith had to borrow a car to pick him up so Scott could make the pregame meal and not lose his starting position for being tardy. Smith was unhappy throughout the game, in which Carolina shot 59 percent from the floor but missed twelve of twenty-two free throws and kept throwing the ball away.

Scott made all eight of his shots; Smith's wrath after the 89–76 defeat was directed at Joe Brown and Bill Bunting, who both played tentatively in their coach's estimation. "I was so upset with the loss and how we played that I stayed on them for close to twenty minutes," Smith wrote in his autobiography. Returning to Chapel Hill and watching the film, he decided he would never again criticize his team right after the game because he might have been too harsh with certain players. "In this case, it wasn't that we played so badly but Vandy playing well," he said.[8]

Wallace, a six foot five center, had eleven points and eight rebounds for the Commodores before a loud but respectful crowd at Memorial Gym. Unlike Scott, Wallace's fame was more modest because he never played in the NCAA Tournament, rarely appeared on television, and was not a pro prospect, going instead to law school.

The daunting schedule continued against No. 4 Kentucky and No. 10 Princeton, both in Greensboro. Carolina broke open close games in the second half to win twice in the final five minutes. Scott, Miller, and Clark set a pattern that continued throughout the season of taking about two-thirds of the team's shots and rarely scoring below double figures. Grubar consistently got the ball to them in position to score and would have easily led the ACC in assists if they had been recorded in 1968. Before beginning the ACC schedule, the team played in the Far West Classic in Portland, where sports promoter Harry Glickman had built a beautiful new coliseum and was lobbying the NBA for a franchise. That would happen in 1970 when he founded the Trail Blazers. The Tar Heels made *Sports Illustrated* as the "BVD Boys" after their uniforms were lost en route and they had to practice in their underwear the day before playing Stanford. Scott was a big hit in that liberal corner of the country and looked on his way to MVP in the tournament, after scoring 17 points against Stanford and 24 against Utah. In the championship game against Oregon State, the capacity crowd of 12,955 roared through a second-half comeback by the Beavers, who continued to send Miller to the foul line, hoping he would miss. He did not miss much, making 19 of 22, to finish with 33 points. Right after the game and before the trophy presentation, Smith talked to tournament committee members who had received some MVP votes for Scott even before the final game ended. Smith made sure the award went to Miller because he deserved it and was a senior. Smith always took care of his seniors first.

Scott's true breakthrough game was the second meeting against N.C. State. A month earlier in Raleigh's Reynolds Coliseum he had heard every bigoted insult imaginable from the Wolfpack fans, courtside to balcony. In that game, Scott turned the ball over 6 times but helped the Tar Heels rally from a halftime deficit to win by 2 points. The rematch at Carmichael was all Scott, however. He hit 14 of 23 shots on his way to a season high of 34 points. *Chapel Hill Weekly* columnist Billy Carmichael III called it a "good lesson for the Wolfpack after having subjected Scott to an abnormal amount of abusive language in the first meeting. Even the longshoremen in the crowd were offended." Carmichael took the opportunity to openly write about race, predicting Scott would be "the first Negro superstar in the ACC, possibly the first Negro All-American at a traditionally white Southern school. He's proved himself on both boards—the backboards and the college boards. He's proved that blacks and whites can work together as a team. He's proved once again that in sports . . . you're judged by what you do, not who you are."[9] It was the first, and perhaps the most pointed, racially charged defense of Scott.

Carmichael's comments had an ironic candor to them, and perhaps purpose, coming just after UNC student government invited Communist sympathizers Herb Aptheker and Frank Wilkinson back for a second time and they were again denied permission to speak on campus. Student body president Paul Dickson finally went to court, and on February 19, 1968, a panel of three federal judges in Greensboro deliberated for less than a half hour before striking down the Speaker Ban Law of 1963 as unconstitutional. A five-year protest had ended in a matter of minutes, coinciding with Scott and the new era of Carolina Basketball.

UNC returned to No. 3 in the polls after winning twelve consecutive conference games and clinching a second straight ACC regular-season championship. However, losing Miller's last home game to Frank McGuire's emerging South Carolina team and then the finale in triple-overtime at Duke left the Tar Heels with a bad taste. Now they headed to Charlotte to defend their ACC Tournament title and secure another NCAA bid. They would appear in three more of the twenty-five televised games Charlie Scott played in during his college career, as America's most prominent black college star next to UCLA's Lew Alcindor.

Carolina's toughest test of the 1968 ACC Tournament, the first ever in Charlotte, was the semifinal against McGuire's Gamecocks, who had already spoiled Miller's senior game in Chapel Hill. Both teams were hot in a first half that ended with the Tar Heels ahead 50–41. South Carolina had a senior-laden team called the Four Horsemen: Yankees Gary Gregor, Skip Harlicka, Frank Standard, and Jack Thompson, plus "The Pony," sophomore Bobby Cremins from the Bronx. Showing the same grit as some of McGuire's UNC teams, the Gamecocks fought back to tie the score before Miller missed a last-second shot in regulation. The Tar Heels wore South Carolina down in overtime, and Clark-Miller-Scott finished with a combined 51 points and 36 rebounds in the 82–79 victory. In the second semifinal, N.C. State held the ball against lumbering

Duke, as Carolina had in the 1966 ACC Tournament, and the Wolfpack pulled off a 12–10 victory that had fans booing and UNC radio announcer Currie crowing, "This is about as exciting as artificial insemination."

So, instead of a rubber match between Carolina and Duke and a rematch of the 1967 tournament final, the crowd got the 24–3 Tar Heels versus the 16–9 Wolfpack. After a lackluster first half in which both teams shot 35 percent, Miller asked Smith, Lotz, and Guthridge to leave the locker room. "Talk it over among yourselves," Smith agreed. "Hold a sort of 'truth' meeting among yourselves."[10] Rarely having a lot to say, Miller ripped into his teammates for not playing as hard as they could—or certainly as hard as he did—and they returned to the court to blow out the Wolfpack and win a laugher, 87–50. The game remains the most lopsided ACC Tournament final ever. Carolina was going back to the NCAA Eastern Regional in Raleigh to play third-ranked and unbeaten St. Bonaventure and likely No. 8 Davidson for another trip to the Final Four. Miller, with 76 points and 26 rebounds in three games, won his second straight Everett Case Award as ACC Tournament MVP. Scott, on the other hand, felt the first tinge of prejudice in the all-tournament voting. He had 16 points and 10 rebounds in the championship game and finished with 49 points, 22 rebounds, and 9 assists for the tournament. Yet he made only second-team all-tourney, as three of McGuire's players joined the clutch Grubar and Miller on the all-white first team. Playing two games, only the Gamecocks' Harlicka matched Scott's statistics for the weekend. It proved a foreshadowing of what would happen to Scott the following season.

After State coach Norman Sloan shook Miller's hand in congratulations and good riddance to the All-American, the Tar Heels took another picture with the team trophy and headed for the locker room. Johnny Harris, from a prominent Charlotte family and Clark's fraternity brother, was throwing a celebratory bash at his family estate called Morrocroft in south Charlotte. Whether invited or not, Scott did not feel at ease going and instead went out to eat with Lotz. He felt he had to find his own party somewhere else, as he so often did.

"I don't blame them; circumstances and society made it impossible," Scott said, looking back. "If you want to be realistic about the whole thing, it was a unique experience for me to be involved in and a unique experience for them to be involved in."

By then, Scott was dating Margaret Holmes, who was a year older and had recently returned to Durham, where she lived with her parents after a time spent working in New York City. They had met on a Sunday the previous

January, when Margaret and a friend were driving around north Durham and saw two young men on the side of the road fixing a flat tire. Margaret's friend said, "That's Charlie Scott, the basketball player at Carolina." Margaret was not a big sports fan and had never heard of him, but they stopped and asked the guys if they needed help. Margaret and Charlie became friends, bonded perhaps by her being one of the first five girls to integrate Durham High School in 1963 or by her time in his native New York, or both. They started dating and, by the spring, were pretty much going steady.

As the 1968 season drew to a dramatic conclusion, sophomore Scott, junior Clark, and senior Miller had established themselves as a sensational "big three." Miller was on his way to bettering his junior average of 21.9 points a game and shooting nearly 100 free throws more than anyone else on the team. And the rugged southpaw led everyone in minutes played by far; he almost never came out of a game. The magnificent athlete Scott was a close second, however, because he rarely tired, effortlessly beating his gasping teammates in sprints at the end of practice. Besides heading for a 17.6-point scoring average, Scott's defense was so deft that he easily led the team in steals (although like assists, steals were yet to be recorded as official statistics). Meanwhile, the towering Clark averaged a double-double (15.8 points and 11 rebounds) and should have joined Miller and Scott on the All-ACC first team (he made second team); he set the UNC single-game rebounding record with 30 (plus 27 points) in a home win over Maryland. Clark, a pre-med student, was at his best in big games. In the Eastern Regional, he had 18 points and 10 rebounds against seven-foot Bob Lanier and St. Bonaventure, and 22 and 17 against Davidson in the championship game, earning the regional MVP award. Scott added 18 points against the Wildcats and an unhappy Lefty Driesell, for whom he nearly played.

Basking in his growing glory, Scott spent most of his down time in Durham with Margaret and other friends. He had become what Smith hoped for: a famous and accepted black athlete in the South. Scott had done it by being visible to thousands during basketball games and a few others who shared the same UNC classes. But he found personal comfort and less stress on another campus, North Carolina Central, ten miles from Chapel Hill. While Margaret felt true devotion for a man she was learning to love without regard to basketball, Scott saw the relationship as a salve for the loneliness and insecurity he felt at Carolina.

"The more famous Charles got, the less time there was for me," Margaret said almost fifty years later. "He had a lot of friends in Durham, both men and women. And he liked all the attention. I was working all day, trying to save up enough money to get my own apartment. He wanted me to be there whenever he needed me."

When Scott went with the Tar Heels to the 1968 Final Four in Los Angeles, and later to the Olympic trials in New Mexico, Margaret remained with her friends and her parents. They all liked Charlie and cheered for him and his team. Scott played well in the semifinal against Ohio State at the Los Angeles Sports Arena, one of five UNC starters in double figures against the unranked Buckeyes. After the convincing 80–66 victory, Smith let his players watch the first half of the second semifinal between top-ranked Houston and No. 2 UCLA. Houston was led by Elvin Hayes, and UCLA had Scott's boyhood friend Alcindor and two others he had played with during the summer, Lucius Allen and Mike Warren. The Bruins lashed the Cougars from the opening tip, avenging their only loss of the season in the "game of the century" at the Astrodome the previous December.

Smith later regretted that he allowed his players to watch the 101–69 slaughter, but he had already anointed UCLA "the greatest college team ever assembled"—Alcindor, guards Allen and Warren, and forwards Mike Lynn and Lynn Shackleford. The 28–1 Bruins had dominated the Pac-8 Conference (14–0) and won just four times by fewer than nine points. They were in the middle of the most dominant run in the history of college basketball: ten national championships in twelve years between 1964 and 1975 under Coach John Wooden, including seven straight.

UNC assistant coach Lotz was among those who knew the 28–3 Tar Heels had notched their final victory of the season when they defeated Ohio State. However, he also thought their most important victories were the second consecutive ACC championship and the Eastern Regional title, which allowed them to play in the NCAA Tournament and return to the Final Four. "Although our biggest goal might have been the ACC championship, we had tremendous motivation to get to the Final Four," he said. "Most of our players had never been to Los Angeles, and it was a tremendous thrill to go there and be in the same field with UCLA."

Smith had already begun making such trips cultural experiences for his players, who visited MGM studios and stayed on Wilshire Boulevard at the plush Ambassador Hotel. The hotel had twice hosted the Academy Awards, and a little more than two months after they checked out, it was the site of Robert Kennedy's assassination on the night he won the Democratic presidential primary in California.

While Smith had intended to open in the Four Corners offense the year before if the Tar Heels had played UCLA in Louisville, he was not planning to slow the ball down in his first national championship game as a coach—that is, until he watched the Bruins demolish Houston from his baseline scouting seat. He went back to the hotel believing, even more so in 1968, that a spread offense might pull Alcindor away from the basket and perhaps frustrate the Bruins in the second half. But Miller and Scott, the two run-and-shoot scorers on the team, challenged the slowdown strategy in a private meeting the next morning. Miller never considered losing to anyone, and Scott relished his first chance to go against another bona fide black star, this time three of them. Scott had played with and against Alcindor in the schoolyard and thought his own quickness to the basket could get the national player of the year into foul trouble. "Coach Smith felt like we could not run with them at the beginning because it was like a home game for them, and they were playing like a runaway locomotive," Scott recalled of the decision.

The other players knew nothing about the plan until the pregame meeting. They were certainly prepared to play that way, having worked on Four Corners at the end of almost every practice. But they, too, believed such a tactic was unnecessary against any opponent from the beginning of the game. "It was kind of shocking that he wanted to do that," Grubar said thirty years later. "After beating Ohio State, everybody was really pumped all day about playing UCLA. As nineteen- and twenty-year-old kids having gone as far as we had, you don't think anyone is better than you are."

Grubar recalled no argument or disagreement between Smith and the other players before the Tar Heels took the court, just a few raised eyebrows and disconcerting glances among teammates. "Some of us may have thought, 'Why are we doing this?' But most of us were good soldiers and went along," Grubar said in *The Dean's List*.[11] They opened the game in Four Corners with Grubar, Miller, and Scott taking turns as the "chaser," or man in the middle. Slowing the tempo of the game was about the only success they had against their overpowering opponent.

The Tar Heels led once, 5–4, and trailed 32–22 at the half, theoretically still in the game. Miller and Scott, who were cocky enough to have been thrown out of practice by Smith during the season, were either too quick to the basket or too tentative. "I was very disappointed," Scott said. "I felt like we could play on UCLA's level. I thought Rusty could hold his own with Lew, and that Dickie and I could play with Lucius and Mike Warren. And with

Miller and Bunting, I thought we were better in the front court." At halftime, Smith said they were about where he thought they'd be and that they could "just play" in the second half because UCLA would be eager to run and might make mistakes. "Of course, that's not what happened," Scott said.

A photo on the sports front of the *Los Angeles Times* on Sunday, March 24, 1968, shows Scott skying for a layup on the right side of the basket and Alcindor coming down the lane to swat it away with his right arm extended high above Scott, five fingers spread like a spider web. At the bottom of that same sports front was a long examination of African American athletes' emergence in college and professional sports. While it did not mention Scott or Alcindor, the story could have cited the differing paths the old acquaintances had taken from the same Harlem playgrounds. Scott chose to follow some of his asphalt idols to prep school in the South and stayed there to integrate a college basketball program. Alcindor headed for the far more open-minded West Coast and already-integrated UCLA, where he turned his curiosity toward the Muslim religion. By the time he and Scott met again in college at the Los Angeles Sports Arena, Alcindor was preparing to embrace the Kalima Shahadat, the Islamic creed that accepted Muhammad as God's prophet, and was choosing his new Muslim name. Although he was officially Kareem Abdul-Jabbar by the next season, he did not force it on anyone and was occasionally referred to by Coach Wooden as "Lewis Kareem."

In his column on the game, Jim Murray of the *Los Angeles Times* dissed the "University of Nicotina" for putting a less-than-capacity crowd to sleep with its slowdown. "North Carolina came out looking like a bunch of guys asked to wash a lion," Murray wrote. "It wasn't a game, it was a Death Watch. No one expected much of North Carolina and they didn't disappoint."[12]

The 78–55 final score was the largest margin of defeat in an NCAA championship game until UNLV (University of Nevada, Las Vegas) routed Duke by 30 in 1990. Alcindor, who finished with 34 points and 18 rebounds, won his second of three consecutive Most Outstanding Player awards, as well as his second of three straight national titles. The out-of-sync Tar Heels shot 35 percent, with Clark, Miller, and Scott combining to go 15 for 42; no one who played looked comfortable in the game.

At this point in his career, Smith was still far from the iconic coach whose moves were rarely questioned in public. Although the circumstances weren't the same, he deserved criticism nine years later in his second national championship game, when he went to the Four Corners after the 1977 Tar Heels rallied to tie Marquette with ten minutes to play. The move backfired.

Had Smith let his horses run against UCLA, it might have been more exciting but with the same outcome. In truth, the Bruins were so dominant that his plan didn't matter, except to his players. The 1967 and 1968 UCLA teams lost once over two seasons, the 71–69 classic at Houston. Alcindor was perhaps the greatest college center of all time.

From a sports trivia standpoint, Carolina lucked out by losing in the national semifinals in 1967 and 1969 or UNC might have been the Bruins' victim in three straight NCAA title games, a dubious distinction Smith and his program were better off avoiding. Being No. 2 and the best in the East wasn't bad, and it finally pushed Smith out of McGuire's shadow. The evidence was the Carolina Blue Cadillac convertible the Rams Club gave him the week after the team returned to Chapel Hill. McGuire had received the same gift of gratification after his perfect season of 1957.

Claiming he was not "the Cadillac type," Smith accepted the car because he was "certain that what you are really expressing . . . is your appreciation for the fine play of our team. And in that spirit, I accept the gift."[13] Assistant coaches Lotz and Bill Guthridge accepted bonus checks for $1,000. "Thanks for doubling my salary," quipped Guthridge.[14]

Scott could not avoid the racial issues of the era in Los Angeles, where he met Harry Edwards, a teacher, activist, and former track athlete at San Jose State. Edwards's Olympic Project for Human Rights (OPHR) was organizing a Black Power boycott of the 1968 Summer Games in Mexico City the following October. Scott was torn, as he would be over similar controversies throughout his life, but he did not want to turn his Olympic effort into a cause. He saw no personal logic in boycotting the Olympic trials, which seduced the three Bruins stars, plus Houston's Hayes, St. Bonaventure's Lanier, and Louisville's Wes Unseld, creating serious concern about whether the United States could win its seventh consecutive gold medal.

"I found out San Jose's track athletes were going to try to qualify for the Olympics," Scott said years later. "And, for me, I had gone to the University of North Carolina to be the first black scholarship athlete there. What sense would it make for me to then turn around and boycott the Olympics?"

Scott's decision was clearly self-interested but also brave. "I wanted to prove I could make the team—that I was just as good as the first-team All-Americans who were trying out," Scott said. "In the ACC, there were two things I was playing against. I had to prove to white players I was good enough to play, and I had to prove to black players that I was good enough not only because I was playing against white players. Going out for the Olympics was for me to prove I was a good enough basketball player to play with and against anybody."

Scott had one week in Chapel Hill and with Margaret before leaving for Albuquerque, where he joined seventy-nine players at the Olympic trials, including LSU's Pete Maravich, the nation's leading scorer, and first-team All-Americans Rick Mount of Purdue and Calvin Murphy of Niagara. All three got cut by the forty-five-man U.S. Olympic Selection Committee, chaired by former UNC and Navy coach Ben Carnevale. Oklahoma State's Hank Iba, the USA coach whose team had won the gold medal in 1964 in Tokyo, made it clear that he wanted athletes who could score *and* play defense, and was apparently unfazed by the lack of star power on the U.S. team.

Lotz had told Scott before he went to New Mexico to "take your shot when it's there, but pass the ball and bust your butt on defense." Scott took the advice to heart, and by the time the trials ended, he was the committee's top vote-getter among collegians. He had averaged 20 points and 7.5 assists in three tryout games, while playing the determined defense he was still learning at UNC. The twelve-man roster included one other well-known college player, Jo Jo White of Kansas, and a young junior college big man named Spencer Haywood. Houston's Ken Spain and Ohio State's Bill Hoskett, both coming off the Final Four like Scott, made the team. Also selected were three members of the Armed Forces All-Stars, who won the national AAU tournament in Denver the week before, and two college grads who played for AAU teams. "I think the main reason I was chosen was due to my all-around play and my defense," Scott said at the time. "I credit Coach Smith for that. He taught me to play defense during our season, and that made me a complete player."[15]

Iba immediately took his new Olympic team to play exhibition games in Finland and Russia. "On the trip, my roommate was a guy named Calvin Fowler," Scott said. "I was nineteen; he was twenty-six. Every day he would sit in that room and tell me about married life. Then we had Jo Jo White and Spencer Haywood always talking about how much fun they had in school. There was a schism there because you had the black ballplayers, me, Jo Jo, Fowler and Spencer, and on the other side, Bill Hoskett and Ken Spain and Mike Barrett and Mike Silliman. All those guys had a life story, and I didn't have one. And I got more and more lonely; in Russia, I became very lonely. And I told myself that when I got back to Carolina I was going to get married and never feel lonely again in my life."

Charles and Margaret eloped on June 1, 1968, and were married by a justice of the peace in Bennettsville, South Carolina. Margaret's sister, Janice, was her maid of honor and Janice's husband, Jessie, stood up as the best man. A few weeks later, after renting an apartment near N.C. Central, the Scotts threw a small party at their new home. Coaches Smith and Lotz dropped by as did manager Randy Forehand and several of Scott's older teammates from the class of 1969, including Dick Grubar and Rusty Clark. No one from his class of 1970 team was there. Most of the players from out of state had gone home for the summer, but revealing their separateness that existed off the court, and Scott's longtime resentment over it, few of those players even remember that Scott was married for the last two seasons of their college careers. "I might have heard it down the road, but I don't think I knew at the time," Eddie Fogler said. "I saw Charlie almost every day with practice, meetings, and games, but I don't remember him being married."

The Scotts did not take a honeymoon for two years, as Margaret had to make enough money to buy a car and cover the apartment rent in Durham. She eventually landed a secretarial job in the UNC Computer Science Department with the help of Smith's recommendation and her ability to type a hundred words a minute. Scott spent the summer playing pickup games almost day and night at the Central gym, where dozens of kids came to watch and cheer. Margaret always had dinner waiting for him, but sometimes Scott didn't make it on time. Sometimes he did not make it at all. Then, he often went back to play or hang out with the group. Rarely, Margaret went with him. A bad pattern was developing.

"About a month after I got married, I knew I made a big mistake; my reason for getting married was totally asinine," Scott said forty-six years later. "I thought I could be married and never feel lonely and still go out and run around. I really didn't want to be married; I just wanted to not be lonely again in life. So I got married for the wrong reason. She was committed to marriage; she came from a family that was very close knit, and they believed in marriage. That was on me and very wrong.

"I stayed with the marriage because I made an obligation; my mother had told me before, I can't go back on my word. I had no idea what marriage encompassed and didn't want to do the things that marriage involved. I wasn't in love; I wanted to make sure I never felt like I was by myself again. I grew up by myself, had raised myself, and went to school by myself; I didn't want to feel by myself anymore."

7

The Push and the Pull

For UNC and the town of Chapel Hill, the 1968–69 academic year proved to be one of the most disruptive ever. The civil rights marches and almost daily demonstrations of 1963–64 were only a prelude. Like the rest of the nation, many North Carolinians were reeling from the assassinations of Martin Luther King Jr. in April and of Robert F. Kennedy (RFK) in June. The Black Student Movement (BSM) protested after King's slaying, burning Confederate flags in front of several fraternity houses.

Meanwhile, Lyndon B. Johnson's landslide election in 1964 was all but forgotten as he continued to deploy ground troops to Southeast Asia. The growing counterculture of radicals, hippies, and yippies, as well as clean-shaven moderates, swarmed into Chicago in the stifling heat of late August. Soon, the 1968 Democratic National Convention turned into one of the most regrettable scenes in U.S. history, as television cameras captured helmeted police and National Guardsmen holding back hundreds of protestors with clubs and tear gas. Inside, two-time Minnesota senator Hubert Humphrey earned the nomination that might have been RFK's; he was swamped by Richard Nixon the following November. Alabama governor George Wallace, in his second of four runs for the presidency, finished a distant third as an Independent.

In Chapel Hill, the images from Chicago spawned antiwar protests that became the new focus, most of them at The Pit and on campus quads. While the Middle East's Six-Day War had flared in 1967, Vietnam was the daily story. It looked to be a prolonged and increasingly bloody battle that would affect college students everywhere. Some began declaring as conscientious objectors, like deposed heavyweight boxing champion Muhammad Ali, others worried about the draft lottery. Unrest over Vietnam was rivaled by ongoing racial tensions, as the BSM raised the temperature at UNC. And Howard Lee's campaign to become the first African American mayor of Chapel Hill kept race at the forefront of debate around the town. On campus, however, the predominant sentiment was reflected in the song lyrics "I don't give a damn. Next stop is Vietnam."[1]

In the midst of these upheavals, by the fall of 1968, Dean Smith had found quiet waters as a coach—fully established through his run of recent success as a regional and national force to be reckoned with. Smith had his hands full, however, not only with managing his program on the court but also with supporting his players during turbulent times. He encouraged Charlie Scott to attend Black Student Movement rallies, and Smith himself occasionally stood in antiwar vigils near the post office on East Franklin Street, often alongside other UNC coaches and athletes. "It was difficult for me to tell a student not to be politically active on campus, when I felt the chief reason they were there was to ask questions and develop their own convictions," Smith wrote in his autobiography.[2]

That previous spring, Smith had signed his second African American player, Bill Chamberlain, who commuted from Harlem each week to attend integrated Lutheran High School on Long Island, which had one of the best teams in the state. Chamberlain very nearly followed his white high school teammate Chris Thomforde to Princeton. But Chamberlain was excited about joining Pennsylvania prep stars Steve Previs and Dennis Wuycik, whom Smith had secured for the Tar Heels. Having attended a largely white high school, and even vacationing with white teammates on Martha's Vineyard, the handsome six foot six Chamberlain was not intimidated by the small number of African American students at Carolina. Indeed, he regarded it as a personal challenge. Chamberlain proved popular and provocative from almost the moment he stepped on campus.

As Chamberlain arrived for the start of school in the fall of 1968, Scott had left Chapel Hill, now practicing with the Olympic team on the way to Mexico City. He had registered for classes, but through a special exception from the ACC and NCAA was allowed to take one correspondence course while away and still be an active member of the Carolina team when he returned in late October.

The U.S. basketball team had automatically qualified for Group Play, having won its sixth consecutive gold medal in Tokyo in 1964. In winning seven straight games before the elimination round, the Yanks had close calls only with Yugoslavia and Puerto Rico. Scott averaged nine points in Group Play, but in the semifinals against Brazil and the finals rematch with Yugoslavia totaled only nine, as fellow collegians Jo Jo White and Spencer Haywood took over offensively. Scott started every game, and as John Lotz had advised him before the Olympic trials, concentrated on making assists and playing good defense. In the 65–50 gold medal victory over Yugoslavia, the United States held a precarious three-point lead at halftime and opened the second half in a full-court press that triggered a decisive 17–0 spurt. Scott was most responsible for holding leading Yugoslav scorer Radivoj Korac to one point.

Scott returned to campus the last week in October to find long-haired students dressed in boots, baggy pants, and Army jackets meeting in groups when they should have been in class. He had some harried Olympic stories about the Black Power salute of sprinters Tommie Smith and John Carlos, who bowed their heads and raised one closed fist with a black glove on the medal podium, after winning the gold and bronze in the 200-meters. They were immediately ushered out of the Olympic Village and banned from the remainder of the Summer Games. After that, Scott said, all black U.S. athletes received stern warnings and some felt like they were on lockdown between practices and events, given an ultimatum by Avery Brundage, president of the International Olympic Committee.[3] "They pooled all the blacks together and told us what not to do," Scott said. "We couldn't show any form of protest or they would reprimand us. I understood this to mean they would strip us of our medals."[4] Those restrictions, even with winning a gold medal, made Scott more eager to get back to North Carolina and Margaret, where he felt at least in better control of the racial landscape.

Scott went right to practice, which had begun two weeks earlier, and took his place as the undisputed star of the preseason No. 2–ranked Tar Heels. The cover of the 1968–69 UNC basketball media guide featured seniors Bill Bunting, Dick Grubar, Gerald Tuttle, Joe Brown, and Rusty Clark at the Old Well on campus, but it also had an inset of Scott in his USA No. 9 uniform. *Sports Illustrated* had come to Chapel Hill to shoot the cover of its college basketball issue and brought in Kentucky star Mike Casey and Davidson's Mike Maloy to be interviewed with Scott, posing them all at the Old Well in their respective warm-ups under the headline "Challenge to UCLA." The magazine had this scouting report focused on Scott stepping into Larry Miller's shoes:

> North Carolina will have to go to another man for the points, leadership and the meal money—6′5″ Charlie Scott, fresh from the Olympic Games with a gold medal around his neck and a new wife on his arm. Scott averaged 17.6 points last year while playing second banana, and he is a gloriously exciting player who can—and will—play all over the

court and do just about everything but paint the ball blue for the Tar Heels. That includes scoring.

Reinforced with Scott's multiple talents, Smith can talk more easily about a schedule that includes early-season games with Kentucky, Vanderbilt and Villanova. "We're the same team as last year," he says. "Except we start every game with Larry Miller having fouled out. Maybe Charles can replace Miller, but then who replaces Charles?"[5]

Having to deal with only one correspondence course, Scott resumed his social life while living with Margaret in Durham. She had gone to work at UNC and bought a car, sometimes waiting for him after practice and sometimes leaving the car and taking the bus back to their apartment. She said her husband's increased fame put even more pressure on their marriage because they were alone less. "It made me feel insecure," Margaret said. "People would always come up to him and didn't even look at me. He expected me to be there for him, at games and award dinners, and it seemed like I was getting nothing out of the marriage."

As the start of basketball season approached, on November 23 Carolina finished its first football season with a black player, Ricky Lanier, on the roster. It was a fine finish, with Carolina upsetting Duke and star quarterback Leo Hart at delirious Kenan Stadium. Coach Bill Dooley and his courageous left-handed quarterback Gayle Bomar saved another losing season by beating the Blue Devils for a second straight year.

That same night, however, a very different event had the attention of campus. Black Power activist Stokely Carmichael spoke to more than seven thousand mostly white students in the arena that coincidentally bore his name, openly advocating "revolutionary violence" and railing against "liberals who are trying to stop confrontation. . . . The role of the liberal is to maintain the status quo. . . . They may say they want change but they really want to keep things the way they are." The words heightened the tension in some corners of campus, much steered by the BSM, which brokered Carmichael's appearance and charged that the university withheld some of the student fees the BSM was promised. Nevertheless, without further disruption, the overwhelmingly white student body remained passive and more interested in the start of basketball season. The 1969 *Yackety Yak* looked back on Carmichael's visit by writing, "Suddenly there was a lot of talk about the Black Student Movement. Who were they? What did they want? Over 7,000 people saw Stokely Carmichael. He scared them a little bit. He also made them think."[6]

As UNC let out for Christmas break, the confluence of some racial friction and the war in Southeast Asia had almost become a part of regular life in a college town. Ed Caldwell, a black Presbyterian elder who would soon announce his candidacy for a seat on the Board of Aldermen, delivered a long Sunday sermon that was reprinted in its entirety in the *Chapel Hill Weekly*, entitled "We Are All Condemned to Live Together." The town was almost empty when the next edition of the paper came out, carrying adjacent front-page stories about the BSM's demands delivered to Chancellor Carlyle Sitterson in December and the first Chapel Hillian to die in Vietnam, UNC graduate and former star high school athlete Joel Leigh. It was a stirring juxtaposition two days before Christmas, 1968.

Scott found himself pulled into the protest over the BSM's demands to Sitterson, which included the establishment of an Afro-American studies curriculum. "I was the only instrument on campus that they thought could have made a difference," Scott recalled, "or something they thought the school would have to respond to, react to. They were always trying to get me to be more vocal about it."

Scott told Smith he was asked to speak at a civil rights demonstration for cafeteria employees claiming low pay and poor working conditions. "Great, go do it," Smith said.[7] Scott was not as outspoken as acknowledged BSM member Chamberlain, who by Smith's freshman policy was not supposed to talk to the media during his first year on campus. Chamberlain wasn't talking—at least about basketball.

By then, Scott and his fellow Tar Heels had won their first six games impressively, all by double figures, defeating Oregon in Greensboro and Chapel Hill. Scott scored thirty-four points in the opener and twenty-eight the next night, with movie star and North Carolinian Ava Gardner watching from the first row at a roaring Carmichael Auditorium. "If any man can make Tar Heel fans forget Larry Miller, it seems it's Scott," wrote Bill Prouty in the *Chapel Hill Weekly*.[8] Smith delighted in UNC's fourth straight victory over Kentucky, and especially in bringing his first black player to Lexington. Longtime segregationist Adolph Rupp watched Scott score nineteen points in the 87–77 win over his third-ranked Wildcats. On the court, everything seemed to be running smoothly. After the Kentucky win, however, Scott gave a telling quote to a North Carolina reporter when asked about his recent marriage and how Margaret served as an anchor. "There is something missing in the life of a black student at an all-white college," he said. "There is some loneliness. Last season, I was ready to give it all up. We had lost back-to-back games to South Carolina and Duke, and when you're losing, your other problems become more vivid. Margaret helped me a great deal then. And now that I'm married a lot of my problems have evaporated."[9]

Two nights later, Carolina evened the score from the year before against No. 12 Vanderbilt in Charlotte. They next blew out Clemson and Virginia in early ACC home games. Then the solidly second-ranked Tar Heels (behind UCLA) went to New York for the three-day Holiday Festival tournament where they opened by facing eighth-ranked Villanova, which featured black star Howard Porter. A likely semifinal would follow against well-coached St. John's before a partisan Madison Square Garden crowd. Then they would almost certainly face two-time defending national champion UCLA in the finals of what was regarded as the premier Christmas-season college tournament.

Scott savored matchups against strong black players because there were so few of them in the ACC, and he wanted to prove his success beyond mostly white teams. In the avenging rematch with Vanderbilt, Perry Wallace had missed 11 of 12 shots and scored only 2 points while Scott produced 14 points and 15 rebounds. He would outscore his old playground pal Norwood Todman 61–24 in UNC's three games against Wake Forest in 1969. And when Maryland led by 19 points in the first half behind black point guard Pete Johnson (who scored 28 points), Scott led the comeback charge to overtake the Terrapins with 26 points.

Villanova's Porter, a bruising six foot eight, 230-pound sophomore post man from Florida, and Scott, who came in averaging 22.5 points a game, did not guard each other. But before a packed house of 19,500, Scott jawed at Porter for how he was manhandling the skinny Bunting, who missed five of his six shots in the first half. In the second half, they nearly triggered a brawl, and both benches emptied before the officials and coaches cleared the court. In one classic *New York Post* photo, Porter (one of Villanova's three black starters) has his right arm raised and fist cocked, with Scott on the floor beneath him. Carolina went on to win 69–61, but the team was physically and mentally spent.

Grubar remembered that Smith had given the players eight days off over Christmas before reassembling in New York for practice on December 26, something Smith never did again. "I don't think we worked out on our own as much as we should have, and some of us came back a little fat and happy," Grubar said. Scott had made half of his 12 shots and scored 15 points against Villanova, while Bunting caught fire to finish with game highs of 26 points and 13 rebounds. Porter, who would be a three-time All-American and play seven years in the NBA, had 12 points and 4 rebounds, and fouled out trying to stop Bunting, who used the game as a springboard to an All-ACC season.

In the semifinals against Lou Carnesecca's Redmen, before another pulsating Garden crowd, Carolina had to play long possessions of defense against St. John's deliberate style in the pre–shot clock era. The Tar Heels fell behind early, drew close a couple of times, and ultimately lost 72–70. Unheralded St. John's went on to the NCAA Tournament that season, losing in the Sweet Sixteen to Davidson, UNC's eventual opponent in the Eastern Regional final for the second straight year. At the moment, however, Carolina's team was stung by its first loss of the season and missing another shot at UCLA.

Against St. John's, Scott had a second straight mediocre game by his standards (15 points), as Clark's 23 points and 12 rebounds and Eddie Fogler's 14 points in his own return to New York were not enough to compensate. Scott shouldered the burden in front of family and friends in his old hometown. In a piece titled "Fall from Olympus," *Charlotte News* columnist Ronald Green called it an "inexcusable performance. In each (game), Carolina turned the ball over 20 times. It hurt all of them but tore the guts out of Charlie Scott." Green, normally a positive, eloquent journalist, wrote, "This was that once-in-a-lifetime moment—New York, Madison Square Garden, some of the best teams in the country. And Charlie Scott bombed."[10] Scott was even harder on himself, sadly proclaiming he "blew this one. Charge it to me. I got called for walking four times against Villanova and three times tonight. We . . . I just didn't do the job Coach told me to do. I had to do certain things to help the team and I didn't do them." Scott denied that he felt any pressure from having his mother, stepfather, sisters, wife, and friends—about twenty in all—watching from seats behind the UNC bench. "No, I haven't felt any pressure because of the Olympics or the Garden, any of that," Scott said. "We weren't looking ahead to UCLA. I played my two worst games of the year here. I don't know why."[11] Despite his denials, the pressure *had* to be enormous on Scott.

He came back with 22 points, 7 rebounds, and 5 assists in the meaningless third-place romp over Princeton. The team then returned to Chapel Hill and continued its winning form, taking out any frustrations in four straight blowouts of Duke, N.C. State, Virginia Tech, and Georgia Tech, all by at least 20 points. Scott rang up another 34 points in the 94–70 rout of the Blue Devils, 26 against N.C. State, and 23 against Virginia Tech, a game in which Bunting had a career-high of 30 points.

Before the team flew to Atlanta on Monday, January 13, for the game at Georgia Tech, manager Randy Forehand had made dinner reservations at a restaurant near the team hotel. When the players walked in, the owner saw Scott and refused to seat them. Smith was furious, remembering traveling as a boy with his father to a tournament in Lawrence, Kansas. That's when the Emporia High School team stomped out of the Jayhawk Hotel after its only black player, Chick Taylor, was refused service.

Of the Atlanta problem, UNC teammate Ricky Webb said, "I had never seen Coach so irate. He gave the managers money for everyone to eat on their own and walked away with the other coaches." Webb said he would not have been surprised if Smith circled back to the racist restaurant and let the bigoted owner have it.

Smith was already upset, having had to defend uncharacteristic comments by Larry Miller that week in Los Angeles, where as a rookie with the American Basketball Association LA Stars he said the UNC team had "voted" to run with UCLA in the 1968 national championship game, but Smith made them play Four Corners. "We run a dictatorship here, not a democracy," Smith told columnist Fox Casey of the *Durham Morning Herald*. "I make every decision. I take the responsibility for defeat, and the players get the credit for victory."[12]

In the Tech game, the proud Scott sparked UNC to a 56–33 halftime lead and had 8 rebounds and a dazzling 5 assists to go with his 30 points in the 101–70 blowout of the Yellow Jackets, perhaps using the restaurant incident as additional fuel. Scott continued his personal tear, scoring fewer than 20 points only once as Carolina completed its longest winning streak of the season with eleven in a row. The streak included defeating Florida State, not yet a conference foe, with Scott outplaying All-American Dave Cowens, his old Davidson summer camp teammate. A month after a 20-point blowout of N.C. State in Chapel Hill, when Scott and sophomore Lee Dedmon combined for 53 points, the Tar Heels went to Raleigh. The measured Smith was not known for his sense of humor, but he quipped to his players before they took the court at Reynolds Coliseum, "State is an improved team; they've stopped biting." The frustrated Wolfpack fans left Scott pretty much alone since State now had its first African American, Al Heartley. Instead, they turned on their own team for making a pathetic 5 field goals in the first half of a 23-point loss, State's seventh of what would eventually be 10 straight to its hated rival.

Then the still second-ranked team in the country bused to Charlotte for the North-South Doubleheaders and a matchup with Frank McGuire's upstart

Gamecocks, who would emerge as a national power and thrust themselves into the center of the first ACC racial controversy.

McGuire, with a reloaded lineup of New Yorkers, had beaten Carolina twice in the teams' last four meetings, and familiarity was already breeding contempt. Smith had stayed in touch regularly with McGuire until the latter thought his protégé had run up the score on him during a thirty-four-point pounding in 1966, McGuire's second season at South Carolina. Since then, the Gamecocks had shocked the nationally ranked Tar Heels at the end of the 1967 and 1968 seasons. And they were ready to do it again.

The North-South Doubleheaders, which matched UNC and N.C. State against Clemson and South Carolina, with the teams swapping opponents Saturday night, had historically been a good weekend for the Tar Heels since the event's inception in 1959. Their overall record was 16–4, with two losses each to Clemson (1964, 1967) and South Carolina (1960, 1962). In alternate seasons, the teams counted them as ACC home games, so UNC visited Clemson and Columbia only every other year. As a sophomore, Scott had played against South Carolina in Charlotte and Chapel Hill, winning in the Queen City and losing in Miller's last home game.

The underdog Gamecocks came in at 15–3, having won eleven of their last twelve games. They were young, starting four sophomores and junior Bobby Cremins in a three-guard lineup with six foot ten Tom Owens and six foot eight John Ribock in the frontcourt. The man in control was John Roche, who seemingly always had the ball in his hands and never rested. He and Owens had played together in New York since they were kids and by then could communicate without saying a word. Cremins and Billy Walsh were also from New York, and Ribock was the interloper from Augusta, Georgia. This was a hungry team, having watched the departed Four Horsemen—Gary Gregor, Skip Harlicka, Frank Standard, and Jack Thompson—upset the Tar Heels in Chapel Hill the year before. The Gamecocks were brimming with confidence that came across as cockiness.

McGuire's pattern during his coaching career was to settle on his first seven and play them almost exclusively, but he carried it to the extreme this time. His starters played all forty minutes, using their time-outs throughout to rest. Roche, a skinny, pasty-faced point guard who played with a smirk and a chip on his shoulder, took the Tar Heels' man-to-man defense apart, scoring thirty-eight points, with Walsh the only other Gamecock in double figures. Smith tried everything on Roche to no avail. Both teams played well and shot well. UNC won the rebounding battle by ten, but the Gamecocks hit 69 percent of their shots and held on for a stunning 68–66 upset.

Roche's performance made him a major ACC star in a league dominated by the four Tobacco Road schools. In the eyes of some fans and sportswriters, it also created an opportunity to pit a white Gamecock Yankee against an African American pioneer. As Roche and McGuire jumped to favorites for ACC Player and Coach of the Year, Scott dropped into the background after the Roche-led upset. A few days later, the *DTH* reported that Roche and Owens wanted to go to college together, but Smith had offered a scholarship only to Owens. Still bristling from the loss, Smith called the reporter to his office and held up the clipping of the story. "Say I'm a lousy coach, criticize my strategy," he said with teeth clenched. "But don't say I can't judge talent. Of course we wanted Roche."

Luckily, the Tar Heels had another crack at South Carolina only twelve days later, but it was in Columbia, where Charlie Scott got his first taste of no-holds-barred racism from fans.

The intervening period was as tense as ever at UNC; a peaceful moment was hard to find on campus in early 1969. Soon after the Tar Heels returned from Charlotte, the Black Student Movement was rallying in anticipation of BSM leader Preston Dobbins's meeting with Chancellor Sitterson on Tuesday morning, February 18. Scott and Chamberlain, a freshman already considered outspoken, were invited to join the meeting. Scott said Smith summoned him to his office and said he understood the circumstances and what Scott was being asked to do. Smith also said some alumni would be upset if Scott took a stand against a university that had given him a scholarship to play basketball. According to Scott, Smith said that he, too, was in the crosshairs with a conservative university administration and had to consider the security of his wife and three small children. In retrospect, it was a perfectly logical priority. "Coach Smith basically told me there were a lot of big alumni who were upset with the stance they thought I was going to take," Scott said, "that I was going to disrupt the university. So they put pressure on Coach Smith. It was the first time I understood that Coach Smith was under pressure, too—that if he supported me, the university might not support him. He wanted me to understand that if he had to choose between me and his own family, keeping his job, he was going to support his family."

The highest-profile African Americans on campus were clearly caught in the middle. Smith had no choice but to remind them of their responsibilities, not only to their race but their own families, their basketball teammates, and the university they represented on the court. Smith encouraged Scott and Chamberlain to attend the meeting but was unhappy when reports came out that they were affiliating with the BSM and would quit the basketball program if the administration did not meet its demands by the end of the week. "I felt like I had to tread lightly," recalled Scott, who attended rallies but rarely spoke and made no such threat. "I wanted to support them but not ruin my career over it. That was a very trying time, a decision-making time for many black athletes. There were times when everyone agreed on the problems; the solutions were harder to come by."

Because race was still the hottest button on campus, Smith was more careful with the BSM controversy in counseling his players than he was about the Vietnam War he so strongly opposed. Having stood silently at peace vigils with fellow members of the Binkley congregation, he had to be consistent when his players were asked to join protests. "Understand you are being used because you're a name," he told them. "That's why they want you to be there. But now tell me what you're being used for. And do you believe it yourself?"[13]

As the varsity team departed for a game at Maryland on Wednesday night, February 19, a week before the South Carolina rematch, freshman Chamberlain remained alone to nervously address the two hundred black and white students who gathered at noon outside South Building to hear about the morning meeting with Sitterson. "I feel that if I am going to represent the university on the basketball court," Chamberlain began, "I think the university should go to bat for me and take some positive action soon."[14] Scott received several calls at his motel room in College Park that night and tried to walk a fine line. "I have not been an active member of the Black Student Movement," he said to reporters. "However, I am concerned about the plight of blacks on this campus or any campus."

Scott said he went to the first meeting "hoping that Bill Chamberlain and I could serve as mediators in helping to close the communication gap."[15] He said he did not speak at the meeting and then heard about what Chamberlain said at the noon rally. Scott denied having threatened to quit the basketball team and added, "I don't think anywhere in that statement by Bill Chamberlain ... [did he say] he would quit basketball. ... There was no mention to the chancellor of quitting the team."[16]

Chamberlain acknowledged years later that he had joined the BSM and seriously considered leaving Carolina if the administration failed to correct what he believed to be oppressive working conditions at Lenoir Hall cafeteria.

According to Chamberlain, when an assistant cook severely cut his finger slicing meat, the cafeteria supervisor sent him home without medical assistance and then fired the employee after he missed work the next day. Chamberlain went to see Smith, who happened to have Sitterson in his office. As was Smith's practice, he asked the chancellor to step outside so he could speak to one of his players. Chamberlain showed his coach the BSM petition against the standard contract for hundreds of nonfaculty employees, which Chamberlain said listed a base weekly schedule at 39.5 hours so UNC would not have to pay health benefits. Furthermore, he said, the cafeteria workers had to be on campus from 6 A.M. to 8 P.M., working split shifts of eight hours in between. Chamberlain said Smith confirmed the veracity of the petition and told Sitterson he was going to sign it, and ask others in the athletic department to do the same. Later that week, Jesse Helms, on one of his WRAL-TV commentaries, said to an audience of thousands that Chamberlain was a "Negra athlete who is challenging the policies of a great university." Chamberlain said he contacted WRAL seeking "equal time" and was refused.

Smith and Sitterson decided that putting out statements would help clarify the basketball program's position on the controversy. Smith said, "Charles Scott, Bill Chamberlain, and I have discussed the Black Student demands on many occasions. We are close enough that we can bring these things out into the open. I am concerned about the pressure that has been put on Charles these past two weeks. He is a young man who is extremely loyal to me, to his teammates, and to the university. He is also called upon to be loyal to his fellow black students and to the black community across America. Therefore, a young man with divided loyalties has a lot of pressure to bear. I personally think he has done an amazing job serving as a mediator between the divided loyalties. Charles Scott is a student-athlete of the university and is entitled to the same privileges as any nonathlete to visit with the chancellor and to have his own beliefs."

Scott said, "Coach Smith and I have discussed the Black Student demands for two weeks. He suggested that I talk with Chancellor Sitterson. I went there, not with any demands. . . . I have not been an active member of the Black Student Movement. My concern grew out of the situation in which black students have found themselves at universities throughout the country."

The Black Student Movement, which grew into the second largest organization at UNC behind the Greek system, did not embrace Sitterson's nineteen-page reply that vowed "to be responsive to the educational needs of . . . all races, colors and creeds" while also asserting that "the University cannot, in policy or practice, provide unique treatment for any single race, color or creed." The BSM said its "tactics will change from reform to revolutionary"[17] if action was not taken by the end of the week. Sitterson promised open discussion and the establishment of a student commission.

The demands unnerved the university and town, which had lived through a half-decade of protests, and Memorial Hospital conducted disaster drills to prepare for the possibility of violence. UNC hoped to avoid anything similar to the student takeover of administrative buildings at Duke in early February, which led to police firing tear gas and a five-hour standoff with demonstrators. C. B. Claiborne, the school's first African American basketball player, was in one of the buildings.

Many UNC students and some faculty considered Sitterson's response dismissive. Led by the BSM, they organized picketing and a strike by the cafeteria workers, which led to Governor Bob Scott having the state police and National Guard sent to the UNC campus. Eventually, with the help of President Friday and Howard Lee, who was running for mayor in Chapel Hill, the food workers negotiated an increased minimum wage to $1.81 an hour. Gradually, most of the BSM's twenty-three demands were met, under threats from the AFL-CIO and other unions. Dobbins, who was a transfer from Chicago City College, was the driving force behind UNC officially recognizing the BSM in 1969, which was one of the demands. The *Yackety Yack* later presented Dobbins with the annual Frank Porter Graham Award for being an "apostle of a new social order."

For students who were paying attention to the strife on campus and who still loved Carolina basketball, Carmichael Auditorium was a place for welcome escape. Scott and the Tar Heels avoided looking ahead to the South Carolina rematch on February 26, 1969, when they posted the second-largest margin of victory in school history to date by blowing out The Citadel, 106–59. Scott hit eight of his ten shots and spent most of the second half with the starters cheering on the reserves in the raucous arena.

Two intense practices preceded the bus ride to Columbia for UNC's first visit to the new downtown Carolina Coliseum, dubbed the House That McGuire Built. When the Tar Heels came out to warm up thirty minutes before the 9 P.M. tip-off, most of what would be a standing-room-only crowd was already inside the building ready to pounce, particularly on Scott. The abuse began long before the regionally televised tip-off and never subsided. Because McGuire had coached at UNC, and left the program to a "no-name" assistant, Smith did not get the respect in Columbia he had earned elsewhere.

Smith learned much from McGuire but did not adopt his habit of staying in the locker room through warm-ups, then staging an anticipated entrance just before the game started. Smith was sitting on the bench to hear "some South Carolina fans hurl the worst possible racial epithets at Charles, taunting him as he warmed up."[18] By the time McGuire made his rock-star entry and embraced his protégé warmly, Smith and Scott and the Tar Heels had heard hundreds more smears and curses. With additional motivation from Smith, the Tar Heels were ready when the ball went up.

A trapping, run-and-jump defense keyed by Dick Grubar made John Roche give up the ball more than he wanted. He took half of his team's 22 shots in the first half and made 3 for the eighth-ranked Gamecocks. Scott pressed and missed 9 of his first 11 attempts but had 11 rebounds at the half as the second-ranked Tar Heels went to the locker room with a ridiculous 27–9 advantage on the glass and a 34–27 lead. Scott heard more "nigger go home!" and other catcalls as he sprinted off the court through the visitors' runway. The starters had scored 30 points in a well-balanced and focused first half, amidst an atmosphere as intense as any of them had ever experienced.

The lead jumped to 10 on Scott's first basket of the second half, but it slowly slipped away as Roche upstaged his new rival. Roche tied the game at 52 with a driving layup midway through the second half, as the building seemed to shake. Answering the challenge, Scott hit two jumpers and bumped the lead back to 4 points before another Roche drive made it 61–60 with less than 3 minutes to play. After Owens goal-tended a Fogler layup that had McGuire jawing at officials Lou Bello and George Conley, Roche made it a one-point game again with a pair of free throws. Lee Dedmon dropped one of two from the foul line, and then came the play that decided the game. Roche turned the corner at the top of the key and drove the lane with 55 seconds left. As he went up to shoot, Bunting blocked his path. Conley blew the whistle as both teams, and the wild home crowd thought *they* had the call. But Conley pointed to Roche for a charge instead of a block as the South Carolina bench exploded in rage. Bunting made both free throws, and after a hurried Owens miss, the Tar Heels hung on to win 68–62. Scott finished with 13 points and 14 rebounds, but the threats went toward Conley and Bello as they left the court.

"There was a lot of contact on that play," McGuire said of the crucial charging call. "Roche was hit from both sides. I'll have to see the pictures before I know if he charged, and it will be too late to do anything about it then. That was the turning point of the game, and I think we would have won if the call went the other way. North Carolina is a tremendous basketball team, but I hope I never see them again, and the same goes for those two fellows who were officiating tonight."

Smith had quickly shaken McGuire's hand and walked off the court patting his right jacket pocket to find his cigarettes. A chain smoker since college, Smith needed a smoke before, at halftime, and especially after every game to help him collect his thoughts and choose his words before meeting the press. This time, he heard a redneck South Carolina fan shout one last insult at Scott, calling him a "big black baboon."

Smith veered toward the seats and went up the row toward the guilty party. He almost got there before two ushers and three other fans stopped him. Bill Guthridge saw what was happening and raced to rescue his boss, but by now several more fans had become so foul-mouthed that the feisty thirty-five-year-old assistant coach started after them. It took a half-dozen ushers and police officers to restrain both coaches.

"That was the first time I'd ever seen Coach Smith get angry like that," Scott recalled thirty-seven years later. "At first I was shocked. Then I was just proud of him."[19]

Smith was always humble in victory, giving praise to the other team, win or lose, but this time he opened his press conference with Scott's performance in spite of what he really believed was a mean-spirited crowd. "He didn't shoot well, but gentlemen, he played some basketball game. His rebounding was tremendous and I thought the key to our victory," Smith began. "Grubar did an excellent job on Roche. I know Roche came back to score (a game-high twenty-two points), but it's a tribute to Dick that he held him as well as he did. Anytime you go on the home court of the eighth-ranked team in America and win, it's quite an achievement. This ranks alongside our victory at Kentucky and beating Villanova at the Garden. It took some kind of pressure play to win."

After he had met with sportswriters outside the South Carolina locker room, McGuire heard about the incident and apologized to Scott and the entire UNC team before they left the building. McGuire had played with black kids in his New York City youth, served with them in the Navy, and coached them at St. John's. He seemed genuinely sorry and particularly embarrassed for his program because he recently had signed South Carolina's first African American player, Casey Manning, who was enrolling the next fall to play on the freshman team.

Manning would have an experience much like Scott. He remembered his days of walking all the way across campus and never seeing a black face. "It was a social revolution across the country, not just in the South," recalled Manning, who went to law school and became a circuit court judge and still does commentary on South Carolina game broadcasts. "Most other teams had one or two African American players, so you were pretty much hated by other fans because you were part of the other team. It wasn't just because you were black. It was because you were on the other team. So it was the same everywhere."

The ride back to Chapel Hill was rowdy at first as the players recounted the game and ate their box sandwiches, but soon the bus quieted, as the physically and emotionally drained team dozed off. With the gutty win, the Tar Heels clinched at least a share of their third consecutive ACC regular-season title. The Gamecocks missed a chance to tie for first when they lost at N.C. State the following Saturday, as UNC was upset at unranked Duke in Vic Bubas's last home game. In Durham, Scott led the Tar Heels with twenty-two points. In many voters' minds, however, he had already lost ACC Player of the Year to the Cinderella Roche, even though it would not be announced until after they both played in the ACC Tournament.

The first sign came the week *before* the ACC Tournament, when the conference released its All-ACC voting results. Roche and Scott made the first team. But only Roche was unanimous, and Scott was left off five first-team ballots. Although privately Smith was livid, he said little about it publicly because, in 1969, school sports information directors were voting members of the Atlantic Coast Sportswriters Association (ACSWA), and he figured the five votes might have come from some of them. Smith often explained, "I always tell the truth but I don't always say everything I am thinking." His players were critical, some openly saying it was racism, and the *DTH* called it a "great injustice."

Smith did open up to the student newspaper: "The five who left Scott off the first team just don't know their basketball. He is justified to be player of the year. How anyone could leave him off the top five of the All-ACC shows there was something else on his mind. Maybe that person is anti–North Carolina or anti-black . . . if race is involved in this thing, it is a sad comment for college basketball today."[20] Years later, in his autobiography, Smith reiterated it was "transparently racist. . . . The awards were voted on by the ACC sportswriters, sportscasters and media relations directors for the schools, all of them, of course, white . . . five voters did not even put Charles on their all-conference team—even though he was an Olympian and first-team all-American. It was a clear insult. In the coming days there was even some acknowledgement among the sportswriters that an injustice had been done."[21]

In retrospect, it is impossible not to agree with Smith. Fans and sports-writers certainly had a case to cast their ACC Player of the Year votes for the unheralded sophomore Roche, who had a slightly higher scoring average than Scott and engineered the biggest upset of the season. However, no one without prejudice could deny that Scott was among the best *five* players in the ACC. So Scott, Smith, and the Tar Heels arrived at the Charlotte Coliseum with extra incentive to earn a third consecutive ACC title and berth in the NCAA Tournament.

Meanwhile, Duke catapulted from upsetting UNC to defeat Virginia and then edge South Carolina in the only game in ACC Tournament annals when the ten starters played all forty minutes. The slumping Gamecocks went on to the National Invitation Tournament on McGuire's home turf of New York City and lost to Army as the Cadets' senior guard Mike Krzyzewski hounded Roche and held him to six points.

Meanwhile, after routing Clemson in the first round of the ACC Tournament, the Tar Heels found themselves trailing Wake Forest by eight points at halftime of the semifinal. Deacons' guards Jerry Montgomery and Charlie Davis, who had followed Scott to Laurinburg Institute from New York City, combined for fifty-seven points in the game, and Carolina needed a second-half surge to pull ahead and win 80–72. Despite losing in Durham seven days earlier, the Tar Heels were heavily favored against Duke in the Saturday night championship game. Then, late in the first half, Grubar suffered a career-ending injury to his left knee. Grubar was the key to stopping Duke guards Dick DeVenzio and Dave Golden, and the Blue Devils moved out to a 43–34 half-time lead as the capacity coliseum crowd buzzed.

UNC still trailed by nine when Bunting, who had joined Scott on the All-ACC first team, fouled out with nine minutes left, forcing sophomore Lee Dedmon into the game to battle forward Steve Vandenberg and help with center Randy Denton, the Duke sophomore who averaged thirteen rebounds a game. Carolina was trying to win its ninth straight ACC Tournament game in three years, which had only been done by N.C. State from 1954–56. Trailing and forced to chase the Duke guards without Grubar, the Tar Heels appeared dead and out of the NCAA Tournament, since only the ACC tourney champion went in those days. "I glanced down at their bench and everyone looked like the game was over," Bubas said afterward. "On the court, one man was shouting, 'Give me the ball, give me the ball!'"

Smith had said on several occasions that Scott turned loose could score 40 points any night. With 12 points by halftime, Scott took complete control and made shots from literally all over the floor to score another 28. He hit pull-up jumpers, turnarounds, and fade-aways; he drove to the basket, hit from long range. He pretty much did anything he wanted, missing only one of his 13 shots in the second half.

"Charlie had more athletic ability than 99 percent of the guys we played against," said Grubar, his closest friend on the team since they met on Jubilee weekend, 1966. "When he got going, you gave him the ball and got out of the way. Sometimes you found yourself passing the ball and just watching."

The once-moribund Carolina bench had come alive, with players and coaches jumping over and over. Even veteran trainer John Lacey, who had been at Carolina since McGuire's undefeated season and usually sat stoically, got into the act. The Tar Heels actually won going away, 85–74, thanks to the most sensational twenty minutes in ACC history, given that Scott carried the team with two starters on the bench. It was also a clear response to the five anonymous voters who had left Scott off the All-ACC first team ballot. Smith, still careful to stay out of a public debate on race, only praised Scott for "one of the greatest individual performances you will ever see" in his postgame press conference.

Grubar, who watched the epic feat from the bench with his knee wrapped in ice, came to Scott's defense by saying, "We're glad for Charlie because we felt he had been slighted in the All-ACC voting." For his performance, Scott received the Everett Case Award as the unanimous tournament MVP, but he bit his tongue when asked about the All-ACC vote. He changed his mind on Monday when ACC Player of the Year was announced.

Still not enough voters waited until after the tournament, or Scott's performance didn't change enough minds. Roche (23.6 scoring average) defeated Scott (22.3) by seventeen votes, and McGuire, who still had a strong sentimental following among the press corps, denied Smith a third consecutive Coach of the Year award by a surprising fifty-six votes. Smith said Scott deserved Player of the Year, citing his long-held belief that individual honors should go to the star players on championship teams.

Nearly forty-five years later, Roche is a lawyer living in Denver. When asked about the season and his memories of the controversy over his selection, he said he believes he earned his awards "by solely appropriate factors." He also had high praise for his then-rival, however, later to become a teammate during the 1979–80 season with the Denver Nuggets. "Charlie Scott was easily the best player in the ACC during my time there," Roche recalled, further commenting on Scott's wit and intelligence during their time together as professionals. And Roche acknowledged that whatever unfolded on the basketball court, there was a wider context. "Past and current racism, bigotry, and intolerance in this country . . . are sadly undeniable," he said.

After days of media mentions, Scott faced some direct questions from the Washington sportswriters once the Tar Heels played their 1969 Eastern Regional semifinal at College Park on Thursday, March 13. Perturbed by scoring only four points in the second half against Duquesne as Carolina almost let a double-digit lead slip away before winning 79–78, Scott did not duck answering. "This is a frustrating thing when you go to the Olympics and represent your country, your state and your conference," he told the *Washington Post*. "They put a guy ahead of me (on the All-ACC team) because he's white. It was the first time I ever felt slighted as a basketball player because of my race."[22]

Two subplots bubbled beneath the surface of the regional championship game against Davidson Saturday afternoon at Cole Field House on the Maryland campus. Lefty Driesell was rumored to be leaving Davidson to take over the Terrapins program, which had fired coach Frank Fellows after two terrible seasons. In fact, Driesell had actually sought the job at his alma mater in Durham in the wake of Bubas's retirement. Duke had considered him along with former Blue Devils assistants Hubie Brown, Chuck Daly, and Bucky Waters (the post went to Waters). Regardless, Driesell had at least one more game to coach at Davidson after the Wildcats had defeated St. John's in the other regional semifinal. And he said, as if he meant it, "I'd rather die than lose to North Carolina again."[23]

The other subplot would go far toward determining whether Driesell got the victory he so coveted. "I played basketball because I enjoyed it," Scott recalled years later, "and at that moment a little joy was taken from me. For a short period, it was completely lost. I was so hurt emotionally that I did not want to play."[24]

On Saturday, Randy Forehand was taking his traditional nap between the team's pregame meal and the bus ride from the Holiday Inn on Route 1 to the arena. The phone rang with Dean Smith on the other end. "Please get the word out that we're having a team meeting at two o'clock in my room," Smith said. Forehand put his feet on the floor to make sure he wasn't dreaming. The meeting was not on the itinerary, and in his two years as a varsity manager, Forehand couldn't remember a time when Smith changed the routine on game day: team meeting, pregame meal, rest up, arrive at the gym ninety minutes before tip-off. Every aspect of Smith's program ran on a strict, consistent schedule. Forehand went from room to room on the outside corridor of the motel, knocking on doors and notifying the players, including Grubar, who limped down the hallway on his crutches. Forehand, however, could not find Scott.

As thirteen players squeezed into Smith's room, Forehand noticed that Bill Guthridge was there, but not John Lotz. Smith told the players that Scott had protested the All-ACC voting to national reporters after Thursday night's game. Smith wanted them to know that whatever happened against Davidson, they would face questions about Scott's charges of racism. Smith said Scott was with Lotz and would meet the team at Cole Field House before the game. He did not share his worst fear: that Scott might act out his protest by sitting out against the Wildcats, which of course would have killed Carolina's chances of reaching a third straight Final Four. If Scott made that choice before the game, Smith planned to tell the team in the locker room that he supported his decision and not argue against it, even though Scott sitting out under protest carried the inherent danger of severely damaging Smith's relationship with the university and how Scott's career would be remembered. After all, this was still 1969 in the South.

"Coach Smith was never one to single out an individual player in front of the team," Scott said. "The only way I knew I was appreciated was through the ACC voting. For two years, Larry Miller was the MVP of the tournament and ACC Player of the Year. I had the same type of season as Larry, the team had the same type of season we had the year before. I didn't think there was a player better than me; it wasn't like I was shooting 42 percent (actually 50.3 percent). I felt like in comparison to what Larry had done, I was going to be Player of the Year. And not only that, Coach Smith was going to be Coach of the Year.

"Then when I said something to a reporter about not being unanimous All-ACC, he wrote that Babe Ruth was not unanimous for the Hall of Fame, which had no correlation to that because John Roche was unanimous for All-ACC. That fed my anger, really pissed me off. They're talking about the Hall of Fame in baseball compared to being unanimous on the All-ACC team, when there were other players who were unanimous. I was frustrated by that, and it wasn't a basketball decision I was making. I thought about the Black Student Movement and now making a statement that there was inequity for blacks. That's when I thought about not playing in the game, and Coach Smith said he understood if I felt that way and he would not try to talk me into playing."

This created a conflict for Smith, who was caught between empathy for Scott and the need for him to play. That morning, before the pregame meal and emergency meeting, Smith had been at the University of Maryland hospital for what the team doctor thought might be an ulcer. It was gastritis, which Smith said came from the Italian food he had eaten the night before but more likely was the result of his dilemma. He popped antacids and went back to the motel.

Lotz was UNC's best chance to change Scott's mind, and the assistant coach appealed to the isolated black player's love of his teammates for having been his refuge on an otherwise unfriendly campus. Lotz made two points as they drove around College Park in Smith's rental car Saturday morning while the team met back at the motel.

"Everybody understands how you feel," Lotz said to Scott, "but you will be hurting your teammates more than the people you want to hurt." And Scott did not want to hurt his teammates and their chances of winning, which were nil without him. Lotz also told him to go out there and prove those racist bastards wrong. "I said, 'Charlie, this game is what you have lived for,'" recalled Lotz, years before his death in 2001. "Although he was upset, Charlie always had a sense of self-preservation; in his mind, he knew what would be best for him. And he had a great feeling for his teammates."

Scott listened, and Lotz's words carried the day. "It wasn't to prove anyone wrong, because the vote was already in," Scott said. "It was the point of not hurting my teammates."

In what would be the last of nine seasons at Davidson, Driesell had his best team and his best chance to not only reach the NCAA Final Four for the first time but to exorcise the demons caused by Carolina, Dean Smith, and the player Lefty missed. The fifth-ranked Wildcats owned a 27–2 record and had captured their fifth Southern Conference championship in the last six years, a stretch when they won 80 percent of their games. They had a veteran, seven-man rotation, led by Mike Maloy, the two-time Southern Conference Player of the Year, still in 2015 the school's all-time leading rebounder. Doug Cook, who missed the 70–66 loss to UNC in the 1968 Eastern Regional final, and Jerry Kroll were the forwards, Dave Moser and Wayne Huckel, the crafty guards. Steve Kirley and Mike O'Neill rounded out the rotation that, like Scott and Carolina, had one black star and a strong white supporting cast. Only this time, the Tar Heels were missing a starter, Grubar, who could only watch from the bench in street clothes.

When the Tar Heels took the court in their road blue uniforms at 3:30 P.M. on Saturday, March 15, 1969, Scott ran out with them. Of course, none in the near-capacity crowd of 13,166 expected otherwise. All they knew was that with the "Great Scott" out there, the team in blue had a good chance. Whereas the 6–10 Dedmon had started in Grubar's place against Duquesne, Jim Delany got the nod because Davidson had a smaller starting lineup. Clearly relieved to have Scott with them, the Tar Heels began hot and made 19 of 33 shots in the first half. Bunting, capping off a sensational senior season, hit 6 of 8 from the floor, Scott 4 of 8, and Clark and Fogler combined to hit all 7 of their attempts. Davidson shot poorly but had 6 more possessions on offensive rebounds and made 4 more free throws. Gerald Tuttle's jumper with 14 seconds remaining gave Carolina a 47–46 lead at halftime.

Smith had little to say in the locker room, other than to keep it up, get on the boards, and take care of the ball, and they would be there at the end. The lead changed hands four times in the second half, and both teams shot well with runs to 5-point leads. Scott, who had 9 points at the half, took control of the offense and gradually built his total to 13, 17, 20 almost midway through the second half. But Maloy's 6 points had stretched Davidson's lead to 73–68 at exactly the 10-minute mark. Then, with the game seemingly going the Wild-cats' way, Scott scored 8 points, Clark, 4, and Bunting, 2, to reclaim the lead at 82–81. Kroll and Cook scored before Delany hit a free throw and Scott dropped in a 13-footer to tie the score at 85 with 1:49 remaining. Smith called a time-out to set up the next defensive possession. Before the game, the five foot eleven Tuttle had studied film on which way the Davidson guards liked to go with the ball, and he jumped in front of Kroll to draw a crucial charging foul with 1:05 left.

Smith called another time-out and had his team run off 52 seconds in the Four Corners, then took a third time-out. He set up a play to win at the buzzer, knowing if they missed, Carolina could still win in overtime. The inbound pass went to Delany, who found Scott between the top of the key and half-court. Scott had been instructed to look down low for Bunting or Clark, who had already combined for 38 points, but he wasn't giving up the ball. He was determined. As the seconds ticked off, he went up, above those racing to guard him, tucked his feet behind his knees, and shot an 18-footer with :02 left on the dying clock.

An unknown photographer smartly kept his camera on the Carolina bench as the ball whipped through the net. Smith and Lotz were on their tiptoes, arms raised. Guthridge and sophomore Dale Gipple were two feet off the ground, Fogler and sophomore Dave Chadwick, a foot off the floor. Forehand, who wore thick black glasses and hadn't played basketball since junior high, elevated above them all, sport coat flapping and mouth agape.

The moment turned back to real time. The bench emptied and the entire team mobbed Scott, the conflicted player who had decided to play at the eleventh hour. He had scored thirty-two points, won the game at the horn, proved his redemption again, and took his team to another NCAA Final Four. Back home, Franklin Street was soon teeming with joyous students toasting the Great Scott's shot. They coaxed President Friday, who had state troopers on campus and was deep into negotiations to end the cafeteria workers' strike, to come out of his house and join the celebration.[25]

"They were trying to force me to the right, so I faked right and cut left," Scott said of his favorite move that Davidson bit on. "I got the ball with seven seconds left. I knew the shot would go in."[26] Owen Davis, sports editor of the *DTH*, wrote, "The game winning shot alone did not make Scott glorious in the eyes of Carolina followers. It made him mystically brilliant . . . what legends are made of."[27]

Smith recounted his own slightly different version years later: "Charles didn't look at anything but the basket. He took the ball thirty feet away, dribbled twice, held it to let the clock go down, and rose in the air. He soared above the defenders and put up an arc with three seconds to play. It settled through the net as the buzzer sounded and we exploded off the bench. We were going to our third straight Final Four."[28]

CHAPTER

8

Endings and Beginnings

"The season lasted a week too long," Dean Smith sighed after his injured and exhausted team suffered blowout losses to Purdue and Drake at the 1969 Final Four in Louisville, where the Tar Heels committed an unimaginable sixty-two turnovers in two games. No one was more exhausted than Charlie Scott, who had played eighteen consecutive months of basketball—including time spent winning an Olympic gold medal between his sophomore and junior seasons. When it came to life on the court, he was happy to have a break.

Some of the players were glad it was over, period. The graduating seniors were all embarking on different paths. Rusty Clark had been accepted to medical school at UNC; Dick Grubar faced a long summer of rehabilitation after his knee surgery and eventually entered coaching; Bill Bunting was on his way to the American Basketball Association, where he would play three seasons before joining Joe Brown and Gerald Tuttle in the business world.

It was less fun playing for Smith in the 1960s than in later years. He was a demanding coach who pushed his players more than some of them wanted to be pushed. The class of 1969, which remained underappreciated for years, made champions out of older star players Bob Lewis and Larry Miller, who had lived through the early criticism of Smith and were not completely convinced that he had all that much to do with the winning when it began.

Some sportswriters who covered UNC shared the view of Lewis and Miller; only a handful—mostly those who had attended UNC—had bought into the idea that Smith's greatness had transformed the Tar Heels into a perennial power. Many in the old guard, as well as longtime fans, still remembered what Frank McGuire had done in the 1950s and what he was, at least in part, replicating at South Carolina. They remained skeptical, wanting to see what Smith would do without the Clark-Grubar-Bunting class. At least Smith would have Scott, however, who had announced he would return for his senior season. With basketball over for the spring of 1969, Scott jumped into helping Howard Lee's pioneering campaign to become the first African American mayor of Chapel Hill. Lee, still a relative newcomer to town, whose population had more than doubled during the 1960s,[1] had little support outside the black community and was considered a long shot to beat lifelong Chapel Hill resident Roland Giduz, a member of the Board of Aldermen and widely regarded as the heir apparent to four-term mayor and close friend Sandy McClamroch.

Giduz, who had degrees from UNC, Columbia, and Harvard, was a newspaperman with a regular column in the *Chapel Hill Weekly*, where he occasionally rolled out his agenda for the future of Chapel Hill. Giduz also had the support of the most prominent black man in town, the Reverend John R. Manley, pastor of the First Baptist Church and the first African American to serve on the Chapel Hill–Carrboro school board. Every local major constituency supported Giduz, including the powerful and conservative Merchants' Association and Jaycees.

Lee believed he had good reason to run for mayor. As a new Duke employee in 1966, he had encountered overt racism when trying to buy a home in a new white subdivision—a painful experience with crank callers threatening the Lees and their children; when friend Dean Smith heard about it, he calmed skittish residents and put pressure on the developer to approve the sale. After the Lees moved in, they endured more hostile phone calls and awoke one morning to a cross burning in their front yard. Two years later, the dismissive Board of Aldermen offended Lee in his attempt to have an open housing ordinance passed.

In the summer of 1968, Lee went back to the Board of Aldermen, asking members to pass an open housing ordinance in the memory of the slain Martin Luther King Jr. Lee took along Buie Seawell, pastor of the Church of Reconciliation and well-known white activist who ran a nonprofit to support the public schools. Giduz said such an ordinance would put too much pressure on realtors and suggested instead a resolution encouraging agents and developers to sell to every qualified buyer. From that position, Giduz found himself cast as the candidate for the white establishment, though he really was more of a moderate who did not intend to send Lee and Seawell away angry.

"Buie and I had breakfast together to talk about what we wanted to do to shake up Chapel Hill," Lee said. "We felt like it needed to be shaken up; it had a good ole' boys system, and while we didn't think we had a prayer of controlling the system, they needed to know we were here." This approach was hardly new to Lee, an Army veteran who had served on the front lines in Korea and twice challenged the military brass over what he considered prejudicial treatment and disrespect. He was not disciplined for doing so. In fact, he wound up with work that benefited both him and the Army before being discharged with honor in 1960.

"Buie Seawell said, 'I think you should run for mayor,'" Lee recalled. "I said, 'You gotta be out of your mind.' Buie wanted to go see Jim Shumaker and tell him I was running for mayor. I said he probably shouldn't do that until we met up with some other folks and decided this was acceptable. So we agreed that nothing was going to happen until we got back together and talked again. Buie went straight to Shumaker's office anyway and told him. The headline in the next issue of the *Weekly* was 'First Negro Is Candidate for Mayor' with my picture. Had that not happened, I would not have felt any pressure to run."

Lee had a bigger problem at home: his wife, Lillian, had no idea he was even thinking about running until the newspaper story came out. When they had met in Savannah, Lillian sensed Howard was interested in politics—and she hated politics at that time. "Before we ever decided to get married, she said, 'I don't like politics, I don't want to be involved in politics, and I want you to promise me you will never run for political office,'" Howard remembered. "I lied and made the commitment so I could get Lillian."

Approaching the holiday party season, among the biggest cocktail receptions was at the home of Alice Welsh, a liberal on the Board of Aldermen. The Lees showed up to a large crowd of people and a divided but friendly house, half telling Lee he was crazy and the other half saying it was a great idea. Lee recalled, "There were a lot of progressives who thought my running would disrupt Chapel Hill, which was recovering from some of the nastiest civil rights battles any town had experienced."

Lee, who still worked at Duke at the time, knew he needed strong local backing to have his candidacy taken seriously. He enlisted the help of the Reverend Robert Seymour, who believed it was the right thing at the right time for Chapel Hill. Seymour's support changed the minds of many doubters. Lee also knew that Smith would endorse him, but due to Smith's position as head basketball coach, it would come in a far subtler way.

"Lillian and I talked about the hard time we had buying a house, and I said, 'Why don't I just play this out and see what happens. I'm probably not going to run because I doubt Duke will even allow me to run for mayor of Chapel Hill.'"

Late in 1968, the Lees invited fifteen people to their home to discuss the possibility of Howard's candidacy. More than fifty showed up, most excited by the prospect. "They came with the express purpose of talking me into running for mayor," Lee said. "I got carried away, stood up, and gave this long diatribe on what was needed in Chapel Hill and how things could change. It turned everybody on, and I could see in Lillian's eyes that she was changing. She was caught up in the whole thing. That night we decided it was the thing to do; if I could work it out with my employers at Duke and it wasn't going to cause any heartaches for the family, she would support me."

Lee had moved over from teaching to administration at Duke, setting up an employee relations program to come up with ideas that pacified workers who were thinking about unionizing. Charles Huestis, vice president of finance and a liberal-leaning power figure at Duke, supported Lee running for mayor of Chapel Hill. However, he predicted Lee would face some resistance from trustees and people on the Duke campus who would be concerned it was taking away from his job. To keep Huestis on his side, Lee promised he would campaign at night and on the weekends, not a single minute during the workday.

At the same time, Lee said UNC had called him about joining the faculty of the School of Social Work. Professor Morris Cohen headed up the community organization program, and Lee had written several articles on the subject. Cohen traveled regularly to South Africa, which made him controversial in his own right because he opposed apartheid. UNC was interviewing candidates for the job, but once Lee was rumored to be running for mayor, Cohen received a call from UNC Chancellor Carlyle Sitterson, who in turn had been contacted by Governor Bob Scott. Lee said Cohen was told not to offer a position to him until the mayor's race was over, and then they would reconsider. Lee said years later that he thought "it might have been a ploy to keep me from running."

After Lee officially entered the race in December 1968 and the campaign got under way, Giduz faced an unprecedented grassroots crusade by Howard and Lillian, who met, shook hands, and spoke with almost everyone in town. One of Lee's first fund-raisers was at the home of Gertrude Taylor, whose husband, Isaac, was dean of the UNC medical school. (Today the Taylors would best be known as parents to their famous singer-songwriter son, James Taylor.) The Taylors had moved to Chapel Hill from Massachusetts, where Gertrude witnessed such deplorable racism that she wanted to help elect a black mayor in Chapel Hill.

As the campaign gathered steam, Howard Lee asked Charlie Scott to use his celebrity and passion for politics to recruit UNC students to knock on doors, hand out fliers, and help get hundreds of mostly black citizens registered to vote for the first time. Volunteers came from as far away as North Carolina A&T, N.C. State, and Duke to help Scott and the Carolina students. Lee had the tour bus of Carrboro bandleader Doug Clark and the black Rolls Royce of local pharmacist George Harris taking dozens of people to register. The same vehicles carried people to vote on Election Day. Either way, Lee felt like he could not lose, since he and Giduz agreed on most issues. One of them would have promises to keep.

In the end, many prominent locals backed Lee, including Clark, who canceled a number of performances for his rhythm and blues rock band, The Hot Nuts, to campaign in the Carrboro neighborhoods. Smith became more open with his support for Lee as well, although he couched it in his existing friendship with Howard and Lillian. He was already introducing black and white recruits to the Lees, who would serve as godparents to his players for thirty years and whose gestures of support included offering to rent their basement apartment to homesick freshman Michael Jordan in 1981. The Reverend Seymour, whose Binkley Baptist congregation worked tirelessly for its first black deacon, had been heavily involved in political, racial, and religious issues since Seymour's arrival almost ten years earlier. These were strong, influential alliances. However, Smith's stepping up for Lee after winning three consecutive ACC championships created a conundrum for the staunchly conservative Carolina fans in town. If there had been any doubt, Smith was now branded a firm liberal.

An outstanding orator, Lee boldly talked about what Chapel Hill truly needed to live up to its reputation. Lee was not shy about pledging to upgrade low-income housing and improve utilities, especially in the black sections of town where many of the streets were unpaved, wells were contaminated, and children played near a massive hole on Mitchell Lane that collected trash and was a breeding ground for insects and vermin. Chapel Hill schools had fully desegregated by this time, but some serious racial issues lingered. The thirty-four-year-old Lee wanted more recreation areas, younger people involved in local government, a stronger bond between the town and gown, and his pet project, free public transportation beyond the UNC campus.

In April, Lee and Giduz spoke to the Jaycees. At the time, most of them were steadfast "Rolandites." They did not know Lee was such a commanding orator with some novel ideas. He gave a resounding speech and sat down to surprising applause. Giduz followed and, according to those who were there, rambled for about twenty minutes. When the meeting ended, Lee had the majority of support from the Jaycees, and Giduz had lost it in one evening.

"That gave us a high degree of confidence that we were onto something and that we were just going to have to out-organize and out-campaign Roland," Lee said. From February through Election Day in May, the Lees went to more than three hundred coffees and teas, all in the evenings from 6 to 10:30, meeting people in their homes in small groups.

The Reverend Manley remained Lee's nemesis, however, especially with the black vote. He had been close to McClamroch since his appointment to the local school board ten years earlier. Manley continued campaigning alongside McClamroch, trying to conjure up votes for Giduz. The election was slipping away, however. Lee staged a large rally at the Baptist student center on campus the Saturday before the election, and people and families from all over town turned out. Giduz was out in the community virtually alone. Jim Shumaker wrote in the next *Chapel Hill Weekly*, "Roland was walking and the only friends he could find were the birds chirping in the trees." The "Rolandites" stronghold had disappeared.

Still, as Election Day of May 6, 1969, approached, Lee was never confident. "I went to our campaign headquarters fully prepared to give a concession speech. I just didn't think we had put it together enough. Doug Clark saw I was as nervous as a cat on a hot tin roof, and took me outside. He had given us his bus to campaign, and we laughed about how we took people to the polls in George Harris's Rolls-Royce and pissed them off by taking them back in the bus." The 4,734 votes cast were the most in town history, and included a record turnout from the African American community, which won it for Lee, whose margin of victory—about 400 votes—was the smallest on record for a municipal election.

"When the votes started to come in, we felt a little comfortable that it was going to be close," Lee said. "And when the last precinct came in, Jim Heavner and the folks from WCHL announced it was over. I did not have an acceptance speech written so I had to grab a paper bag and write out what I was going to say. Tom Horton, the pastor at St. Joseph's, was all teed off with John Manley, so we went to his church on Rosemary Street, and people packed in there and were hanging outside coming from all over Chapel Hill. Every seat was full. Amazing."

Charlie Scott came. Dean and Ann Smith stopped by briefly to offer their congratulations after having voted and reminding friends, with whom they were close enough to do so, to vote. Smith might have also identified with Lee, suddenly having been named head basketball coach almost eight years earlier when he never expected it to happen—at least at UNC.

Lee turned to Lillian and said, "Now that I got it, what the hell am I going to do with it?" She said, "You asked for it, you got it, and it's yours."

Scott might have been the most prominent athlete in North Carolina and the ACC to break the color barrier, but Lee made national and international news as the first black mayor of a predominantly white southern community. Newspapers from his hometown of Lithonia, Georgia, to the *New York Times* and *Wall Street Journal* carried stories on Lee's victory. When a reporter from the *Christian Science Monitor* came to town for an in-person interview, Lee purposely took him to the College Café on East Franklin Street, one of the restaurants regularly picketed during the civil rights protests of 1963. In April of that year, the restaurant "desegregated" when the black head cook quit and joined the picket line. With no one to cook for the customers, the owners pledged to serve everyone if the cook went back to work. He did.

Lee's election was astounding on several fronts. Of the town's 20,000-plus residents, less than 10 percent were black and most of them hadn't voted before in their lives because, according to Lee, "they never thought their vote meant anything." And the Lees and their two children had lived in Chapel Hill less than six years, the first black family since 1939 known to have moved there without any ties to the town. While Lee had been a social worker, probation officer, and aspiring community organizer, he had never run for or held public office. (He had made that wedding vow to Lillian that he never would.) To top it off, Lee worked at Duke University and some people wondered whom he rooted for. After being sworn in on May 12, 1969, Lee took little time to demonstrate that he would not be a figurehead like many previous Chapel Hill mayors, who deferred to the town manager and what was then called the Board of Aldermen (later the Town Council). Prior to Lee's arrival on the scene, the mayor held a ceremonial position paying one hundred dollars a year and did not have an office. With a referendum approaching whether to renovate or expand the municipal building, Lee successfully pushed to have a mayor's office included. As the 1969–70 school year began, however, he wanted to work in Chapel Hill and his teaching position in the UNC School of Social Work still had not been approved by the Board of Trustees.

As a speaker in demand, Lee gave a speech to the NAACP in Washington, D.C., on September 12, 1969, and during a question and answer period that followed, he called Bob Scott a "Southern Democratic bigot governor." Lee assumed Scott had nixed his appointment to the UNC faculty. A reporter from the *Charlotte Observer* was there and when the event ended, asked Lee whether he meant what he said. "Yeah, I guess so," Lee responded, and the story broke the next day in Charlotte and quickly spread across the state.

"My election gave a lot of people a pause to understand that Chapel Hill showed great courage electing me as its mayor," Lee said. "This [the Bob Scott accusation] was a few months after I was elected, and it almost derailed my political beginning even among my liberal supporting core, who didn't think that was smart at all and called my judgment into question."

Ironically, at almost the very moment Lee was calling the governor a bigot, the trustees were approving his position at the UNC School of Social Work. "I have never felt lower, more irrelevant, and more stupid than living through that experience," he said. "I went public with my apology and they kept my faculty approval, but I said, 'I don't deserve it, I shouldn't have done it.' That was just plain stupid, and I got lucky. I got through it, apologized to Governor Scott (who accepted and said he had been called a lot worse), and we developed a very cordial and strong working relationship." That certainly was not the last controversy surrounding Howard Lee, however.

As summer turned to fall and the start of the 1969–70 academic year, new beginnings also held signs of some significant endings—and not just the close of Charlie Scott's UNC career. On the personal front, Scott and Dean Smith both began the school year in troubled marriages. Charlie and Margaret were expecting a child, but Charlie wondered how he would handle that role. Meanwhile, Dean and Ann Smith were spending less and less time communicating about anything beyond their three children, and Dean agonized over how a divorce might affect the kids. "The guilt was incredible," his sister, Joan, said in 1998. "You stayed married, no matter what, the way we were brought up. That ordeal made him search himself even more." Nevertheless, Smith moved into an apartment with assistant coach John Lotz, who was a bachelor at the time. Lotz, a tall, handsome, impeccable dresser from New York, was not much of a housekeeper. Smith joked that it was so bad that "I almost moved back into the house." He would return home at least twice before the marriage finally ended in 1973. "He didn't divorce lightly," Joan said, "it was long, drawn out, and a painful thing."

Scott and Margaret continued living together in Durham, but they grew further apart. Margaret and her family were ecstatic over the impending arrival of the baby, and Scott was torn between the excitement of having a child but not being committed to his wife. "Charles wanted to have a family," Margaret said in a 2015 interview, "but because of his childhood, he wasn't sure how to get there."

Scott's life of self-preservation kept it hard for him to worry much beyond himself. He made the hard decisions about his future, but he made them even more difficult by lacking trust in other people, or sometimes questioning their motives. When he realized he was good enough to have a professional career in basketball, the most individual of all team sports, his decisions began and ended with his best interest. He was convinced that was the only way he would get where he wanted to go.

Despite being slighted in the All-ACC voting as a junior, as a new season loomed, Scott was a bona fide All-American, recognized as one of the best players in college basketball alongside some other greats such as Pete Maravich, Bob Lanier, Rudy Tomjanovich, Rick Mount, and Dan Issel. Had his Olympic teammate Spencer Haywood already filed and won his 1971 lawsuit against the NBA, allowing players to turn pro in fewer than four years out of high school, Scott would have been a prime candidate to go after his junior season. He had averaged 22.3 points a game and shot 50 percent, led the team in assists, and was third in rebounding, behind big men Rusty Clark and Bill Bunting. Both the latter had departed, along with the rest of Dean Smith's terrific turnaround class of 1969, heading into Scott's senior year.

Scott had a close eye on his future as he began his final season of college basketball. And, even with a baby coming, he was spending less time at home with Margaret and more time with his friends from N.C. Central and North Carolina A&T. An entourage was beginning to follow Scott since everyone around him expected he was headed for professional fame and fortune.

"Some nights he came home late and some nights he didn't come home at all," Margaret recalled. "We had about one good year. After that, it was something different that he wanted to do every day."

Determined not to damage his pro career before it began, Scott stayed removed from the UNC campus and the pressures being created by the growth of the Black Student Movement. And he noticed that, between the war protests at The Pit and McCorkle Place and the ongoing strikes at Lenoir Hall, the students were not especially fixated on the start of another basketball season.

On campus, Howard Lee delivered the cooperation and assistance he had pledged during the mayoral campaign. He and Bill Friday worked long hours in November 1969 trying to resolve the cafeteria crisis for good. Governor Scott again sent the Highway Patrol and National Guard to Chapel Hill when he heard that three thousand African Americans would assemble on December 9 for what had been termed Black Sunday. Lee boldly convinced Governor Scott to remove the troops in a good faith gesture to settle the strike, and at 3:30 A.M. on December 10, a final resolution included another wage increase and more benefits for full-time, nonfaculty employees.

With that crisis resolved, tensions seemed to quiet around the university, and anticipation grew for the Tar Heels' next campaign on the court. Smith had reason to be confident with three highly regarded sophomores moving up to the varsity team. Forwards Bill Chamberlain and Dennis Wuycik were competing to start alongside junior center Lee Dedmon and guard Steve Previs, set to join Scott and fellow senior Eddie Fogler on the perimeter of what was a very good, albeit young, 1970 Carolina team.

Scott was so much better than anyone else, and in such great shape from having played basketball almost non-stop for two years, that Smith often rested him during practice to give the other team members a chance to catch up, at least in conditioning, and create even competition for the unsettled starting positions. Scott enjoyed his senior status and flippantly attributed UNC's stylish new uniforms with V-neck jerseys to Smith's fondness for the sophomores, who as freshmen found their way to most varsity road games, slept on Randy Forehand's motel room floor, and cheered wildly behind the bench. "The Dream Team," Scott called the highly touted recruiting class.

The Tar Heels won nine of their first ten games, losing only to second-ranked Kentucky in Charlotte, to climb all the way to No. 4 in the polls. They were overrated, however, since all the victories had come over unranked opponents. On January 5, 1970, they played their first ACC road game at powerful and third-ranked South Carolina, which had four starters back and added six foot ten sophomore Tom Riker, making the Gamecocks bigger and stronger than the year before. With the 1970 Eastern Regional to be played in Columbia, this team was clearly Frank McGuire's best shot at his second national championship—and his first ACC title at South Carolina. The jammed-packed Carolina Coliseum wanted light blue blood when the Tar Heels took the floor against a team confident of avenging the bitter defeat of 1969.

Smith tried a slowdown strategy against the Gamecocks' towering front line, but it backfired. Carolina fell behind early and was never in the game, which allowed the vicious home crowd to focus on Scott's unusually poor play. He made only four of his ten shots and added a single free throw for nine points, only the second time in his college career—ninety-one games—that Scott did not score in double figures. South Carolina's massive 2-3 zone, with Tom Owens, John Ribock, and Riker underneath, and John Roche and Bobby Cremins up top, held UNC to one of its poorest shooting performances of the season. The Tar Heels ended as 65–52 losers.

Smith's ninth UNC edition stumbled the rest of the season, beating top-ten-ranked N.C. State twice (to make Scott 7–0 versus the Wolfpack in his career) but only winning three consecutive games once. Scott took more than twice as many shots as any teammate, his 611 attempts the second most in UNC history, behind Lennie Rosenbluth (631) in 1957. Plagued by injuries and inconsistency, the Tar Heels' best hope was to give the ball to Scott and get out of the way. And while he did average 27.1 points, leading the ACC over his old New York playground rival Charlie Davis of Wake Forest, Scott shot 44 percent in Carolina's nine defeats against constant double-teams.

Scott's last chance to upstage Roche was the late-season rematch at Carmichael Auditorium, when Smith considered holding the ball to pull the Gamecocks out of their zone. It was Scott's senior game, however, and he wanted to run and shoot with the fourth-ranked team in America. The strategy failed. Scott missed 15 of his 25 shots, and South Carolina swept the home-and-home series for the first and only time, 79–62.

Over the course of the season, Scott scored more than 30 points in seven different games and went over 40 twice, losses to Wake Forest at home and Virginia in the first round of the ACC Tournament, when he made 12 of 30 shots and went to foul line 21 times. Scott easily finished more than half of Carolina's possessions in a 95–93 loss to a bad Virginia team that went 3–11 in the ACC and 10–15 overall. When Player of the Year was announced, Scott again lost to Roche, this time by four votes.

"We had so many players playing hurt that I told Charles to start throwing it up," Smith said. "He shot 40 percent for his last three games and that was the end of that." After losing three games in February, the team did not care as much and seemed resigned to not making it back to the NCAA Tournament. When Smith boarded the bus for the short ride to Duke on February 28, 1970, the players began to serenade him on his thirty-ninth birthday. He waved them off with a smile and said, "Wait till next year, when I will be the big 4-0." It was a concession for more than a birthday, and the Tar Heels lost the first of what would be three straight to end the season.

Some of Scott's teammates were already moving in different directions. The other seniors were worried about the military draft; Scott, with a pending young family (3A) deferment, was more concerned where the ABA and NBA would draft him. There were no other sure-shot pros on the 1970 Tar Heel roster, especially because of how the season played out. In addition, the body language on the court and the off-the-record comments from teammates showed some resentment over the freedom Smith had given Scott, and how it sometimes backfired when he had a poor shooting game.

The Tar Heels finished tied for second in the ACC regular season with a 9–5 record, but far behind South Carolina (14–0), which became the third team in ACC history (after UNC in 1957 and Duke in 1963) to go undefeated in conference play. The Gamecocks lost to N.C. State in the ACC Tournament championship game, however, with Roche hobbling on a severely sprained ankle. Roche not winning the ACC championship and averaging almost five points less than Scott made the ACC Player of the Year voting seem inconsistent with the previous season.

By then, it seemed fans had grown tired of the controversy and the court demeanor of both players. Some African Americans even believed that Scott had gone too far with his charges of racism and his increased chirping at opponents. According to Wake Forest's Charlie Davis, who was soft-spoken on and off the floor, Scott "wasn't the most beloved person. I can assure you that if Charles was as arrogant as he tended to be back then, but couldn't play as well, he wouldn't have spent four years at Carolina. They wouldn't have tolerated him."[2] Those who watched from afar saw a different story between Scott and his coach. Ernie Jackson, the Duke All-American safety and the first black football ACC Player of the Year in 1971, hated the racial attitudes on his own campus and admired how Smith guided Scott through UNC. "I think that helped Smith for years to come," Jackson told Barry Jacobs in *Golden Glory*. "There was a good amount of loyalty toward him for what he did."[3]

After the loss to Virginia in the ACC Tournament, UNC played in its first NIT (National Invitation Tournament) and was embarrassed on opening day by Manhattan College at Madison Square Garden. The 1970 Tar Heels finished with an 18–9 record, the only time in Smith's final thirty-one seasons they failed to win at least twenty games. Tellingly, he gave that team virtually no mention in his autobiography, *A Coach's Life*. The season was one of the most challenging for Smith, who used the failed experiment of turning Scott loose to reaffirm his belief in basketball as a team game with all five players filling specific roles. With the injuries and Smith avoiding any strategy that cut into Scott's pro draft status (as he did with Bob Lewis in 1967), the Tar Heels had played out the string, living and dying on Scott's ability to beat double-teams to get open. Besides the two wins over N.C. State, Carolina did not defeat a team that ended the season ranked.

In a strange outcome that might have been a wakeup call for the questionable voting of the press corps, essentially the same voters named Scott ACC Athlete of the Year. That award also included academics and citizenship, for which he generally got good grades. By the time he had played his last college game, Scott had adjusted to the Carolina campus, which had more than two hundred black students and was pulled into more protest by the Nixon-ordered invasion of Cambodia and the Kent State killings, which were certainly traumatic events but not Scott's fights. Later that spring, Scott won the Patterson Medal at UNC, the most significant academic-athletic honor bestowed on any Tar Heel athlete; Scott, of course, was the first African American winner. He called it "a very gratifying moment . . . a great honor for me. It felt good to be recognized for more than what I accomplished on the basketball court."[4]

After losing Scott, some observers around the ACC expected Smith to fall back into his teams' mediocrity of the mid-1960s. Instead, the Tar Heels unleashed a balanced approach of selfless stars who won or shared 12 ACC regular-season titles, captured six ACC Tournaments and reached four more Final Fours over the next twelve years. Smith teams shot between 51 and 56 percent for an astonishing eighteen consecutive seasons. Only when the three-point shot became a permanent part of the game in 1987 did they barely drop below the 50 percent mark.

Holly Francena Scott was born on May 3, 1970, as her father was getting ready to sign one of the largest contracts offered by the new American Basketball Association. The ABA had survived its first three seasons well enough for rumors to swirl that four of its teams would be absorbed by the established NBA, where Scott had long dreamed of playing. Scott could have turned pro with the ABA after his spectacular junior season, but anyone circumventing the NBA eligibility rules was considered a "scab" who might never be accepted in the more traditional league. The ABA, which played with a red, white, and blue ball and introduced the three-point shot to the game, was already a refuge for players banned from the NBA, such as Carolina's Doug Moe and Iowa's Connie Hawkins, two New York City kids touched by the college point-shaving scandals of the late 1950s.

Scott said Smith advised him to sign with the agent for former Tar Heel All-American Billy Cunningham, who had just jumped to the Carolina Cougars of the ABA. Cunningham's move and Scott's signing helped legitimize the new league and expedite a merger with the NBA. Scott's contract included a bonus of $38,000 to play for the Washington Caps team that had just relocated from the Bay Area, where it began as the Oakland Oaks. The Caps looked to be a power with former college All-Americans Rick Barry (Miami) and fellow Tar Heels Larry Brown and Moe.

"Larry Brown talked me into going to the ABA," Scott said many years later. "I went to a school where I didn't have any goddamn friends. Larry Brown [his freshman coach in 1967] was the guy I connected with from a basketball standpoint. For friendship, it was John Lotz. For basketball, it was Larry. And he was telling me how his team had Rick Barry, Doug Moe, and him, and there was going to be a merger, and when it happened, they would be one of the teams that went into the NBA."

Scott signed before the NBA draft in June, but his contract with the Caps did not stop the Boston Celtics' shrewd general manager Red Auerbach from drafting his rights in the seventh round, in case the ABA folded or Scott wanted to jump leagues. Scott said he did not find out until he eventually played for the Celtics in 1975 that Auerbach was trying to talk to him before he signed with the Caps; according to Scott, his agent had rebuffed the Hall of Fame coach while he was working out the ABA deal.

Scott spent a chunk of his bonus money and took Margaret on the honeymoon they never had. The new parents traveled to Montego Bay in Jamaica, leaving infant Holly back in Durham with Margaret's parents. "We had a wonderful time, just the two of us, where a lot of people didn't know who Charles was," Margaret recalled. But when they returned, Scott found out his new team had suddenly been moved from Washington to Norfolk and had been renamed the Virginia Squires. It turned out that Abe Pollin, who owned the NBA Baltimore Bullets, did not want another pro team in his geographical territory, exemplifying how unstable and unpredictable things were in the wheeling-and-dealing ABA.

The backroom nature of the events frustrated Scott deeply. "It seemed like the day after I signed, they were the Virginia Squires," Scott said. "If they told me they were going to Virginia, I never would have signed. They never told me."

Initially, Scott tried to look on the bright side. "Larry and Doug and Rick Barry were still on the team," he recalled, thinking optimistically of a nucleus for success. Even that possibility ended before it began, however. "Barry found out what I was making," Scott reported. Soon after, Barry "said he didn't want his son to grow up in the South, saying, 'Hi, you all,' and [he] demanded a trade to the New York Nets. I still thought we were going to the NBA, but it turned out that the Nets were going (along with the Denver Nuggets, Indiana Pacers, and in 1976, the San Antonio Spurs)." Scott got there, too, in 1972, when Phoenix acquired his rights by trading Paul Silas to Boston.

Upset but with more money in his pocket than he had ever had, Scott spent the summer of 1970 playing every day with stars from CIAA schools at McDougle Gym on the N.C. Central campus and going back to the Rucker Tournament in August, before heading for training camp in Virginia. He left Margaret and Holly in Durham, saying he would be practicing and traveling to games once the season started and they would be better off with Margaret's family during his rookie year. The travel part was true, as the Squires were a regional franchise that played home games in Hampton, Richmond, and Roanoke, as well as Norfolk. He said he would come back to Durham every chance he got—and he did whenever he had a break—but Scott wanted it that way for another reason. "I was in Norfolk living by myself, and Margaret kept asking to move up and I kept putting her off," Scott said. "I said I had to concentrate on my game, but I was already going out with another girl, Vivian Ford, who was a Squires cheerleader."

Margaret remembered "fighting tooth and nail over it and there was a lot of conflict." When Scott returned to Durham, he was an attentive father to Holly but also a celebrity star in the ABA, averaging 27.1 points and on his way to sharing the 1971 Rookie of the Year award with Dan Issel of the Kentucky Colonels. The Squires won the ABA Eastern Division by eleven games, losing to the Colonels in the play-offs.

After the season, Margaret thought it was the right time for her and Holly to move, but Scott again rejected the idea. "I knew I didn't want to be married, that I was a bad husband, and being with another girl gave me the impetus to say, 'Okay, let's get a divorce,'" he said. "She gave me the ultimatum, and I felt guilty about it, so I told her to get a lawyer and send me the papers, whatever it is, and I will sign them."

Margaret did not know any lawyers. Uncertain of her options, she went to see Dean Smith in the UNC basketball office one day during her lunch hour. He set her up with Travis Porter, a prominent Durham attorney, Carolina alum, and major donor to the Rams Club. Porter also happened to be Smith's lawyer, and occasionally helped former Carolina players in their legal matters.

To an outside eye, this might have seemed like some sort of conflict of interest. For Smith, however, it was likely another case of trying to take care of everyone at the same time by adjudicating a fair outcome for both parties. "He gets caught up sometimes in the masculine image of being the supplier of everyone's needs, the one in control of every situation," Linnea Smith said in 1982. "One of his old friends who had read the book on Dean that's out said, 'What's it like living with God?' "[5]

Margaret met with Porter, told him what she wanted, and waited to hear back. Porter put a separation agreement together and mailed it to Scott in Norfolk, assuming he would sign it as he had told Margaret he would. "I knew I had done her wrong, so I was going to sign whatever it was," Scott said. "Until I got the papers from her lawyer; it was (asking for) like every goddamn dime I was making and fifty cents on the dollar I made after that."

Scott said he called Smith and told him, "Coach, I'm not upset about you getting her a lawyer, but the lawyer you got her sent me some papers—I don't even have a lawyer—and what they are asking for is out of this world."

As Scott recalls, "Coach Smith said, 'Send me the papers and let me look at them.' " Scott mailed the separation agreement to Smith and a few weeks later got a new set of papers from Porter, this time with much more reasonable demands, at least in Scott's estimation. "It was like 10 percent of what he had asked for the first time." Scott signed the agreement and sent it back to get Margaret's signature and move on with the divorce. Margaret wanted more, however, because she knew he would continue to command a big salary from playing professional basketball.

"Charles said if I didn't sign the papers, I would get nothing," Margaret remembered. "I was intimidated, so I signed them and we got divorced. It called for me getting $100,000 in cash—$50,000 right away, $25,000 the next year, and $25,000 the year after that. I also got $200 a month in child support, which stayed the same until Holly was in the eleventh grade."

Scott thought the settlement was fair. "I had been married two years before we separated, gave her alimony, child support, the car and town house in Durham," he said. "I gave her $50,000 right away, which was a lot of money for that time. I thought it was fair and Coach Smith thought it was fair, and Margaret thought it was fair when she got it. She never argued about it."

Margaret recalls it differently. She said she remained angry for a few years but laughed when told by mutual friends that "Charles says he ruined your life."

"He didn't ruin my life," she said. "I have a beautiful daughter and grand-child. I had moved on." As the years passed, Holly, age forty-six and the principal of a middle school in Durham, grew closer with her father and developed a friendship with Scott's three sisters (her aunts), two of whom lived and worked in New York and one who had moved to Barbados. She also spent time with her stepmother, Trudy, and her three half-siblings, Simone, Shaun, and Shannon Scott. It wasn't the perfect ending, but it worked out.

Scott had met Trudy, an actress and model, after he finished playing and moved to Los Angeles. They were married in 1986 in a formal ceremony. John Lotz, who had left coaching after seven years at Florida, flew out to be Scott's best man. Bill Chamberlain and Kareem Abdul-Jabbar, his college and pro teammates, were members of the wedding party.

Scott had finished his career with the Lakers and Nuggets before retiring in 1980. He played eleven seasons in the ABA and NBA, averaging 20.7 points, slightly less than his 22.1 career mark at UNC. He made all-pro his first five years and, in his sixth season, won the NBA championship with the Celtics. Scott jumped right into business, opening an exclusive imported shoe store on Sunset Boulevard; he and Trudy bought a spectacular home not far away in Laurel Canyon. However, after a large business investment with nine other NBA players, including Abdul-Jabbar and Ralph Sampson, went south,[6] the Scotts eventually moved to Atlanta, where, with Smith's recommendation, Scott went to work for Champion products in marketing and fought his way through the toughest financial time of his adult life.

Lotz, who had moved back to Chapel Hill, steadfastly stood by Scott as a friend and confidante, and reminded him often that while fame and fortune might be gone, Trudy and their family were most important in his life. Scott proudly attended the graduations of Shaun and Simone from UNC, and he and Trudy moved to Columbus, Ohio, for four years to watch Shannon play for Ohio State, retuning to Atlanta after Shannon graduated.

In the meantime, Margaret worked as a guidance counselor in the Durham school system, retiring after thirty years. She says she had chances to marry again but decided to live out her senior years modestly with her daughter and granddaughter. Only her family and closest friends know she was married to a man who was once the most famous black athlete in North Carolina, and to her, that is all part of a past life. She can even laugh about it now. "If he feels so guilty," she said, smiling, "tell him he can give me some more money. I need a new car."

Dean and Ann Smith also divorced, finally. He saw his children, who all graduated from UNC, as much as possible, but it took him years of studying theology and praying with Bob Seymour to deal with leaving what he believed to be a sacred institution. The Smiths had been living separate lives, Dean's revolving around basketball while Ann worked as an occupational therapist at Memorial Hospital and ran the household. So intensely private, Smith could not bring himself to talk about the divorce with any of his three kids until years later. "It was the one time I saw him cry," daughter Sandy recalled in 1998. "He felt so guilty—he thought he had messed up our family."

In 1975, Smith built a home on a secluded five-acre lot south of town, and later that year, on a flight back to Raleigh-Durham International Airport, met psychiatrist Linnea Weblemoe, a Californian fourteen years younger than him who had come to Chapel Hill to attend medical school. They were married in 1976 and eventually had two daughters. The blended Smith family, including Ann, got along well enough to vacation together at the beach during several summers over the next three decades.

As the first African American of so many to follow him at UNC, Scott was especially moved by Smith's death, which almost everyone who had followed the story knew was coming. "While you played for him, he was your coach, your disciplinarian, your teacher," Scott reflected. "But more important, after we all graduated, he became a friend, a father, and a mentor, which was even better. And I'm not talking about just the guys who played professional sports, but every single person who played for him."[7]

The Test of Yesterday

Linnea Smith thinks her late husband would have enjoyed being at the White House for the Presidential Medal of Freedom ceremony—even more than their first three trips to 1600 Pennsylvania Avenue. The first two followed the national championships of 1982, when Ronald Reagan was in his first term, and 1993, after Bill Clinton had stunned incumbent George Herbert Walker Bush. But the third, Linnea recalls, made her and Dean "feel like kids." In June of 1998, eight months after Smith retired, a last-minute cancellation at a state dinner for new South Korean president Kim Dae-jung resulted in an invitation for Coach and Mrs. Smith to attend and stay over in the Queen's Bedroom at the White House. "We didn't know why we were there," Linnea said. "We thought it was because of Erskine Bowles (the UNC graduate and White House chief of staff at the time), but he didn't know anything about it. Then we thought it was because President Clinton knew Eddie Sutton (Smith's friend and the basketball coach at Arkansas while Clinton was governor of the state)."

It turned out that Dae-jung had lived in the United States during the early 1980s and had become a UNC basketball fan. "So we went up there," Linnea said, "they gave us badges, we had a tour of the White House, and that night we went across the hall to the Lincoln Bedroom and saw one of the original copies of the Gettysburg Address."

During her last trip, all those memories came flooding back, and Linnea naturally found it bittersweet. She couldn't help but think about how her husband would have relished hobnobbing with such distinguished guests, most of whom he would have deemed much more important than a college basketball coach who got altogether too much attention. "That's where Dean would have been comfortable with the recognition—that part of it he would have loved—the pageantry, the opportunity to be with the Clintons again and Obama," she said.

The sixteen to receive the medals were seated in alphabetical order, and much to Linnea's delight, on her right was Gloria Steinem, the longtime activist for women's equality and a leader in the women's liberation movement. Smith, a psychiatrist by profession, for many years campaigned against *Playboy* and other publications that she believed depicted women and girls as sexual objects, and her husband backed the controversial stance. "I told her how much I appreciated her, that she was a real pioneer, and her resilience for doing it so long because so many people burn out," Linnea recalled. "So that was a real treat for me."

The president's well-researched comments on the honorees lasted approximately three minutes each. Dean Smith was second for no apparent reason other than he followed another sports figure, baseball Hall of Famer Ernie Banks, the first African American to play for the Chicago Cubs. As he began to speak about Smith, President Obama looked up and noticed Roy Williams sitting on the back row of the left-hand section of chairs. Obama made a slight hand gesture toward Williams and nodded.

"That was pretty neat, the President of the United States giving me what the kids would call a shout-out," Williams said. "Then he started talking about what Coach Smith had meant to college athletics, what he meant to African American kids in the South, what he meant to kids throughout his entire career. That's when I about lost it. I had drastically mixed emotions, being so proud of Coach Smith and so sad because he wasn't there. I've always thought it was so great to be able to honor someone while they were there. And it was so much different than the times you are at the White House to celebrate winning a national championship."

Besides Banks, Smith was the only sports figure honored, but he had much in common with several other recipients. Bayard Rustin, who, with astronaut Sally Ride was honored posthumously, had been an advisor to Martin Luther King Jr. and as a younger man rode buses through Chapel Hill with a group of African Americans on a dangerous mission to protest segregated bus and train travel. The work of Rustin, who died in 1987 at age seventy-five, remains an important piece of the fight against segregation in North Carolina, as his group was threatened and beaten on various stops there. And of course, honoree Oprah Winfrey became the first African American female billionaire after a childhood of poverty and abuse by building a media empire in Chicago where she befriended former Tar Heel legend Michael Jordan. Smith knew Winfrey, and he would have surely savored that reunion.

Smith joined renowned basketball coaches John Wooden and Pat Summitt as Presidential Medal winners and was the fourth North Carolina resident to receive the honor, after Dr. Billy Graham, Andy Griffith, and Richard Petty. Dr. Francis Collins, a physician-geneticist who taught at UNC and has been director of the National Institutes of Health since 2009, also received the Presidential Medal in 2007. Smith's hardware has been hidden away in a safe deposit box until his family and UNC decide how it should be exhibited. "I think it should be displayed at the university outside of the athletic department," Linnea Smith said, "because it is more than an athletic honor."

Dean Smith had been gone eight months when he was feted at a small ceremony at Peace and Justice Plaza in Chapel Hill as a champion of social justice, his name engraved on a stone plaque with fourteen others who had also been cited for their roles in fighting against segregation and for all civil rights. Had he been alive and had his say, Smith might have insisted that Charles Scott's name be there instead of his because he knew that living through it was more difficult than merely championing it. Nevertheless, it was an honor well deserved.

Without Scott and his lonely journey through a difficult decade for a black man, there might not have been a Bill Chamberlain, Robert McAdoo, Walter Davis, Phil Ford, James Worthy or Michael Jordan, and all who have followed them wearing Carolina light blue. They had it much easier because of what Scott endured. Through the years, Smith gradually increased the number of African Americans on his rosters; in 1983, he had more black players than whites, and in 1989 he started an all-black lineup for the first time when Jeff Lebo missed five games with a sprained ankle. By then, the rest of the ACC also had fully integrated athletic programs.

The transformative 1960s both inspired and scarred many people who lived, worked, and studied in Chapel Hill and the University of North Carolina during that decade. Some longtime, older residents who are alive have chosen to forget, or remain in denial, about what happened in the so-called Southern Part of Heaven, where racism and separatism were not as spiteful as other places in the Deep South but were nevertheless present. Disbelief is prevalent among those who have since arrived and think whatever stories they hear are exaggerated or simply do not apply to their new hometown and university. The Reverend Robert Seymour, the Baptist preacher and longtime friend of Dean Smith, has continued his crusade to reestablish a local museum that closed in 2010, primarily to tell the civil rights story.

UNC's African American undergraduate population has grown to 9 percent compared to the infinitesimal fraction when Scott arrived in 1966. And while the university has been hailed as one of the best major colleges for minorities, it continues to face racial issues all over the campus, most visibly surrounding athletics. On November 10, 2015, retired Georgetown and Hall of Fame coach John Thompson received the first annual Dean Smith Award from the U.S. Basketball Writers for his lifelong fight against social injustice. A month later, the ninety-two-year-old Seymour and seventy-four-year-old former civil rights activist Fred Battle, who marched and protested side by side in the 1960s, shared the Lifetime Achievement Award from the Chapel Hill–Carrboro Chamber of Commerce, which did not dare give it to one without the other. Dean Smith was right between them in more than age.

Operating quietly and carefully, and never a braggart, Smith was neverthe-less proud of how he rebuilt the UNC basketball program and helped it cross the segregation barrier to reach his goal of simply bringing the best combination of athletes and students to the university. That began with Charles Scott, who repre-sented both his race and his school on the basketball court. Reggie Hawkins, cofounder of the Black Student Movement at UNC with Preston Dobbins, said the BSM considered Scott a member whether he acknowledged it or not because "his accepting a scholarship to play basketball at Carolina was as important, if not more, than anything the BSM did." Hawkins, who lives in Maryland and goes by the name of Abdullah Salim, said Scott's purpose was making sure African Americans had the opportunity to play at UNC and in the ACC. "He didn't need to hold picket signs or be on the forefront," Salim said. "We wanted more opportunities for our race, and so did he." Salim also called Smith "a civil rights activist in his own right by not punishing Scott for supporting us."

As for Scott, his recollections bring understandably mixed emotions. Catch him on a good day, and he can swell with pride over his role as a trail-blazer for so many black athletes and students who now attend UNC. He did so in 2015 during a long meeting with new UNC Chancellor Carol Folt, who was charmed and impressed by Scott's continued dedication to the university without her knowing the full extent of his travails. For years, Scott had admit-ted, "it was very difficult at times, but I am very proud of my time at UNC. It's a legacy my kids can be proud of."

On other days, Scott looks back on the experience with some bitterness and expresses a feeling that the university still owes him something. Like several players from those first ACC championship teams of the late 1960s, he may resent that his era does not get as much credit for launching the Carolina basketball dynasty as do the teams of the 1970s and 1980s. Or he might have seen the 1997 *Carolina Alumni Review* issue commemorating Dean Smith breaking the all-time record for major college coaching victories. The front and back covers are artist renderings of twenty-one of the fifty-two jerseys that hang in the Smith Center, but do not includes Scott's No. 33. Smith long badgered the North Carolina Sports Hall of Fame to make an exception and induct Scott, who did not meet the criteria of being born in the state or living there for ten consecutive years. The selection committee said one exception would only lead to others. Such obvious slights can make a lonely pioneer feel unappreciated and minimized. However, Scott's friends remind him that attitude diminishes the hard truth—that it *was* lonely and exclusionary, and he survived and paved the way for those black students, among them two of his children, who now enjoy a completely different experience at Carolina.

One can hardly blame Scott if he harbored resentment toward his alma mater. Although Dean Smith and John Lotz championed him throughout their lives, the University of North Carolina took forty-five years to celebrate Charles Thomas Scott during Black History Month for his courage as a trailblazer, following a trend with other racial barrier breakers in the South.

After Perry Wallace's revealing autobiography, *Strong Inside*, was published in 2015, athletes who played with him at Vanderbilt began an academic scholarship in his name. Davidson did the same for the late Mike Maloy, plus paid him an emotional tribute in 2011 attended by his family and his coaches Lefty Driesell and Terry Holland.

Scott was about fifteen years too early for the big-money contracts and endorsement deals that have made multimillionaires of much lesser or less-involved athletes, such as Michael Jordan and Tiger Woods, who chose commerce over cause. Nevertheless, his 2015 induction into the College Basketball Hall of Fame gives Scott a permanent place in the game he played so spectacularly on championship Tar Heel teams, and cements his status as a pathfinder whose courage transcended even his immense talent. Trudy, Simone, and Shaun were with Scott in Kansas City (Shannon and Ohio State had a game that weekend) for the induction ceremony, a long-overdue honor given his contributions to college basketball—in Chapel Hill, in the ACC, and all through the Deep South. He is an unforgettable character in the story of how a town in turmoil and a conflicted university coped together and made it through to a new millennium.

Today, both Dean Smith and Charlie Scott have their rightful roles in the challenges of the past. Thanks to trailblazers such as Smith, Scott, and Seymour, and the likes of Chancellor William Aycock, Police Chief William Blake, and Mayor Howard Lee meeting the tests of yesterday, Chapel Hill and UNC were able to become what they are today.

Chapel Hill may be more deserving of its progressive reputation now than it was fifty years ago, with a university campus and town where residents of all races and backgrounds live and work side by side closer than ever. But tensions remain as UNC's flagship campus continues to wrestle with certain legacies, and the community it calls home still grapples with persistent economic and racial divides. Progress does not mean perfection.

Clearly, the transformation of this southern college town is not yet complete.

Notes

Acknowledgments

1. Greg Barnes, "A Game Over Grades," FayObserver.com, April 4, 2010, http://www
.fayobserver.com/news/local/a-game-over-grades/article_fb30506b-6a80-52cd-83a0
-8d91a55adb6e.html.

Prologue

1. Unless otherwise noted, all direct quotations are from the author's interviews or
personal communications.

Chapter 1

1. Barry Jacobs, *Across the Line: Profiles in Basketball Courage: Tales of the First Black
Players in the ACC and SEC* (Guilford, Conn.: Lyons Press, 2007), 105.

2. Ibid., 105.

3. "Earl Manigault," *Wikipedia*, last modified April 23, 2016, https://en.wikipedia.org
/wiki/Earl_Manigault.

4. Jacobs, *Across the Line*, 105.

5. Ronnie Flores, "Elite 24: Rucker Park Legends," ESPN, June 21, 2012, http://espn.go
.com/high-school/boys-basketball/story/_/id/7939736/rucker-park-legends.

6. Mary Brown, "Killer Crossover," *SLAM Magazine*, June 1990, 108.

7. Dean Smith, *A Coach's Life* (New York: Random House, 1999), 42.

8. James Vickers, *Chapel Hill: An Illustrated History* (Chapel Hill, N.C.: Barclay
Publishers, 1985), 167.

9. Mark Pryor, *Faith, Grace and Heresy: The Biography of Rev. Charles M. Jones* (Lincoln,
Neb.: iUniverse, 2002), 85.

10. Vickers, *Chapel Hill*, 167

11. Smith, *A Coach's Life*, 45.

12. Ibid., 53.

13. Billy Prouty, "McGuire Resigns at UNC to Join Basketball Pros," *Chapel Hill Weekly*,
August 8, 1961, 1.

14. Ibid.

15. Curry Kirkpatrick, "Never Forget: Dean Smith Was the Best, and I Was There from the Start," *Sports Illustrated*, February 15, 2016, http://www.si.com/college -basketball/2015/02/17/dean-smith-north-carolina-tar-heels-duke-blue-devils-curry -kirkpatrick.

16. Prouty, "McGuire Resigns at UNC to Join Basketball Pros," 1.

17. Ibid., 8.

18. Max Mulheman, "Dean Smith—Young Man Happily On the Hot Spot," *Charlotte Observer*, August 7, 1961, 5A.

19. George Cunningham, "Smith Eyes Future," *Charlotte Observer*, August 7, 1961, 7B.

Chapter 2

1. Gerald Unks, *The Town before Brown* (Chapel Hill: University of North Carolina Department of Education, 2007).

2. David E. Brown, "A Grudging Acceptance," *Carolina Alumni Review* (May/June 2002): 20.

3. Harvey Beech, "First and Wishing He Wasn't," *Carolina Alumni Review* (May/June 2002): 22–23.

4. Dick Creed, "Two UNC Negro Students Living in Segregated Steele Rooms," *Daily Tar Heel*, October 5, 1954, 1.

5. Bruce Kalk, interview with Floyd B. McKissick, *Documenting the American South* (DocSouth), May 31, 1989 (Southern Oral History Program Collection [#4007], Southern Historical Collection, Wilson Library, University of North Carolina at Chapel Hill).

6. Beth McNichol, "First Black Students Recall Open Wounds, Opening Minds," *Carolina Alumni Review* (January/February 2000): 67.

7. Ibid.

8. Unks, *Town before Brown*.

9. Dean Smith, *A Coach's Life* (New York: Random House, 1999), 10.

10. *Klansville USA*, PBS documentary (2015).

11. Mark Pryor, *Faith, Grace and Heresy: The Biography of Rev. Charles M. Jones* (Lincoln, Neb.: iUniverse, 2002), 99.

12. Ibid., 101.

13. Ibid., 102–3.

14. Chapel Hill Historical Society, *Town Treasures*, Chapel Hill Historical Society recognition program (2010).

15. Robert Seymour, *Whites Only: A Pastor's Retrospective on Signs of the New South* (Chapel Hill, N.C.: Chapel Hill Press, 2012), 104.

16. UNC Archives, Student Affairs, Vice Chancellor, Wilson Library, University of North Carolina, Series 6, Box 1.

17. *Chapel Hill News*, February 3, 1999, 1.

18. Seymour, *Whites Only*, 2.

19. Smith, *A Coach's Life*, 95.

20. Charles L. Thompson, "Standing Up by Sitting Down," *Carolina Alumni Review* (March/April 2006): 36–38.

21. David McReynolds, "A New Kind of Christmas in Chapel Hill," *Village Voice,* December, 1963, reprinted in the *Daily Tar Heel,* January 7, 1964, 2, 4.

22. Smith, *A Coach's Life,* 95.

23. Ibid., 98.

24. Joe Menzer, *Four Corners* (New York: Simon & Schuster, 1999), 141.

25. Ibid.

26. Barry Jacobs, *Across the Line: Profiles in Basketball Courage: Tales of the First Black Players in the ACC and SEC* (Guilford, Conn.: Lyons Press, 2007), 13.

27. Ibid., 95.

28. Ibid., 73.

29. Mike Organ, "Christie Hauck Leads Perry Wallace Scholarship Effort at Vanderbilt," *The Tennessean,* October 10, 2015, http://usatodayhss.com/2015/christie-hauck -leads-perry-wallace-scholarship-effort-at-vanderbilt.

Chapter 3

1. Alfred Hamilton Jr., "Everything Good about Life," *Carolina Court* (Chapel Hill, N.C.: Four Corners Press, 1987), 86.

2. Dean Smith, *A Coach's Life* (New York: Random House, 1999), 95.

3. Larry Keech, "Laurinburg's McDuffie Put Scott on Road to Success," *Greensboro Daily News,* March 11, 1969, B3.

4. Barry Jacobs, *Across the Line: Profiles in Basketball Courage; Tales of the First Black Players in the ACC and SEC* (Guilford, Conn.: Lyons Press, 2007), 105.

5. Hamilton, *Carolina Court,* 86.

6. Bill Livingston, "Charlie Scott Has Much of Which to Be Proud," *The Plain Dealer,* January 15, 2012.

7. Jacobs, *Across the Line,* 107.

8. Smith, *A Coach's Life,* 69.

9. Karen L. Parker Diary, Letter, and Clippings #5275, Southern Historical Collection, Wilson Library, University of North Carolina at Chapel Hill.

10. The Alien Registration Act of 1940 (Smith Act), 76th United States Congress, a United States federal statute enacted June 29, 1940, set criminal penalties for advocating the overthrow of the U.S. government and required all noncitizen adult residents to register with the government; "Smith Act," *Wikipedia,* last modified March 10, 2016, https://en.wikipedia.org/wiki/Smith_Act.

11. Reprinted in *Chapel Hill Weekly,* July 7, 1965.

12. Jim Shumaker, "Gag Law Vastly Overrated," *Chapel Hill Weekly,* July 9, 1965.

13. Thad Mumau, *Dean Smith: A Biography* (Winston-Salem, N.C.: John F. Blair, 1990), 53.

14. John Montague, "The Crucial Week," *Daily Tar Heel,* January 7, 1964, 6.

15. William B. Aycock's personal correspondence.

16. Eulogy for Bill Aycock, UNC professor Gene Nichols, June 23, 2015.

17. Smith, *A Coach's Life*, 74.

18. John Kilgo, *Carolina Blue* column, November 1997.

19. Al Amon photo, Southern Historical Collection, Wilson Library, University of North Carolina.

20. Kelli Boutin-Nicole White, "Making a Name: Four Local Men Broke Barriers and Continue to Fight for Civil Rights," *Daily Tar Heel*, February 26, 1998.

21. Ibid.

22. John Ehle, *The Free Men* (New York: Harper & Row, 1965), 49.

23. Jim Wallace, *Courage in the Moment: The Civil Rights Struggle, 1961–1964* (Mineola, N.Y.: Dover Publications, 2012).

24. Gary Blanchard, "Segregation's Last Stand," *Carolina Alumni Review* (March/April 2006): 46.

25. Professor James W. Prothro, "A Case Study of a Community's Needs in Relation to the (Civil Rights Act)," 8, Daniel H. Pollitt Papers #5498, Southern Historical Collection, Wilson Library, University of North Carolina at Chapel Hill.

26. Ibid.

27. *Chapel Hill Weekly*, January 12, 1964, 2–3.

28. "Town Won't Be Coerced—Sanford," *Chapel Hill Weekly*, January 12, 1964, 1.

29. Carolyn Edy, "Town and Gown," *Carolina Alumni Review* (March/April 2006): 46.

30. Ibid.

31. Robert Seymour, *Whites Only: A Pastor's Retrospective on Signs of the New South* (Chapel Hill, N.C.: Chapel Hill Press, 2012), 122.

32. "Demonstrators Doused with Ammonia," *Chapel Hill Weekly*, January 2, 1964, 1.

33. Ibid.

34. Jim Shumaker, "Meeting Demonstrators with Violence an Animal Act Deserving Contempt," *Chapel Hill Weekly*, January 5, 1964.

35. "Two Hundred Attend Meeting on Racial Situation," *Chapel Hill Weekly*, January 2, 1964, 6.

36. Ibid.

37. Charles L. Thompson, "Standing Up by Sitting Down," *Carolina Alumni Review*, (March/April 2006): 42.

38. Joseph Mosnier, "The Demise of an 'Extraordinary Criminal Procedure': *Klopfer v. North Carolina* and the Incorporation of the Sixth Amendment's Speedy Trial Provision," *Journal of Supreme Court History* 2 (1996): 143.

39. Thompson, "Standing Up by Sitting Down," 43.

40. Edy, "Town and Gown," 42.

Chapter 4

1. Dean Smith, *A Coach's Life* (New York: Random House, 1999), 99.

2. Ibid., 100.

3. Ibid.

4. Caption, *Daily Tar Heel*, February 28, 1966 (photographer unknown).

5. Gary Smith, "The Relentless Scrimmage of Dean Smith," *Inside Sports* (March 1982): 56.

6. Barry Jacobs, "Campus Atmosphere Helped Bring Charlie Scott Here," *Daily Tar Heel*, May 5, 1966, 5.

7. Ibid.

8. Larry Keech, "Laurinburg's McDuffie," *Greensboro Daily News*, B3.

9. Hannah Lebowitz, "UNC: Different Stories of Charles Scott; Newspaper Coverage of the First Black Scholarship Athlete at the University of North Carolina" (bachelor's thesis, University of North Carolina, May 2014), 10.

10. Ibid.

11. Chapel Hill–Carrboro City Schools, "History of Desegregation" (video, 2010), http://www.chccs.k12.nc.us/about/district-history.

12. Ibid.

13. Ibid.

14. Jim Shumaker, "Token Integration," *Chapel Hill Weekly*, June 21, 1963, 2.

15. Jim Shumaker, "Sit-Ins and Chapel Hill's Traditions," *Chapel Hill Weekly*, May 18, 1964, 2.

16. Beth McNichol and David E. Brown, "Where Freedom Should Be Spoken," *Carolina Alumni Review* (November/December 2002): 18

17. Carolyn Edy, "Town and Gown," *Carolina Alumni Review* (March/April 2006): 46.

18. Karen L. Parker Diaries, "1963–66, Ross Barnett," Southern Historical Collection, Wilson Library, University of North Carolina at Chapel Hill.

19. Blake Hodge, "Speaker Ban Protests 50 Years Later," *Chapelboro.com*, March 16, 2016, http://chapelboro.com/featured/speaker-ban-protests-50-years-later.

Chapter 5

1. David Rothman, "UNC Needs Larger Negro Enrollment," *Daily Tar Heel*, May 13, 1966, 3.

2. Vice Chancellor of Student Affairs, UNC Archives, Series 6, Boxes 22 and 23.

3. Rothman, *Daily Tar Heel*, 3.

4. Charles Cherry, "UNC Should Help Negroes," *Daily Tar Heel*, October 6, 1967, 4.

5. Personal correspondence from Dean Smith, April 30, 1968.

6. Ibid.

7. Dean Smith, *A Coach's Life* (New York: Random House, 1999), 88.

8. Smith Barrier, ". . . The Winner: Duke," *Greensboro Daily News*, March 6, 1967, B2.

9. Ed Hodges, "Sophomores Can Win," *Durham Morning Herald*, 1B.

10. Gordon Beard, Associated Press, "Smith, Staff Set Sights on Dayton," *Durham Morning Herald*, March 30, 1967.

11. Alan Banov, "The Fraternity-Racial Relationship," letter to the *Daily Tar Heel*, February 22, 1967, 3.

12. Ibid.

13. Smith, *A Coach's Life*, 101.

14. Joseph Epstein, *Master of the Game: Essays on Sports* (Latham, Md.: Rowman & Littlefield), 78.

15. "Fraternity Pledges Negro at Carolina," *New York Times*, February 26, 1967.

16. Lee W. Purser, letter to the *Daily Tar Heel*, February 15, 1968.

Chapter 6

1. Turner Walston, "Tar Heel Trailblazer: Ricky Lanier," GoHeels.com, February 6, 2014, http://www.goheels.com/ViewArticle.dbml?ATCLID=209397974.

2. Elizabeth Hull, "Black History at UNC: Charles Scott," *A View to Hugh*, February 6, 2009, 2.

3. Wayne Hurder, "Smith Will Have Closed Practices," *Daily Tar Heel*, November 19, 1965, 4.

4. Rick Brewer, "Frosh Legacy Challenging," *Daily Tar Heel*, November 27, 1967, 4.

5. Larry Keith, "Basketball Is Here at Last," *Daily Tar Heel*, November 4, 1967, 4.

6. Larry Keith, "Rah for the Good Guys," *Daily Tar Heel*, December 5, 1967, 4.

7. Ibid.

8. Dean Smith, *A Coach's Life* (New York: Random House, 1999), 106, 107.

9. Billy Carmichael III, *Chapel Hill Weekly*, February 13, 1968, 5.

10. Hugo Germino, "The Behind-the-Scenes Story," *Durham Sun*, March 11, 1968, 1B.

11. *The Dean's List* (New York: Warner Books, 1996), 43.

12. Jim Murray column, *Los Angeles Times*, March 25, 1968, 1B.

13. Associated Press, *Dean Smith Presented Auto by Supporters*, March 28, 1968.

14. Ibid.

15. Dick Woodward, " 'Modest' Scott Making It 'Big,' " *Greensboro Daily News*, April 9, 1968.

Chapter 7

1. Country Joe McDonald, "I Feel Like I'm Fixin' to Die" (The Fish Cheer; 1967).

2. Dean Smith, *A Coach's Life* (New York: Random House, 1999), 112.

3. "Killer Crossover," *SLAM Magazine*, June 1990, 110.

4. John C. Manuel, "Scott Started It All: All-American Was UNC's First Black Scholarship Athlete," *Daily Tar Heel*, February 12, 1993, 1, 5.

5. "College Basketball Preview," *Sport Illustrated*, November 28, 1968.

6. *Yackety Yack*, Yearbook of the University of North Carolina at Chapel Hill, 1969, N15.

7. Smith, *A Coach's Life*, 112.

8. Bill Prouty, "Mature Is the Word for Scott," *Chapel Hill Weekly*, December 10, 1968, 9.

9. Ibid.

10. Ronald Green, "Fall from Olympus," *Charlotte News*, December 29, 1968, 1B.

11. Ibid.

12. Fox Casey, "To Whom It May Concern," *Durham Morning Herald*, January 14, 1969, 1B.

13. Smith, *A Coach's Life*, 114.

14. Jerry Adams, "Blacks Press UNC to Act This Week," *Charlotte Observer*, February 19, 1969, 14A.

15. United Press International (UPI), "Cagers May Join UNC Protesters," *Winston-Salem Journal*, February 19, 1969.

16. Ibid.

17. Ibid.

18. Smith, *A Coach's Life*, 115.

19. Brett Friedlander, "Glory (Tobacco) Road," *Fayetteville Observer*, February 26, 2006, 1C.

20. "An Extreme Injustice," *Daily Tar Heel*, March 19, 1969.

21. Smith, *A Coach's Life*, 115.

22. William Gildea, "Great Scott Faces Magnificent Maloy," *Washington Post*, March 15, 1969.

23. Owen Davis, "Heels 'Cats Engage in Rematch," *Daily Tar Heel*, March 15, 1969.

24. "Killer Crossover," 112.

25. Rick Gray, "Students Elated in Celebration," *Daily Tar Heel*, March 16, 1969, 1.

26. Owen Davis, "Scott's End-of-Game Bucket Leads Carolina to Regional Title," *Daily Tar Heel*, March 16, 1969, 1.

27. Ibid.

28. Smith, *A Coach's Life*, 117.

Chapter 8

1. (James) Vickers, *Chapel Hill: An Illustrated History* (Chapel Hill, N.C.: Barclay Publishers), 180.

2. Barry Jacobs, *Across the Line: Profiles in Courage* (Guilford, Conn.: Lyons Press, 1999), 116.

3. Barry Jacobs, *Golden Glory: First 50 Years of the ACC* (Greensboro: Mann Media, 2003), 95.

4. Bert Woodard, "Charlie Scott," *Carolina Blue*, April 15, 2006, 22

5. Gary Smith, "The Relentless Scrimmage of Dean Smith," *Inside Sports*, March 1982, 54.

6. Gordon Edes and James Granelli, "Adviser's 'Family' Torn Apart as Losses Total in the Millions," *Los Angeles Times*, April 8, 1987, 1B.

7. Greg Logan, "Charlie Scott Recalls His Journey with Dean Smith to Desegregate the ACC," Newsday.com, February 8, 2015, http://www.newsday.com/sports/columnists /greg-logan/charlie-scott-recalls-his-journey-with-dean-smith-to-desegregate-acc-1 .9917991.

Index